Return of the Black Death

Der Krämer.

'Death and the Pedlar', from 'The Dance of Death' by Hans Holbein.
Reproduced by permission of Bridgeman Art Library.

Return of the Black Death
The World's Greatest Serial Killer

Susan Scott
and
Christopher Duncan

WILEY

Published in the UK in 2004 by   John Wiley & Sons Ltd, The Atrium, Southern Gate, Chichester, West Sussex PO19 8SQ, England Telephone   (+44) 1243 779777

Email (for orders and customer service enquiries): cs-books@wiley.co.uk Visit our Home Page on www.wileyeurope.com or www.wiley.com

Other Wiley Editorial Offices

John Wiley & Sons Inc., 111 River Street, Hoboken, NJ 07030, USA

Jossey-Bass, 989 Market Street, San Francisco, CA 94103-1741, USA

Wiley-VCH Verlag GmbH, Boschstr. 12, D-69469 Weinheim, Germany

John Wiley & Sons Australia Ltd, 33 Park Road, Milton, Queensland 4064, Australia

John Wiley & Sons (Asia) Pte Ltd, 2 Clementi Loop #02-01, Jin Xing Distripark, Singapore 129809

John Wiley & Sons Canada Ltd, 22 Worcester Road, Etobicoke, Ontario, Canada M9W 1L1

British Library Cataloguing in Publication Data

A catalogue record for this book is available from the British Library

ISBN 0-470-09000-6

Typeset in $10\frac{1}{2}/13\frac{1}{2}$pt Photina by Mathematical Composition Setters Ltd, Salisbury, Wiltshire. Printed and bound in Great Britain by T.J. International Ltd, Padstow, Cornwall.

Endpapers: 'The Dance of Death' by Holbein. Engraved by Deuchar, 1786. Reproduced with permission of Mary Evans Picture Library.

This book is printed on acid-free paper responsibly manufactured from sustainable forestry in which at least two trees are planted for each one used for paper production.

10 9 8 7 6 5 4 3

Contents

Preface

Serendipity played a large part in the genesis of this book.
Thirteen years ago, Sue Scott was searching for a suitable
parish in which to conduct an in-depth demographic study and
settled on Penrith in Cumbria. When she analysed the parish
registers, she discovered that this community suffered from a
plague epidemic at the end of the sixteenth century. One look at
the facts was sufficient for a biologist to realize that this was not
an outbreak of bubonic plague, the conventional and accepted
view of the cause of the plagues in Europe. However, we had other
research programmes on hand and did not return to the question
'What caused the plagues?' for a number of years. And so began
the cooperation of a historical demographer and a zoologist, each
bringing their own expertise. What we uncovered as we dug
deeper and deeper greatly surprised us: our initial suspicions
were amply confirmed and the repercussions were far-reaching.

We wrote an academic monograph, *Biology of Plagues*, which
covered many aspects of the subject. When this was published,
we were amazed at the response from the media. Reports were
carried in newspapers throughout the world; we were invited
to give radio interviews in many different countries; television
companies rang to enquire about the possibility of making a film;
we were inundated with telephone calls and e-mails asking
questions and making suggestions. Among our correspondents
was a 12-year-old girl who said that her Mummy had suggested
she write for reassurance that the Black Death would not
reappear. A war veteran from the Far East rang to say that his
platoon had been stricken by a viral haemorrhagic fever and
only he had survived; a fascinating first-hand account of this
gruesome disease. A correspondent from Kent described the
collapse of a main road on the site of the burial ground for the

Black Death at Blackheath. People living in the nearby houses were hurriedly rushed away by armed police who announced a bio-hazard in the immediate vicinity. We had lengthy correspondence with a screenwriter who was working on a script for a feature film dealing with an imaginary virus that wipes out most of humanity. He thought that haemorrhagic plague 'would be the perfect disease for his story' and wanted detailed predictions of how such an epidemic would spread.

It was all very exciting and convinced us that there is enormous public interest worldwide in the subject of plagues. This book is our attempt to tell the story and to satisfy this thirst for knowledge of the most infamous disease of past times and of its possible repercussions for the future.

We gratefully acknowledge the support and encouragement that we have received from so many people.

We salute Dr Graham Twigg, who was the first to recognize that the Black Death was not an outbreak of bubonic plague; he has been a stalwart friend for a number of years.

Dr Debora McKenzie, European Editor of the *New Scientist*, has supported our idea that the plagues were in fact caused by a haemorrhagic virus from the start and has kept us in touch with recent developments.

We thank a multitude of correspondents throughout the world who have sent valued e-mails and letters giving news, reports, comments, unpublished data and suggestions.

Dr Stephen Duncan at the University of Oxford introduced us to the intricacies (and delights) of time-series analysis and then produced all the mathematical models for our work. Without this fundamental assistance, there would have been no research programme.

Mrs Jennifer Duncan provided invaluable assistance in reading documents in Secretary Hand and in translating original articles.

We are particularly grateful to Sally Smith, Senior Publishing Editor at Wiley, for whole-heartedly backing this project and also thank Nicky McGirr, Julia Lampam and Jill Jeffries for their enthusiastic support.

Introduction

For over 600 years, the word 'plague' has struck terror in the hearts of men and women: it engenders a nightmare scenario of an unstoppable and highly infectious disease for which there is no cure and from which an agonizing death is certain. For the people of Europe in the Middle Ages who lived daily with the threat that it would visit their community, this fear was completely understandable. Since it disappeared from the scene in the mid-seventeenth century, this reign of terror has continued to hold a fascination and to evoke more than a frisson of fear. Even the most inattentive schoolchild relishes lessons on the Great Plague of London, fire and devastation in the perilous years of 1665–66.

In the twenty-first century, we have a far greater knowledge of diseases than ever before, a number of effective vaccines and treatments, experts trained in epidemiology and molecular biology, a battery of diagnostic tests and modern techniques that can sequence the genome of a new virus within months of its first appearance – yet the horror that a new disease, perhaps another plague, could emerge and threaten our existence is as strong as ever.

The emergence of SARS (Severe Acute Respiratory Syndrome) in 2003 showed all too well the havoc that a new disease could cause. It was reported in Asia in January of that year and dominated the headlines over the next few months. Could SARS be the new deadly plague? There was widespread panic and people fled from the afflicted areas, which helped to spread the illness further afield. Before too long, cases were being reported in Europe as well as North and South America. Compared with the plagues of the past, it caused relatively few deaths overall: a total of some 8000 cases in 27 countries, of which only 780 died. In spite of this, health authorities struggled to cope, whole nations were quarantined from nonessential travel, airlines faced bankruptcy, national economies were disrupted and there was real fear of the collapse of international financial markets. In the USA, sales of paper face masks soared even though the country had only 192 cases of SARS and all recovered.

Why did a relatively insignificant health scare cause international alarm and panic, even in countries that had no or few cases of SARS? In April 2003, Dr Stuart Derbyshire wrote that we live among a 'population thirsty for panic, and eager to hear the message of doom, demanding these warnings. The warnings blend with our self-conscious expectation of disaster and fear for the planet. Even the seemingly balanced Professor Oxford appears only to be waving away distractions from the anticipated real thing. Neither of the two [potential SARS] viral families would really make my hair stand on end like a virulent new flu virus would.'

In April 2003, Declan McCullagh, a political correspondent living in Washington, wrote:

> SARS is the first epidemic of the Internet age, preying on the fact that as information becomes more communicable, rumours become more communicable too. A teenager's Web hoax claiming Hong Kong's borders would be closed prompted runs on canned foods and toilet paper. A supermarket owner in Sacramento spent two weeks arguing that, contrary to rumours, neither he nor his family was infected with SARS, and his stores were entirely safe. On Tuesday, a Sacramento city councilman tried to quell panic by bravely chewing a ceremonial Granny Smith apple from the produce section in front of reporters.

But to some people, a worldwide health threat might herald the 'Apocalypse now' scenario, the return of the next 'Big One', when a major epidemic of a deadly infectious disease, for which there is no treatment and no vaccine, will cause global catastrophe and threaten the existence of humanity.

What do we know of plagues?

This fear of unknown disease has a sound basis in history. Possibly the oldest reference to plagues appears in the biblical book of I Samuel. In about 1320 BC, the Philistines stole the Ark of the Covenant from the Israelites and returned home:

> the Lord's hand was heavy upon the people of Ashdod and its vicinity; he brought devastation upon them and afflicted them with tumours. And rats appeared in their land, and death and destruction were throughout the city ... the Lord's hand was against that city, throwing it into a great panic. He afflicted the people of the city, both young and old, with an outbreak of tumours in the groin.

We were all taught in school and read in books about the most famous disease of all time – the Black Death – a ferocious killer that appeared from nowhere, spread quickly and wiped out nearly one half of the medieval Europeans. We have heard the following children's nursery rhyme, which is said to commemorate the terrible plagues:

> Ring-a-ring of roses,
> A pocket full of posies,
> Atishoo, atishoo,
> We all fall down.

The first line of the rhyme depicts the round red rash that appeared on the victim's skin. The sweet-smelling posies were what people held to their noses to ward off infection. Sneezing was an early symptom of the disease, and this was closely followed by 'falling down' or sudden death.

In the middle of the seventeenth century, a great plague struck London and killed up to a fifth of the population. Samuel Pepys recorded the events in his diary, and we can follow this outbreak more closely and identify with the victims because of his graphic accounts.

Some people may also be familiar with the most famous plague story of all: the epidemic in the little upland village of Eyam in Derbyshire on the edge of the Peak District in northern England. When the epidemic broke out, the Rector and his parishioners made a heroic sacrifice by agreeing to draw a *cordon sanitaire* around the village and voluntarily putting themselves into quarantine. Nobody was allowed to flee to escape infection and certain death. In this way, they hoped to contain the outbreak and prevent its spread to neighbouring communities. Throughout their ordeal, food was brought to the parish boundary by nearby villagers. Imprisoned, they could only wait and watch as they died, slowly at first, although at the height of the outbreak the Rector was burying several of his flock each day. The terrible epidemic lasted 15 awful months and at the end Eyam resembled a ghost village. Nevertheless, their sacrifice was not in vain – the infection did not escape and spread to any other community.

However, is this the extent of our knowledge of plagues? For instance, how many of us could put an accurate date on these cataclysmic events? Would we be able to say whether they were explosive epidemics of the same disease? We should probably be able to say that the Great Plague of London was the result of bubonic plague, a disease spread by infected rat fleas, but would be unable to say why we believed it to be so, except that in the far recesses of our minds, we recall being told in school that the Great Fire of London in 1666 killed all the rats and saved England from further outbreaks of plague.

Our quest

In 1990, this was also the extent of the authors' own knowledge of the plagues of historic times. We knew as little as anyone, until we accidentally stumbled on a brief record of a catastrophic epidemic that broke out in a small English market town towards the end of the Elizabethan era. It was the first time we had come across the plague in our research on the history of populations, and it sparked an interest that soon became a fascination and a determination to discover as much as we could about this greatly feared disease.

Little did we realize when we started on our quest that this would eventually lead to a debunking of the popular misconceptions of this ancient terror. We were to turn history on its head. To our surprise, and even more importantly, we uncovered a chilling message for us today – this medieval killer may be lying dormant, waiting for the right moment to strike again.

This is our story.

The beginnings

Sue Scott had been carrying out an in-depth historical study of the community at Penrith from the sixteenth to the nineteenth centuries. This little town lies in the valley of the river Eden in Cumbria in northern England, quite close to the Scottish border. Its people were cut off from the rest of England, being hemmed in by the picturesque mountains of the Lake District to the west, the rugged Pennine range to the east and the more gentle Westmorland fells to the south. However, the road to Scotland ran right through the centre of Penrith and for centuries along this came travellers, traders and cattle drovers. Potentially, they could all bring lethal infectious diseases like plague and smallpox from afar, even from London, which was situated some 280 miles (450 kilometres) to the south-east, a journey that would take several days by horseback.

From Sue's studies, we knew that at the end of the sixteenth century the land of the Eden valley was regarded as remote from large industrial and trading centres. Outsiders viewed it with repulsion: it was inaccessible to travellers, landowners were frequently absent and brigands roamed unhindered. At the centre of this area was the small market town of Penrith, which, as shown by a map published 200 years later, was grouped around St Andrew's church and adjacent to the ruins of a long-abandoned castle that had been erected to defend the town from frequent incursions by marauding Scots. Life was difficult for the inhabitants of Penrith and frequently they had to exist under near-famine conditions. As a consequence, fertility was low and usually only four children were born to a family. Of these only two, on average, would survive to the age of 15.

And so it began, with Sue sitting at one of the large mahogany tables in the Record Office at Carlisle. More pleasantly located than most, this two-storey brick building is situated to one side of the courtyard of the castle at Carlisle, where Mary Queen of Scots was held prisoner, and houses all the records that pertain to the old county of Cumberland, now included in Cumbria. Sue was studying original parish registers, the official documents of the Church of England, some dating back to 1538, which have mostly been placed for safe-keeping in the various County Record Offices dotted around the country. As well as a resource for genealogists and family historians, these carefully preserved documents of baptisms, marriages and burials also provide valuable data for the professional researcher, because they give a unique insight into family and community history over three centuries.

Although the people of Penrith thought that they were safe, being so cut off from the rest of the country, Sue discovered that there was no hiding place from the plague. The parish registers record:

A sore plague in Richmond, Kendall, Penreth, Carliel [Carlisle], Apulbie [Appleby] and oth[i]er plac[es] in Westmorland and Cumberland in the yere [year] of oure Lord God 1598.

The parish registers were fully maintained during this period and, sure enough, when Sue turned up the appropriate entries she found:

Penrith Burial Registers, 1597
September
22   Andrew Hogson, a stranger
HERE BEGONNE THE PLAGE (GOD PUNISMET) IN PENRTH

Those that are noted with thys letter P dyed of the infirmity and that those that are noted with F are buried out on the fell.

At that time, vicars were required by law to note the burials of plague victims by adding Pest (an abbreviation for pestilence, the common name for the plague) or simply P after their names.

Obviously, the infection was brought into the little community by a stranger who presumably came via the main road running through the town. The result was catastrophic: Andrew Hogson's entry is followed by a terrible wave of burials marked with a P. This severe epidemic lasted for 15 months but, in spite of what must have been a horrific time for the local vicar (he lost his wife and young son), the events during this dreadful visitation were faithfully recorded in the parish registers. As was the custom, the vicar told people that it was God's punishment for their sins.

One puzzle that we discovered straight away when studying the registers was that after the death of Andrew Hogson, there were no plague burials for 22 days. Wasn't this a very long interval for a normal infection?

At some point, when the outbreak was finally over, an inscription was placed on the walls of the church at Penrith relating the number of people in the Eden Valley who had died:

PENRITH	2260
KENDAL	2500
RICHMOND	2200
CARLISLE	1196

This dedication was transferred to the chancel wall when the church was rebuilt in 1720, but it was apparently covered up during restoration. It was replaced by a brass plate and Sue verified the figures during one of her visits to Penrith. From her earlier studies, she had already obtained a firm estimate of only 1350 people living in Penrith immediately before the start of the plague so, obviously, the 2260 deaths on the inscription was a wildly inaccurate figure. We returned to the registers and counted 606 burials marked with a P. However, there is a gap in the burial records of 11 days when the epidemic was at its peak and we estimated that the final death toll was probably closer to 640. While this was nearly 50 per cent of the population of this small community – an awesome concentration of death in a 15-month period – it was obviously well short of the figure of 2260 on the inscription. So what was going on here? We were intrigued and chose to look more deeply.

It was obvious from the inscription in the church that this strange and fearsome epidemic was not confined to Penrith but had spread further in the Eden Valley. Searching the registers and records of other parishes in the area revealed that the infection moved from its focus in Penrith to Carlisle 20 miles (32 kilometres) to the north and Kendal 32 miles (51 kilometres) to the south. What was interesting was that the first deaths at both towns occurred *on the same day, 11 days after the first burial at Penrith*. We were amazed at our findings and were staggered to learn that this disease could travel so far and so quickly. It came as no surprise, however, to learn that once again, a terrible death toll was recorded at both Kendal and Carlisle.

Discovering this little-known epidemic that struck three market towns in north-west England at the very end of the sixteenth century set us thinking. The vicar and the locals had immediately identified this as a case of the plague or pestilence – they had experience, presumably first-hand, of this disease. But there were a number of puzzling features about this epidemic. Was Penrith typical? Was the disease the same as other outbreaks of plague throughout Europe? Was it the Black Death? We decided to investigate.

The first clues

As any good detective will tell you, identifying a killer involves a thorough investigation of the scene of the crime and a detailed knowledge of all the evidence. Today, epidemiologists studying a newly emerged disease have a battery of modern scientific techniques; they can actually examine their patients and make on-the-spot observations. However, historical epidemiologists have a much more difficult task because there is almost no information on which they can rely to make a diagnosis. The scent has gone cold and they must use all their wits to distinguish between fact and fiction.

So, our first task was to summarize what we had learnt so far about this mysterious disease at Penrith:

- It was lethal. We did not trace evidence of anyone who caught the infection surviving.

- It was very infectious. The disease spread like wildfire, particularly during the summer of 1598.

- The infection was brought into the community by a travelling stranger.

- After the first death, there was a break of 22 days before the next victim was buried. Surely this was remarkable.

- The epidemic quickly jumped considerable distances to Carlisle and Kendal, with the first victims there dying simultaneously 11 days after Hogson's burial.

The next step on the trail was to go back to the original accounts of the plagues that ravaged Europe, discarding all the interpretations and false anecdotes that have been added over the last 100 years, and to search for further clues. We start with the fateful year of 1347 when the plague first appeared completely out of the blue and struck European civilization, with catastrophic effects.

1

Birth of a Serial Killer

'Then a boil developed on their thighs, or on their upper arms a boil ... This infected the whole body, so that the patient violently vomited blood. This vomiting of blood continued without intermission for three days, there being no means of curing it, and then the patient died.' So wrote Michael of Piazza, a Franciscan friar, describing the torment of the first victims of the Black Death.

In October 1347, all that the people of the time knew was that a deadly and hitherto unknown infectious disease had appeared from nowhere on the island of Sicily. They could have had no way of understanding the nature of their adversary.

The scale of the catastrophe was unprecedented. There was no cure and anyone who was infected died a truly awful death. This was the first manifestation of a plague that would blight Europe for the next 300 years and claim countless millions of victims – the worst serial killer of all time and the most tragic event in human history.

The first victims: their story

Contemporary accounts of the plague's first appearance speak to us across the centuries, conveying something of the utter terror and despair that afflicted whole populations. Michael of Piazza described how 12 Genoese galleys said to have come from the

Crimea entered the harbour of Messina in Sicily and the crews who carried such a virulent disease 'in their bones that anyone who only spoke to them was seized by a mortal illness and in no way could evade death. The infection spread to everyone who had any intercourse with the diseased. Those infected felt themselves penetrated by a pain throughout their whole bodies.'

It appears that the crews of the galleys were healthy and were not displaying any symptoms, and yet the inhabitants of Messina were rapidly struck down. When the authorities decided that the galleys were responsible for bringing this dreadful disease, they expelled them from the port, forcing them to put out to sea again. The crews, who were still perfectly healthy, must have been perplexed and indignant.

Onward they are said to have sailed to Genoa and, on arrival, a new outbreak of the pestilence began, the disease spreading rapidly almost as soon as the galleys had docked. Again, the reports suggest that the crews escaped the plague and yet:

> The infection appeared in Genoa in its most deadly form a day or two after the arrival of the ships, *although none of those on board were suffering from the plague* [our italics], for we know that there were no cases of plague on board the ships, although the very atmosphere or smell of the new arrival seemed sufficient to taint the air of Genoa and to carry death to every part of the city within a couple of days.

These reports have obviously been greatly embroidered and our conclusion was that the epidemic was already up and running by the time the galleys arrived at Messina. Since the crews were completely healthy after a voyage of at least a month as well as on the further voyage to Genoa, they cannot have been carrying the infection. Their arrival at the time when the people of Messina realized that they were experiencing an epidemic must have been merely coincidental. We decided that, most probably, unrecognized victims had been dying from the plague in Messina for some weeks before the galleys arrived.

In the throes of the ensuing epidemic, the citizens of Messina believed that the slightest contact with the sick guaranteed rapid infection. Michael of Piazza wrote:

> Soon men hated each other so much that, if a son was attacked by the disease, his father would not care for him. If, in spite of all, he dared to approach him, he was immediately infected, and could in no way escape death, but was bound to expire within three days. Nor was this the end of it: all those belonging to him or dwelling in the same house, even the cats and other domestic animals, followed him to the grave. As the number of deaths increased in Messina, many wished to confess their sins to the priests and to draw up their last will and testament. But ecclesiastics, lawyers and attorneys refused to enter the houses of the diseased. If one or the other had set foot in such a house to draw up a will, or for any other purpose, he was condemned to sudden death. Minor friars and Dominicans and members of other orders who heard the confessions of the dying were immediately overcome by death, so that some even remained in the rooms of the dying.
>
> Soon the corpses were lying forsaken in the houses. No ecclesiastic, no son, no father and no relation dared to enter, but they paid servants high wages to bury the dead. The houses of the deceased remained open, with all their valuables, with gold and jewels; anyone who decided to enter met with no impediment, for the plague raged with such vehemence that soon there was a shortage of servants and finally none were left at all.

This account may be exaggerated in places, but it does convey vividly the horror and terror that everyone felt when this new plague first struck. They were overwhelmed by the ferocity of this mysterious disease which was completely outside their experience. One thing is quite clear – and this is an important clue – they realized immediately that transmission was directly by person-to-person infection.

With hundreds dying and the merest contact with the sick apparently guaranteeing infection, the remaining Messinians panicked and fled. Nevertheless, although they thought they were perfectly healthy, unbeknown to them they were unwittingly carrying the plague with them.

One group of refugees settled in the fields and vineyards of southern Sicily, but many fell down on the road and died. Others sought refuge in the neighbouring port of Catania, where they were tended in the hospital until death overcame them, but the Catanians rapidly realized their mistake – they should not have introduced this appalling infection into their town. The corpses were quickly pitched into trenches outside the walls and further immigration was strictly controlled.

Michael of Piazza relates that 'the population of Catania was so godless and fearful that no one among them would have intercourse with or speak to the fugitives, but each fled hastily on their approach'. Whether this was a sign of 'godlessness' or plain common sense, it was too late and the Black Death ravaged the town: 'The town of Catania lost all of its inhabitants, so that it ultimately sank into complete oblivion.' Michael of Piazza was probably exaggerating again, but the picture is unmistakable.

Fleeing in uncontrollable terror, the people from Messina spread the plague all over Sicily; the death toll was high in Syracuse and the port of Trapani was said to be completely depopulated.

What were the symptoms?

What was it like to contract the Black Death? Michael of Piazza's graphic description of the symptoms is not for those with weak stomachs:

The 'burn blisters' appeared, and boils developed in different parts of the body: on the sexual organs, in others on the thighs, or on the arms, and in others on the neck. At first these were of the size of a hazelnut and the patient was seized by violent shivering fits, which soon rendered him so weak that he could no longer stand upright, but was forced to lie on his bed, consumed by a violent fever and overcome by great tribulation. Soon the boils grew to the size of a walnut, then to that of a hen's egg or a goose's egg, and they were exceedingly painful, and irritated the body, causing it to vomit blood by vitiating the juices. The blood rose from the affected lungs to the throat, producing a putrefying and ultimately decomposing effect on the whole body. The sickness lasted three days, and on the fourth, at the latest, the patient succumbed.

This account may be supplemented by the following description, given by the Florentine humanist Giovanni Boccaccio when the plague ravaged Florence:

Unlike what had been seen in the east, where bleeding from the nose is the fatal prognostic, here there appeared tumours in the groin or under the armpits, some as big as a small apple, others as large as an egg; and afterwards purple spots in most parts of the body: in some cases large and but few in number, in others smaller and more numerous – both sorts were the usual messengers of death. Neither medical knowledge, nor the power of drugs, was of any effect to cure this illness ... nearly all died on the third day from the first appearance of the symptoms; some sooner, some later, without any fever or other accessory symptoms. What made this plague so virulent was that, by being transmitted from the sick to the hale, it spread daily ... Nor was it caught only by conversing with or coming near the sick, but even by touching their clothes.

It was soon obvious that there was no cure: once the dreaded symptoms appeared, the agonizing end seemed to be inevitable. When 'God's tokens' – haemorrhagic spots caused by blood seeping from damaged blood vessels beneath the skin – were found on the body, this was the death certificate and a prelude to four or five days of agony, frenzy and delirium. The victims' thirst was unquenchable and some of them ran naked through the streets, screaming, and plunged into water cisterns. Others went completely mad with the pain and even threw themselves out of windows. There was internal bleeding and, in the final days, the vital organs began to liquefy. Death was truly a merciful release.

The terror spreads throughout Italy

From its starting point, the plague was carried abroad in two ways: by ship, when it could jump over many miles and appear in a completely new port, and on foot, advancing slowly but surely over land.

Sicily occupies a pivotal position in the Mediterranean, and Messina and Catania were important stop-over ports for sea trading. It was trade that spread the plague and from Sicily the

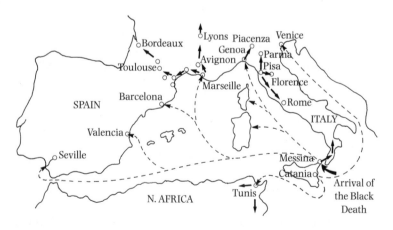

The arrival of the Black Death at Messina in Sicily and its subsequent spread across the Mediterranean by boat.

disease expanded to North Africa via Tunis, to the Balearic Islands and Cyprus, and to Corsica and Sardinia. If it had been confined to these areas, the epidemic would probably have fizzled out and perhaps even been forgotten by history. However, the plague then made some critical strikes almost simultaneously.

It arrived in the northern Italian port of Genoa in January 1348 (some three months after the galleys had docked in Messina). It also made the short jump across the strait to southern Italy.

In January 1348 the disease also arrived in Venice, probably having come by sea from Sicily. A contemporary estimate of the death toll was 100 000, though this is probably an overestimate. One Venetian wrote:

A certain man bled me, and the blood spurted onto his face. On that same day he was taken ill, and the next day he died; and by the mercy of God I have escaped. I record this because, as by mere communication with the sick, the plague mortally infected the healthy ... so the healthy man studiously avoided the sick. Even priests and doctors fled from those who were ill, in fear, and all avoided the dead. In many places and houses when an inmate died, the rest quickly expired, one after another. And so great was the overwhelming number of the dead, that it was necessary to open new cemeteries everywhere.

Can we learn something here? Was the man who was being bled suffering from the pestilence and yet recovered?

A stranger (obviously a person who was already infected) is believed to have brought the disease to Padua and the resulting devastation was great: an astounding two-thirds of the population died. If one person in a household fell sick, the whole family quickly succumbed. Was this an important clue concerning the nature of the disease?

Pisa was struck, probably via the port of Leghorn, in March 1348. From here the plague spread northwards to Tuscany and southwards to Rome. Italy was truly overwhelmed.

Europe was now fighting a war with the plague and the struggle seemed hopeless; this disease was completely outside people's experience or understanding. The enemy was invisible and nobody knew when or where it would next appear. When it did strike, people could not defend themselves and many were overcome. The more they panicked and fled, the more the disease was spread. The plague held all the trump cards.

From Genoa it was carried to Piacenza, about 60 miles (100 kilometres) to the north-east, and Gabriele de Mussi, a resident of Piacenza who practised as a notary, wrote:

> But as an inhabitant I have been asked to write more of Piacenza, so that it may be known what happened there in the year 1348. Some Genoese who had fled from the plague raging in their city betook themselves higher. They rested at Bobbio, and there sold the merchandise that they had brought with them. The purchaser, together with all his family and many neighbours, were quickly stricken with the sickness and died. One of these, wishing to make his will, called a notary, his confessor, and the necessary witnesses. The next day all these were buried together. So greatly did the calamity increase that nearly all the inhabitants of Bobbio soon fell victim to the sickness, and only the dead remained in the town.

In the spring of 1348 another Genoese who was infected with the plague came to Piacenza. He sought out his friend Fulchino della Croce, who took him into his house. But he died almost immediately afterwards and Fulchino was also quickly carried off, together with his entire family and many of his neighbours.

Gabriele de Mussi clearly believed that this disease was directly infectious. He continued:

> The plague was rife throughout the city in a brief space of time. I do not know where to begin: everywhere there was weeping and mourning. So great was the mortality that men hardly dared to breathe. The dead were numberless,

and those who remained alive gave themselves up as lost and prepared for the tomb.

His account brings home to us the terrible scale of the disaster:

The cemeteries failing, it was necessary to dig trenches to bury the corpses. Whole families were frequently thrown together in the same pit. It was the same in the neighbouring towns and villages. One Oberto de Sasso, who had come from an infected place to the church of the Friars Minor to make his will, summonsed a notary, witnesses, and neighbours. All these, together with sixty others, died within a short space of time.

Florence, situated only some 40 miles (60 kilometres) from Pisa, was one of the greatest cities in Europe, a democratic centre of culture, art and learning, its treasures including the works of Dante and Giotto. It did not escape and was badly hit by the Black Death, in spite of all sensible precautions and supplications to God. Boccaccio wrote in the *Decameron* a very memorable account of Florence during this time:

Some shut themselves away and eschewed all social contact and every kind of luxury; others drank, sang and revelled freely, believing this way of life to be the sovereign remedy for so great an evil.

Citizen avoided citizen, few showing any fellow feeling for another, people held themselves aloof and never met their kinsfolk, and 'what is more and scarcely to be believed, fathers and mothers abandoned their own children, untended, to their fate, as if they were strangers'.

No woman, however dainty, fair or well-born, shrank, when stricken by the disease, from the ministrations of a man, no matter whether he were young or not, nor did she scruple to expose every part of her body to him, with no more shame than if he had been a woman, submitting of necessity to that which her malady required.

Many died by day or by night in the public streets; the departure of many others, who died at home, was hardly observed by their neighbours until the stench of their putrefying bodies carried the tidings; and what with their corpses and the corpses of others who died on every hand the whole place was a sepulchre.

It was the common practice of most of the neighbours, who were moved more by fear of contamination by the putrefying bodies than by charity towards the deceased, to drag the corpses out of the houses and to lay them in front of the doors; afterwards biers were brought up or, lacking them, planks on which the dead were laid.

Corpse carriers, known as *becchini*, performed their offices for hire and hurriedly carried the biers to the burial places. They dug huge trenches 'in which they laid the corpses as they arrived, hundreds at a time, piling them up in the same way that merchandise is stowed in the hold of a ship, tier upon tier, each covered with a little earth, until the trench would hold no more'.

The *becchini* were not nice people; apparently they were brutalized monsters who also had a more sinister role, which added to the general misery. They would force their way into the houses of people who were still alive and drag them away to join the ranks of the dead unless the men gave over money for their safety and the women paid with their virtue.

It has been estimated that between 45 000 and 65 000 people died in Florence, probably roughly in line with a general 50 per cent mortality in the towns and cities of Italy. Again, the story was the same. In the plague at Siena, Agnolo di Tura (who buried five of his children) described how father abandoned child and so they died, one after another. No one could be found to bury the huge heaps of the dead in the great pits; they were so sparsely covered with earth that the dogs dragged them out and ate their bodies. A gruesome picture.

The Petrarch endured the plague in Parma and he describes it in his letters. The inhabitants attempted to quarantine themselves by forbidding any contact with cities that were already stricken and the plague did not arrive there until June 1348. But when it did, it was the usual grim tale; about 40 000 people are estimated to have died in six months.

The epidemic raged in Italy for about a year before it began to peter out. The Petrarch wrote mournfully to his brother, the only survivor out of 35 people in a monastery at Monrieux:

> Sorrow is on all sides; fear is everywhere. I wish, my brother, that I had never been born, or at least had died before these times. How will posterity believe that there has been a time when well-nigh the whole globe has remained without inhabitants? ...
>
> When has any such thing ever been heard or seen; in what annals has it ever been read that houses were left vacant, cities deserted, the country neglected, the fields too small for the dead to be buried, and a fearful and universal solitude over the whole earth?
>
> Will posterity ever believe these things when we, who see them, can scarcely credit them? We would think we were dreaming if we did not, with our own eyes, when we walk abroad, see the city in mourning with funerals, and on returning home, find it empty, and thus know that what we lament is real.

We may have discovered an important clue here. The Petrarch's brother was the only person to escape in a closed monastic community and yet he must have been in close proximity to his fellows. How did he avoid infection? Is this an indication that some people in Europe showed a form of resistance to this terrible disease?

The invasion of France

When the plague arrived in France in late 1347 or early 1348, the estimate of 57 000 people dying in Marseille and its hinterland is probably inflated, but the tale of terror and mortality there is just what we have come to expect. Simon de Covino, a doctor from Paris, set down his recollections in 1350. They make grim reading:

> Faces became pale, and the doom which threatened the people was marked upon their foreheads. It was only necessary to look in the faces of men and women to read there the blow that was about to fall; a marked pallor announced the approach of the enemy and, before the fatal day, the sentence of death was written unmistakably on the face of the victim. No climate appeared to have any effect upon this strange disease. It appeared to be stopped neither by heat nor cold. High and healthy situations were as much subject to it as low and damp ones. It spread during the cold of winter as rapidly as in the heat of the summer.

We can learn some important points about the nature of the disease from this valuable account. Covino also noted that the plague appeared to be so contagious that a single breath of an infected person, or an item of their clothing, was sufficient to transmit it.

The plague spread westwards, from Marseille to Montpellier, Narbonne, Perpignan and Carcassone, which it reached by May 1348. From there it travelled to Toulouse and Montaubon, arriving at the port of Bordeaux on the Atlantic coast between June and August 1348. Its average rate of spread was between 1 and 5 miles (2 and 8 kilometres) a day, which suggests that it was mainly carried by infected people travelling on foot rather than on horseback.

The Black Death also spread northwards from Marseille and arrived at Avignon in March 1348, where it struck with particular ferocity. The recorded numbers of deaths, although surely exaggerated, are staggering: 1800 in the first three days and a total of 150 000 in the city and surrounding countryside. Many people fled from the city, but Pope Clement VI remained in seclusion nearby, surrounding himself with large fires that were supposed to purify the air.

One anonymous canon wrote a letter to his friends giving a full account of the plague at Avignon. He began by giving a valuable description of the characteristic course of the disease and of the investigations ordered by the Pope:

> The disease can appear in three different ways. Firstly, men suffer in their lungs and breathing, and these victims, even if they are slightly attacked, cannot by any means escape, nor live beyond two days. Examinations have been made by doctors in many cities of Italy, and also in Avignon, by order of the Pope, in order to discover the origin of this disease. Many dead bodies have been opened and dissected, and it is found that all who had died suddenly in this way have had their lungs infected and have spat blood. The contagious nature of the disease is indeed the most terrible of all the terrors, for when anyone who is infected dies, all who see him in his sickness, or who visit him, or do any business with him, or even carry him to the grave, quickly follow him thither, and there is no known means of protection.
>
> There is another form of the sickness, which is running its course concurrently with the first; that is, certain swellings appear under both arms, and people also quickly die by these. A third form of the disease – like the two former – is that from which people of both sexes suffer from swellings in the groin. This, likewise, is quickly fatal.

The canon, like everyone else, assumed that this illness was directly infectious and he reiterates the writings of others:

> The epidemic has already grown to such proportions that, from fear of contagion, a doctor will not visit a sick man, even if the invalid would gladly give him everything he possessed; neither does a father visit his son, nor a mother her daughter, nor, in fact, does anyone go to another, no

matter how closely he may be related to him, unless he is prepared to die with him, or quickly to follow him.

Evidently, complete avoidance of even near relatives was a standard practice and no one questioned the idea that the disease was directly infectious. The canon continued:

One-half, or more than a half, of the people at Avignon are already dead. There are now more than 7,000 houses shut up within the walls of the city; there is no one living in these, and all the inhabitants have departed; the suburbs are almost empty. A field near Our Lady of Miracles has been bought by the Pope and consecrated as a cemetery, and 11,000 corpses have been buried in this. This number does not include those interred in the cemetery of the hospital of St Anthony, nor in cemeteries belonging to the religious bodies, nor in the many others that exist in Avignon. I must not be silent about the neighbouring parts, for all the gates at Marseille, with the exception of two small ones, are now closed, because four-fifths of the inhabitants are dead.

Clearly, the mortality was as high in France as it was in Italy.

I can give the same account of all the cities and towns in Provence. Already the sickness has crossed the Rhône, and ravaged many cities and villages as far as Toulouse, and it steadily increases in violence as it proceeds. There is such a fear of death that people do not dare to speak even with anyone whose relative has died, because it is frequently remarked that in a family where one dies nearly all the relations follow him, and this is a common belief among the people. The sick are now not served by their kindred, except as dogs would be; food is put near the bed for them to eat and drink, and then the healthy fly and leave the house. When a man dies, some rough countrymen, called *gavoti*, come to the house, and after receiving a sufficiently large reward, carry the corpse to the grave. Neither relatives nor friends go to the sick; the priests do not even hear their confessions nor give them the sacraments; but everyone who is still healthy looks after himself. It happens daily that some rich man dying is borne to the grave by these ruffians without lights, and without anyone to follow him, except these hired mourners. When a corpse is carried through the streets everyone goes into their houses. Nor do these said wretched *gavoti*, strong as they are, escape; since most of them become infected by this contagion after a time and die.

It seems that people sought scapegoats for the plague, because the canon says:

Some wretched men have been caught with a certain type of dust, and, whether justly or unjustly only God knows, they are accused of having poisoned the water, and men in fear do not drink the water from wells; for this crime many have been burnt and, daily, continue to be burnt.

Rough justice indeed for the innocent. He concludes with some commonsense advice:

I write this to you, my friends, that you may know the dangers in which we live. And if you desire to protect yourselves, the best advice is to eat and drink temperately, to avoid cold, not to commit excess of any kind, and above all, to converse little with others, at this time especially, except with the few whose breath is sweet. But it is best to remain at home until this epidemic has passed.

The plague raged on at Avignon through the long summer of 1348 and continued until winter. Bodies littered the streets and the burial grounds were full, so that Pope Clement VI was forced to consecrate the River Rhône and the corpses were thrown into it. The resulting putrefaction, decomposition and pollution can scarcely be imagined. Worse was to come. Many of the sick, considered certain to die, were buried alive.

Meanwhile, the plague had continued its reign of terror and had advanced northwards, arriving in Lyons early in the summer and in Paris soon afterwards. The chronicle of Guillamme de Nangis describes the epidemic of Paris:

> There was so great a mortality of people of both sexes, and of the young rather than the old, that they could hardly be buried. Further, they were ill for scarcely more than two or three days, and some often died suddenly, so that a man today in good health, was tomorrow carried as a corpse to the grave ... And the multitude of people who died in the years 1348 and 1349 was so great that nothing like it was ever heard, read of, or witnessed in past ages. And this same death and sickness often sprang from the imagination, or from the society and contagion of another, because a healthy man visiting one sick rarely escaped death. So that in many towns, small and great, priests retired through fear, leaving the administration of the sacraments to religious men who were bolder. Briefly, in many places, two did not remain alive out of every twenty [i.e. a staggering 90 per cent death rate]. So great was the mortality in the Hôtel-Dieu of Paris that for a long time more than fifty corpses were carried away in carts to be buried each day ... It lasted in France the greater part of 1348 and 1349, and afterwards houses in many towns, country places and cities remained empty and without inhabitants.

This chronicle reinforces the view that the scale of the disaster was unprecedented; nobody had ever seen anything like it before. Death quickly followed the appearance of the symptoms.

The Abbot of St Martin's at Tournay wrote of the ghost towns that were left after an epidemic had burnt itself out:

> It is impossible to credit the mortality throughout the whole country. Travellers, merchants, pilgrims and others who have passed through it describe how they have found cattle wandering without herdsmen in fields, town and land laid waste, houses empty, and few people to be found anywhere. So much so that in many towns, cities and villages, where

before there had been 20,000 people, scarcely 2,000 remain; and in many cities and country places, where there had been 1,500 people, hardly 100 are left. And in many different lands, fields are lying uncultivated.

He continued by saying that later ages would hardly be able to believe the horror of it.

The Black Death moved north-west from Paris to the coast, which it reached in August 1348. The winter again slowed the violence of the infection (was there a clue here?), but it returned to full and deadly virulence. At Rouen, an eye-witness calculated that 100 000 died – which, again, may be an overestimate – and the Duke of Normandy donated land for a new graveyard.

At La Graverie, 4 miles (6 kilometres) from Vire, 'the bodies of the dead decayed in putrefaction on the pallets where they had breathed their last'. A black flag flew above the church as it did in all the worst-affected villages of Normandy.

Spain succumbs

Meanwhile, trading vessels had ensured the spread of the disease throughout the Mediterranean. The mortality in the ports was so great that the bodies were thrown directly into the sea. The plague struck Cyprus with devastating ferocity. Confronted with this calamity, the Cypriots assembled all the Muslim slaves and prisoners and devoted one entire afternoon until sundown to massacring them, because of their fear that the Muslims would gain control of the island when so many Christians were dying and fleeing in panic.

The Black Death caused Pedro IV of Aragon considerable alarm when it reached Majorca in April 1348. He instructed the Government of the island to take steps to stop the further spread of the disease, but its leaders were powerless and the death toll was put at an incredible 15 000 in a single month. Eighty per cent of the island's population are said to have died and soon the Government was protesting that people were so weakened by the disease that they could no longer protect themselves from attacks by pirates and by the Bey of Tunis. Instead, however, the Governor of Majorca was instructed in June 1349 to send troops to the neighbouring island of Minorca, where the devastation was even worse, to assist in its defence against an enemy attack.

The plague invaded the Iberian peninsula through the Mediterranean ports of Barcelona and Valencia, where it arrived in May 1348. At first, through the autumn and winter, the epidemic spread only slowly, killing about 70 people a day. The disease spread southwards to the Arabs who were attacking Alfonso XI of Castile, causing consternation, and Philip Ziegler records in his book *The Black Death* that many of them were so desperate that they considered adopting Christianity as a form of preventive medicine. However, the disease was soon raging among the troops of Castile and 'When they learned that the pestilence had now reached Christian men their good intentions died and they returned to their vomit'.

The Castilian army survived intact at Gibraltar and then was struck by the plague in March 1350. The army officers suggested that King Alfonso leave his troops and seek safety in isolation, but he refused to desert his post and so died during the epidemic. He was the only ruling monarch to perish during the Black Death, although King Pedro lost his wife, youngest daughter and niece.

Law and order eventually broke down in Spain. Bands of armed brigands strayed over the countryside and an ordinance was published ordering severe punishment for anyone found looting the houses of plague victims.

Three deadly years

The Black Death moved relentlessly northwards through Europe like a giant wave. It took about eight months for an epidemic

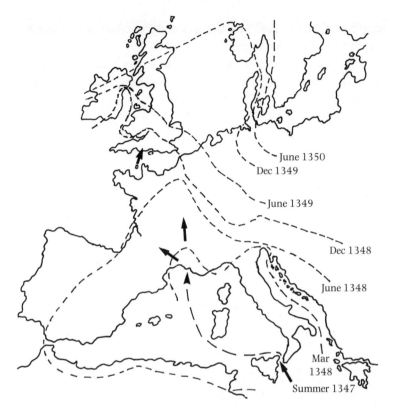

The wave-like spread of the Black Death northwards across Europe, 1347–50.

to clear each town after the initial strike and it never moved backwards. Its progress was most rapid in the early stages, from December 1347 to June 1348, during which time it spread through Italy and much of France, Spain and the Balkans. Crossing the Alps and Pyrenees, it continued its movement northwards, eventually reaching Sweden, Norway and the Baltic by December 1350.

Curiously, a few places escaped the disease completely and these included Milan, Liège, Nuremberg, a small area east of Calais, a very large area north of Vienna and a small area at the north-west end of the Pyrenees (although the disease was present over the rest of the mountain range).

There was panic throughout Europe as the plague advanced on a broad front, engulfing everything in its path. Nobody knew of any way to avoid it except to flee. To run away ahead of it must have seemed an obvious defensive strategy, but it brought little reward and most probably exacerbated the advance of the pandemic. Tragically, if everyone had stayed put the plague might have been confined to Italy and southern France and might have been eliminated.

It was then the turn of the Low Countries to suffer and, true to form, the Black Death caused its customary horror and devastation. Gilles Li Muisis wrote:

> It is almost impossible to credit the mortality throughout the whole country. Travellers, merchants, pilgrims and others who have passed through it declare that they have found cattle wandering without herdsmen in the fields, towns and waste-lands; that they have seen barns and wine-cellars standing wide open, houses empty and few people to be found anywhere ... And in many different areas, both lands and fields are lying uncultivated.

The Black Death reached Tournai in present-day Belgium in the summer of 1349 and the Bishop was one of the first to die. Then came a lull before the epidemic started raging.

> Everyday the bodies of the dead were borne to the churches, now five, now ten, now fifteen, and in the parish of St Brice sometimes twenty or thirty. In all parish churches the curates, parish clerks and sextons, to get their fees, rang morning, evening and night the passing bells, and by this the whole population of the city, men and women alike, began to be filled with fear.

The Town Council acted firmly to restore public confidence: bells were not to be rung at funerals, no mourning was to be worn and there were to be no gatherings in the houses of the dead. New graveyards were opened outside the city walls and all the dead, irrespective of their standing in the city, were buried there.

Thus the plague continued remorselessly northwards through Germany, bringing tragic loss of life on the same scale as before and often causing a breakdown in law and order and in civic responsibilities. The terrible toll of deaths included 2000 people in 72 days in Frankfurt-am-Main; over 50 per cent of the inhabitants of Hamburg; 6000 in Mainz and 11 000 in Munster. Some 12 000 perished in Erfurt and nearly 7000 in Bremen, perhaps 70 per cent of the population. Furthermore, it is said that 200 000 small country towns in Germany were cleared of all their inhabitants. The terror and horror of those faced with certain death are unimaginable.

The *Neuberg Chronicle* recorded in November 1348:

> Since this deadly pestilence raged everywhere, cities which hitherto had been populous became desolate. Their inhabitants were swept off in such numbers that those who were left closed their gates, and strenuously watched that no one should steal the property of those departed ... The pestilence came to Carinthia, and then took possession of Styria so completely that people there, rendered desperate, walked about as if mad.

The frighteningly infectious nature of the plague is again confirmed:

> Pestilential odours proceeded from so many sick, infecting those visiting and serving them, and it happened frequently that when one person in a house died, all, one after the other, were carried off ... As a consequence of this overwhelming visitation cattle were left to wander in the fields without guardians, for no one thought of the future; and wolves came down from the mountains to attack them. Property, both movable and immovable, that sick people leave in their will, is carefully avoided by all, as if it were certainly infected.

The Black Death struck Vienna in spring 1349 and every day during the long summer it was said 500–600 victims died. Nearly 1000 people died in one dreadful day. Probably about half the population perished in all.

The corpses were buried, as usual, outside the city in huge pits, each of which contained 6000 bodies. Because of the odour and horror inspired by the dead bodies, burials in the church cemeteries were not allowed; as soon as life was extinct, the corpses were carried outside the city to a common burial place called 'God's acre'. There the deep and broad pits were quickly filled to the top with the dead.

The lands of the Vikings

Tradition has it that the plague was carried to Norway in the summer of 1349 on a boat from London, but it is more likely that it made the short jump across the strait from Copenhagen. The disease then spread quickly 'over all Norway' and is reported to have reached Archangel, a port on the White Sea in north-west Russia just south of the Arctic Circle. Incredibly, two-thirds of the population of Norway are said to have died; many villages were completely depopulated and disappeared.

Philip Ziegler tells in *The Black Death* the old story that when the pestilence reached Bergen several of the leading families fled to Tusededal (Jostedal) in the mountains and there they started to build a town where they hoped they would be safe. It was not to be; probably one of their number was already infected. An epidemic broke out and the entire community died with the exception of one girl. She was discovered years later still living in the area, but running wild and shunning human company. However, she eventually returned to society and married happily. All the land that had been appropriated by the community became her property and her family were among the large landowners in the neighbourhood for several centuries.

When we uncovered this story, we were puzzled by the question of why this girl had escaped infection. She must have been in close contact with her family and the other members of the community as they died one by one and probably had to bury some of them. We had seen this before and wondered if it was another example of a person who was resistant to the disease.

The plague probably arrived in Sweden in 1350 by crossing from Denmark, and also by a voyage across the Baltic from the port of Gdansk, where an epidemic was raging. King Magnus II of Sweden announced that God had struck the world with a great punishment of sudden death and that most people to the west of his country were dead: 'It is now ravaging Norway and Holland and is approaching our Kingdom of Sweden'. He commanded his people to abstain on Fridays from food except bread and water, to walk to their churches with bare feet and to process around the cemeteries carrying holy relics to appease the divine anger. Again, it was no use. When the epidemic reached the capital, the streets were once more soon littered with the bodies of the dead and Hacon and Knut, the king's brothers, were among the victims.

The Black Death had moved across continental Europe in less than three terrible years. Unfortunately for these hapless men and women, this was to be its home and favourite hunting ground for the next three centuries. Nevertheless, there were still more territories for it to conquer.

2

The Black Death Crosses the Channel

The English Channel has saved Britain from invasion throughout history, from the Spanish Armada to the Second World War. Rabies is endemic on the continental mainland but, even with the Channel Tunnel, it has still not spread to England. Nevertheless, it was no barrier to the Black Death.

In 1348, the people of England lived in a feudalistic society whereby the peasants worked the land provided by their overlords. The villages consisted of single-storey, one-room, thatched, daub-and-wattle huts. They would be damp, cold and dark because there were no chimneys or windows, and the floor would be strewn with straw and dirt. Furniture consisted of a trestle table, a couple of three-legged stools, and beds of straw or leaves.

People's diet consisted mainly of porridge, cheese, black bread and a few home-grown vegetables. However, the summer that year had been abnormally wet, and oats, wheat, hay and straw lay rotting in the fields because of the almost continuous rain. Fears abounded that the harvest would be poor and that a hungry winter awaited them. Little did they know that a far worse enemy was set to appear.

The plague probably arrived in Britain at Melcombe Regis (now called Weymouth), in Dorset, then an important town and port on the south coast – although Bristol and Southampton have also been suggested as the entry point. It may have come from the Channel Islands, where it was already rampant and the fishermen were unable to pay their taxes because they were all stricken. Its arrival has been variously dated between June and early August 1348.

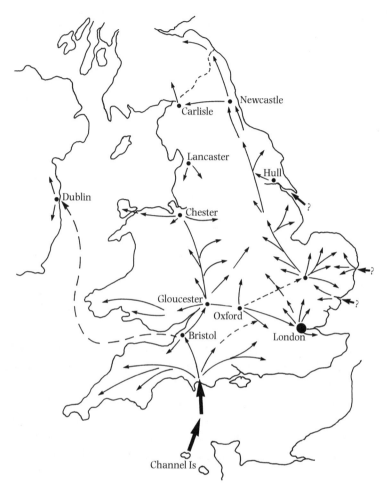

Movement of the Black Death through England following its arrival at Weymouth in Dorset in 1348.

Although there are few contemporary accounts of the plague in Britain (unlike continental Europe), the prevailing sense of desolation and despair comes through in this chronicle of passing events.

And I, friar John Clyn, of the Order of Friars Minor, and of the convent of Kilkenny, wrote in this book those notable things which happened in my time, which I saw with my eyes, or which I learned from persons worthy of credit. And lest things worthy of remembrance should perish with time, and fall away from the memory of those who are to come after us, I, seeing these many evils, and the whole world lying, as it were, in the wicked one, among the dead waiting for death till it come – as I have truly heard and examined, so have I reduced these things to writing; and lest the writing should perish with the writer, and the work fail together with the workman, I leave parchment for continuing the work, if haply any man survive, and any of the race of Adam escape this pestilence and continue the work which I have begun.

The general direction of the spread of the Black Death can be determined from ecclesiastical records describing how the bishops in each diocese hastily had to appoint new clergy to replace those who had died. It first ravaged Dorset and then put out spearheads westwards throughout Devon and Cornwall, causing the usual high mortality, and eastwards to Southampton and the southern counties. But the thrust northwards was the killer punch. It moved through Somerset (where most towns were infected) to the port of Bristol, where the 'people died as if the whole strength of the city were seized by sudden death'. 'Here in Bristol in 1348 the plague raged to such a degree that the living were scarcely able to bury the dead.' The epidemic then spread onwards to Gloucester where the inhabitants had tried to isolate themselves, but to no avail: the death toll has been estimated at a staggering 90 per cent.

This devastating prong of the attack continued into Oxfordshire and thence via the Thames Valley to London, which it reached by November 1348. In the following January the King prorogued Parliament on the grounds that the 'deadly pestilence had suddenly broken out in the said place and neighbourhood, and had daily increased in severity, so that grave fears were entertained for the safety of those coming there at the time'.

Robert of Avesbury reported that more than 200 corpses were buried almost every day in one cemetery in London, where there was a memorial cross recording that more than 50 000 bodies were interred therein, although this was probably another exaggeration after the event. And so the terrible mortality continued. The existing cemeteries were soon full and new burial grounds were opened and consecrated at Smithfield and Spittle-Croft.

Fearful of being infected themselves, carters refused to carry food supplies to London from the surrounding countryside and consequently many people left the city in search of food – taking the disease with them. William Dene, a monk living at Rochester in Kent, wrote when the plague arrived there:

A plague such as had never before been heard of ravaged England in this year ... Alas, for our sorrow! This mortality swept away so vast a multitude of both sexes that none could be found to carry the corpses to the grave. Men and women bore their offspring on their shoulders to the church and then cast them into a common pit. From these there proceeded so great a stench that hardly anyone dared to cross the cemeteries.

It was the all-too-familiar story of death, suffering and grief.

Historians disagree about the total number of people who died from the plague in London. Some have suggested a figure of 100 000, but a more reasonable estimate would probably be between 20 000 and 30 000 deaths, out of a population of 60 000 to 70 000, which would be in line with the death rates in other English cities.

The Black Death now spread northwards on two major fronts, to the eastern and western sides of England. The two fronts converged on central England, which suffered appalling loss of life.

The western front advanced into southern Wales. In Cardigan, so great was the mortality and the fear of infection that it proved almost impossible to find anyone to fill such offices as beadle, reeve (bailiff or overseer) or serjeant. Out of 104 rent-paying tenants, 97 died or fled before midsummer. The Black Death also moved up the Marches and thence into Snowdonia, eventually reaching the island of Anglesey. Meanwhile the eastern front, probably starting from Cambridge, ravaged East Anglia and further introductions through the ports on the east coast may have exacerbated the spread there. The plague also travelled up the Great North Road, reaching York, Durham and Newcastle. It probably crossed the Pennines by the Roman road alongside Hadrian's Wall and so reached Carlisle.

Sir William de Wakebridge had fought beside Edward III in the Hundred Years War with France and he inherited the Manor of Crich (known as Cardale in the television series *Peak Practice*) in Derbyshire. After the Black Death arrived, within three months he had lost his father, wife, three brothers, two sisters and a sister-in-law. Once the pestilence was gone, land values became very depressed and Sir William was able to pick up a number of bargains, which he used to endow two chantries at Crich Church. These were small chapels that were maintained for daily masses for the soul of the founder.

There is a story that a peasant living in County Durham lost all his family in the plague, and the poor man was seen for years wandering around the countryside looking for them.

Hitherto, the plague had advanced steadily into northern England via separate fronts along the trade routes, with a rate of spread that indicates that transmission was probably mostly by infected travellers on foot. We deduced from a study of the ecclesiastical records that once it had reached a town it would remain there for about nine months. This pattern then changed, however, and epidemics now began to appear unpredictably at widely separated places. It seems that there were two types of transmission: one slow and progressive, the other erratic and able to jump long distances. The latter type of spread was probably by an infected person travelling on horseback.

The plague may have reached Scotland from both Newcastle and Carlisle, but little information survives. The Scottish army may have brought the infection upon themselves:

> Thinking that God's terrible vengeance was wreaked upon the English, they joined forces in the forest of Selkirk and planned to invade the Kingdom of England. However, a cruel mortality intervened, and the Scots were suddenly struck by the cruelty of death. About five thousand quickly perished; and the remainder, both those that were sick and those that were well, decided to return home, but the English pursued them and killed a multitude of them.

The panic-stricken soldiers dispersed throughout Scotland, dying by the side of the road or carrying the infection with them to their homes.

John of Fordun, who was living during the Black Death, wrote:

> there was, in the kingdom of Scotland so great a pestilence and plague among men ... as from the beginning of the world even unto modern times, had never been heard of by man, nor is found in books, for the enlightenment of those who come after. For, to such a pitch did that plague wreak its cruel spite, that nearly a third of mankind were thereby made to pay the debt of nature. Moreover, by God's will, this evil led to a strange and unwonted kind of death, insomuch that the flesh of the sick was somehow puffed out and swollen, and they dragged out their earthly life for barely two days ... Men shrank from it so much that, through fear of contagion, sons, fleeing as from the face of leprosy or from an adder, durst not go and see their parents in the throes of death.

Androw of Wyntoun, a contemporary of John of Fordun, confimed that Scotland suffered badly:

> In Scotland, the first Pestilens
> Begouth, off sa great wyolens,
> That it was sayd, off lywand men
> The thyrd part it dystroyid then

Efftyr that in till Scotland
A yhere or more it was wedand
Before that tyme was nevyr sene
A pestilens in oure land sa kene:
Bathe men and barnys and women
It sparryed noucht for to kille them.

The infection was also carried into Ireland, probably on a boat from Bristol in the autumn of 1348. The historical evidence is inconclusive, but Dublin was hit hard and the plague moved from there inland and along the west coast.

John Clyn wrote:

in the months of September and October [1348], bishops, prelates, priests, friars, noblemen and others, women as well as men, came in great numbers from every part of Ireland to the pilgrimage centre of that Molyngis. So great were their numbers that on many days it was possible to see thousands of people flocking there; some through devotion but others (the majority indeed) through fear of the plague, which there was very prevalent. It began near Dublin at Howth and at Drogheda. These cities were almost entirely destroyed and emptied of inhabitants so that in Dublin alone, between the beginning of August and Christmas, 14,000 people died.

John Clyn's chronicle also describes the symptoms displayed by the victims: 'For many died from carbuncles, and boils, and botches which grew on the legs and under the arms; others from passion of the head, as if thrown into a frenzy; others by vomiting blood.' It was so contagious, he says, that those who touched the dead, or even the sick, were at once infected and died and 'both penitent and confessor were borne together to the same grave'. Such was the fear and horror of it that 'men scarce dared exercise the offices of pity, namely, to visit the sick and bury the dead'.

Another contemporary account describes the small black pustules and livid spots on the chest. These came to be considered the peculiar and distinctive mark of the plague and were known as God's tokens. Death invariably followed their appearance. The disease 'was swift in doing its work; one day people were in high health and the next day dead and buried'.

A common thread runs through all these accounts; it was certainly the same disease that literally spread everywhere.

A world in fear

The accounts quoted above by survivors of the Black Death may be colourful in places, but they speak clearly to us across the intervening centuries, conveying a vivid sense of the fear and panic that gripped Europe. People's horror on finding dreaded haemorrhagic spots or God's tokens on their chest can readily be imagined – this was their death certificate and a prelude to four or five days of agony, frenzy and delirium.

This plague was to ravage their entire known world. Little did they know it, but the pestilence was to stay with them for the next 300 years. It was a terrible, overwhelming strike at their civilization, where the Renaissance was getting under way, the like of which had never been seen before – or since. It was truly the greatest tragedy in the history of humanity and the world was going to change forever.

One thing is obvious: right from the word go everybody realized that it was an awful, infectious disease. They were well used to mysterious and fatal illnesses, but they had never seen anything like this before. They immediately took steps to protect themselves: they fled; individuals and whole towns tried to isolate themselves; and they avoided contact with anyone suspected of infection.

We read repeatedly that parents even left their dying children untended, something that we find almost unimaginable. But we have never come face to face with anything like the full horror of the Black Death, an apparently wildly infectious disease that struck from out of nowhere. There was no cure, no way of alleviating the agony, no clean hospitals in which to die peacefully, no painkillers, absolutely nothing anyone could do. They were fearful and completely helpless and doomed if they came into contact with an infected person.

There were also many tales of heroism and sacrifice, of people standing at their posts and not fleeing, of doctors and nuns tending the sick and dying. Remarkably, with a few notable exceptions, there were no complete breakdowns in law and order in England.

The journal *New Scientist* suggested in February 2002:

> AIDS is set to put the Black Death in the shade as the worst pandemic in history. In the fourteenth century, the Black Death swept through Europe and Asia, killing about 40 million people. Now, nearly 700 years later, history is repeating itself. HIV will have claimed 65 million lives by the end of the decade. Although malaria and tuberculosis currently affect more people than HIV, they have less of a social and economic impact than AIDS.

This underplays the impact of the Black Death. We have been aware of AIDS for 20 years, during which time it has slowly spread across the world. A total death toll after this time of 40 million is only a small fraction of the global population today, which is counted in billions. Furthermore, thanks to modern science and medicine, HIV/AIDS is completely understood and it can be tested for in blood samples. There is no panic and no mystery about this disease. We know that it is spread by unprotected sexual intercourse, and AIDS could have been stopped in its tracks by an informed change in social behaviour.

In contrast, in a single strike the Black Death killed about half the population of Europe and it struck again and again for the next 300 years. People were completely powerless against it.

Because the devastation of the Black Death was outside their comprehension, people accepted unquestioningly the doctrine of the Pope and the Church that the visitation was God's punishment for their manifold sins, as we saw at Penrith. This unhelpful doctrine prevailed for the next 300 years and beyond. Presenting the Pope's message for Lent in February 2002, Archbishop Paul Cordes, the head of the Vatican's agency for humanitarian aid, maintained that there was scriptural authority for the idea that those who contract illnesses do so because they have sinned. He asserted that illness is the result of sin and that people have a natural desire to be healthy and good-looking.

What of the survivors of the Black Death?

After they were sure that the plague had left their town – probably about eight months after it had arrived – the survivors must have breathed a sigh of relief and looked out on a different world. Perhaps half or three-quarters of the population of their town had perished and, so far as they could see, the same story was true for everywhere else. There was an endless series of ghost towns where people were deeply grieving but, at the same time, they were trying to pick up the pieces and start their lives again.

The old order was gone and there was much work to do. First people had to find food, because agriculture had been largely disregarded during their ordeal. Fields were unploughed or not sown and there would be little to harvest that year. There were no reapers for hire and what little produce there was rotted in the fields. Animal husbandry had been neglected and many beasts had strayed or been lost.

Next, the appalling mess had to be cleared. Burial of the corpses, some still rotting in their houses or in the fields, had to continue. Were these bodies still infectious? Could the disease be caught from their clothes or from the houses in which they had died? It was no use hoping for help from outside – everyone was in the same boat, and it would be a long time before anyone in authority could begin to sort things out.

Remarkably, after nearly 50 per cent of its population had been so summarily eliminated, Europe made a speedy recovery. People crept in from the countryside where the plague had not touched, took up the vacant spaces and workable land and occupied the empty houses. Soon everything was back to normal – superficially.

What can we deduce about the nature of this calamitous epidemic?

What clues can we enter in our detective's notebook? There is relatively little objective and quantitative information that can be accepted without question, but some conclusions about this first strike are clear. The Black Death moved from the most southerly point of Europe northwards to the freezing, inhospitable Arctic Circle, some 2200 miles (3500 kilometres), in less than three years – a prodigious rate at a time when the means of transport were extremely limited. It crossed the sea to the North African coastlands, to England and Ireland and to offshore islands. It remained active in England through the winter, although, from our studies of the ecclesiastical records, it appeared to spread more slowly at that time of year.

The plague was unstoppable. During its progress it killed nearly half the population of the known western world, leaving behind a completely devastated European civilization. It never moved backwards, attacking again the towns that it had already afflicted, although a certain amount of infill work continued behind the front lines. Instead, it marched remorselessly forwards and northwards.

It was the same story everywhere. Each epidemic in every town ran an identical course and understandably brought panic and terror among the citizens. This hideous disease was completely outside people's experience – but they recognized at once that they caught it when they came in contact with an infected person.

We have recorded a number of reports of people dying or stricken almost immediately they came upon an infected person.

This does not square with any known infectious disease, nor with what we saw at the beginning of the outbreak at Penrith, where 22 days elapsed after the burial of Andrew Hogson and the death of the next victim. At this stage in our investigation, we thought it best to discount these stories provisionally and to assume that these victims were infected some time previously and happened to be struck down by chance when they were in contact with a dying person.

Small villages and large towns were equally affected, and in this respect this first epidemic was to differ sharply from later outbreaks. Dr Charles Creighton, a distinguished expert on infectious diseases, wrote in 1894,

> But plague henceforth is seldom universal; it becomes more and more a disease of the towns, and when it does occur in the country, it is for the most part at some few limited spots.

There is no doubting the horrific infectivity and lethality of the disease during its remorseless spread, but there is no evidence to answer the question of why a few people, who were obviously exposed to infected persons, survived. Were they resistant or did they recover? This was just one of the strands of investigation we were going to follow.

One essential clue came from studying the ecclesiastical records of replacements for the clergy who had died during the plague in England. They are only a rough-and-ready measure, but highly significant: in all 11 of the dioceses analysed, the epidemic persisted in each locality for a remarkable eight or nine months. No wonder it was such an effective killer.

When the plague apparently disappeared forever in the seventeenth century, it left many unanswered questions about the most cataclysmic event in our history, which had dominated the lives of our ancestors from the fourteenth to the seventeenth centuries. What exactly was this mysterious infectious disease? Where had it come from – and why did it disappear in 1670 when it was apparently at the height of its power, remorselessly dominating Europe?

3

After the Black Death: The French Connection

Once the Black Death had burned itself out on the fringes of the Arctic Circle and apparently disappeared, it might have been expected that it was gone forever. Sadly, this was not the case. In the following year, 1351, plagues were reported in at least 11 places (including Venice) that were spread throughout the landmass of continental Europe. Indeed, when we examined the records, we found that it was present somewhere in France – even if only in a few scattered towns – every year for the next 300 years. All this was a complete mystery to us because, by all the rules of infectious diseases, when the Black Death was finished it should have disappeared. We felt that hidden here was the next vital clue that would explain why the plague was so horribly successful in dominating Europe for three centuries. We decided to investigate thoroughly its behaviour in France in our search for answers.

A background of warfare

France suffered less severely during the period from 1450 to 1520, which saw the end of the Hundred Years War, a rise in prosperity and the general reconstruction of places that had been ravaged by battles, food shortages and natural disasters. The worst widespread epidemics of plague in this period occurred in 1464, 1478–84, 1494, 1502 and 1514–19.

However, the sinister effects of the plagues were far-reaching and a common belief arose, because they seemed to appear from nowhere, that they were conjured up by sorcerers and sorceresses. Suspected individuals were put on trial and many men and women were put to death, allegedly for practising the black arts. A plague in Paris in 1466 was particularly ferocious – 40 000 people died – and, as usual, the inhabitants sought scapegoats, including sorcerers, Jews and lepers, or astronomical phenomena. Exceptionally high August temperatures were also blamed. The citizens used religious supplication and made a great and solemn procession through the streets, but it was no use – the epidemic was still in its rising phase and increased in violence, spreading to the outskirts of the city.

France lagged behind Italy in the introduction of preventive measures. The authorities in the town of Brignoles in Provence were the first to appreciate in 1451 the critical role of travellers. And it was a major step forward in controlling the spread of the disease when people were denied entry if they had come from a town that had suffered previously. Subsequently, the authorities of Brignoles also expelled those whom they suspected were sick of the plague and who must have died a lonely death. Later, in addition to inspecting travellers on arrival, the authorities also required proof that all the towns through which they had travelled were completely free of plague. They had obviously identified the main danger: *plague was brought into a town by a long-distance traveller.* We remember that the plague was brought to Penrith by Andrew Hogson, a stranger who came 'from a place at a considerable distance'.

Further public-health measures were introduced progressively in France through the fifteenth century. The sale of the furniture and clothes of victims was prohibited and there were attempts to disinfect houses in which someone had died of plague. Surgeons and hiring men were recruited; they were called crows because they wore masks shaped like the beak of a bird and were clothed in special black cloaks that gave them an evil appearance. This was sound practice and was the first form of protective clothing; it confirms that people at that time believed that the plague could be spread from one person to another. The job of the crows was to inspect, carry and bury the dead. These surgeons were considered to be infectious and their strange clothing warned off others.

Hospitals were set up for the isolation of victims, the first being at Bourg-en-Bresse in 1472. These hospitals later became known as pest houses and were simply waiting rooms for death, with a high turnover. Special bureaux were established in many towns to enforce the anti-plague regulations.

Funerals often had to be conducted at night or were prohibited completely, in order to reduce public panic. Later the poor were banished and beggars and vagabonds were ordered to leave the town, under pain of whipping. Rough justice again. Eventually, France followed the precepts of the medical authorities in Italy and a 40-day quarantine was introduced.

With the benefit of hindsight, we can see that not all of these measures would have been equally effective, but it is clear that even in the fifteenth century, people understood the rudiments of infectious diseases, distinguishing them from the prevailing blind superstitions. They tried hard to combat the terrible pestilence and sensible public-health measures were introduced very early on in the age of plagues.

The unstable sixteenth century

Between 1520 and 1600, against a background of food shortages, famines, flooding, peasant uprisings and religious wars, there were increasingly frequent and virulent outbreaks of plague in France. The health bureaux often hired armed men to enforce regulations and to maintain civic order. The appearance of the disease in a town always caused social unrest and angry crowds attacked travellers, sorcerers and lepers, as well as pillaging houses. Terrible punishments, even death, were meted out to those who disobeyed the rules.

Because of its central position in Europe and its early adherence to the principles of the Protestant Reformation, Geneva had become, at the beginning of the sixteenth century, a refuge for the persecuted and a starting point for missionaries. It was crowded with immigrants and intending emigrants and was a focus for the plague. The Government of the Genevese was aware of this state of affairs and took some precautionary measures accordingly. It had established a pest house early on, with male and female nurses. Plague attendants or *cureurs* were employed as the officially appointed removers of the sick and dead and the notifiers of new cases of the illness. Plunder and petty blackmail probably came naturally to them, but in 1530 the sober Genevese citizens accused some of these attendants of deliberately spreading the plague when they were conducting their business. One of those arrested confessed under torture, and two were then tortured with red-hot pincers before being beheaded. Don Dufour, a priest, was unfrocked, handed over to the secular arm and executed. Two women had their hands cut off in front of the houses of their supposed victims, and then shared the fate of the men.

We discovered the following historical note in the *British Medical Journal* of 1869. During the early part of 1563, Havre, a port on the north French coast, was occupied by English troops under Lord Warwick. It was under siege and the troops, 7000 strong, were closely packed together, ideal conditions for the spread of an infectious disease. On 7th June, Warwick reported that a strange disease had broken out and that nine men had suddenly died. By the 27th, the men were dying at the rate of 60 a day and those who fell ill rarely recovered. By the 29th, 500 had died. The disease principally attacked the common soldiers; the officers for the most part escaped. The physicians died. The troops were not only crowded but suffered much privation: they could not obtain fresh water, were restricted to wine and cider and they had neither fresh vegetables nor meat.

When June ended, out of his 7000 men Lord Warwick had only 3000 who were fit for duty. Bodies were unburied and lay floating in the harbour. Fresh troops were sent out, but these men also rapidly fell victim to the disease.

By 11th July, only 1500 men remained and Warwick reported that, in 10 days more at the present death rate, he would have no more than 300 alive. By special permission of Queen Elizabeth, he surrendered Havre to the French on 29th July. Afterwards Lord Clinton, Admiral of the English Fleet, said that 'the plague of deadly infection had done for them that which all the force of France could never have done'.

The English troops who remained alive returned home. When they landed in England, Elizabeth issued a proclamation, exhorting all people to receive them with honour. But the soldiers, returning to their homes, spread the infection throughout England and both towns and villages suffered.

The eruption on the skin, which was usual with the plague, does not seem to have attended this visitation of it. The first symptom was violent fever, burning heat, alternating with fits of shivering. The mouth then becomes dry; the tongue parches; with a pricking sensation in the breast and loins. Headache followed, and languor, with a desire for sleep; and, after sleep, came generally death.

To prevent the spread of the contagion, the houses, staircases and streets were cleaned thoroughly; windows were set wide open and hung with fresh green boughs of oak or willow; the floors were strewn with sorrel, lettuce, roses and oak leaves, and frequently sprinkled with spring water or with vinegar and rosewater. From cellar to garret, six hours a day, houses were fumigated with sandalwood and musk, aloes, amber and cinnamon. In the poorest cottages, there were fires of rosemary and bay. Yet no remedy was of any use.

Lyons was a wealthy city with several major industries, including silk weaving and printing, and had a population of 60 000. It was situated at a crossroads on the international trade routes and had four annual trade fairs; it suffered regularly from epidemics brought in by travellers and traders. The one of 1564 was particularly deadly and, within two months, the town was almost paralysed and a third of the houses were closed. Even the few victims who recovered sometimes died of hunger afterwards. Corpses piled up in the streets: there was nowhere to bury them and not enough money to pay the gravediggers. The bodies were simply thrown into the River Rhône and, as a consequence, the fishing industry had to be closed.

By the summer of 1564, Provence and Languedoc had been infected and also Nîmes by mid-July. Autumn brought a lull, although local outbreaks were reported as late as mid-December until, finally, a severe winter brought their suffering to an end. This is an important clue because it shows that the plague was sensitive to winter temperatures, even in southern France. We discovered that epidemics could continue in very cold weather but transmission of the disease was much more difficult under these conditions. Infection was probably impossible out-of-doors.

The peak of the epidemics

The French suffered most grievously during the period 1622 to 1646, in contrast with the situation in England where the most serious epidemics occurred later, between 1620 and 1666. The misery in France was compounded by peasant revolts, pillaging by soldiers and virulent occurrences of other diseases. More and more cemeteries had to be opened but, even so, the dead often had to be buried in gardens or other makeshift sites. The financial costs of an epidemic were enormous: care for the sick; salaries for doctors, guards and police; burials; food; medicines and the construction of pest houses. All had to be paid for by taxes and borrowing.

Anti-plague regulations and measures were by now properly established and the poor were more generously treated. In 1636,

Bourg-en-Bresse paid young boys and girls to be shut up in newly fumigated houses for 40 days, the standard quarantine period, to test the efficacy of the disinfections – an early example of the experimental testing of public-health measures.

Lyons was struck again in the summer of 1628 and passing soldiers were accused of having carried the pestilence with them 'as their baggage', probably because one of the first reported deaths was of a soldier lodging in a nearby village. Again, it seems that an infected person travelling from afar brought the plague into the community. The usual regulations were brought into force: guards were posted at the city gates, health certificates were required from anyone seeking entry to the city and, again, a 40-day quarantine was imposed. An isolation pest house was prepared into which 4000 dying were crowded at any one time. Turnover was quick. But many victims had to build themselves small huts and remain in them until they died and others were forced to shelter from the wind behind piles of corpses, awaiting their own deaths – a macabre picture of an awful and agonizing end to life. The town essentially became a vast hospital: the streets and houses were strewn with corpses that were sometimes buried hastily in gardens and cellars, and monks and nuns had to climb over corpses lying on floors and staircases to bring succour to those who were still breathing.

The death toll abated towards the end of December, but rose again with great force early in the following year, before gradually diminishing through the spring and summer. Staggeringly, an estimated 35 000 people died in Lyons during the 12-month epidemic.

Trade: the lifeblood of the plague

Some towns in France were attacked only rarely, whereas others repeatedly experienced plague epidemics. In the worst hit, generation after generation lived in almost continual fear for over 100 years. However, the pattern did change gradually and, whereas during the second half of the fourteenth century Strasbourg and Paris were the towns most often struck, in the fifteenth century this dubious honour went to Bourg-en-Bresse, and by the seventeenth century Luxembourg was recording the greatest number of outbreaks. What caused this changing preference of the plague for certain places?

The Black Death arrived at Strasbourg in 1349, but thereafter the city was free of the disease until 1358, after which it was repeatedly attacked for the next 150 years. Strasbourg was a prosperous city, its wealth stemming from the activity of its merchant class and also from its situation at the centre of numerous waterway and road communications. These factors were also its undoing, because it received regular visits from infected traders and travellers.

Bourg-en-Bresse was the gateway to Geneva and to one of the Alpine passes. It lies some 38 miles (60 kilometres) north-east of Lyons, on the western edge of the Jura mountains, close to the Rhône, Saône and Ain rivers. It was on the trade route connecting Troyes, Lyons and Marseille, and all of these towns were regularly visited by the disease.

Luxembourg was strategically placed on the borders of what are now Belgium, France and Germany. It was once a Roman crossroads and lay at the centre of a network of trade routes linking the Holy Roman Empire and France. It suffered an incredible 20 epidemics in 50 years.

It is apparent from these examples that the pestilence was carried around France each year by infected people travelling along the main long-distance trade routes, often using horse or barge. Once established in one of these major trade centres, the plague could then make the jump to nearby towns by local traffic.

After the progressive, wave-like spread of the Black Death in 1347–50, the pattern changed completely and plague became established in its home and base in France. It was never present everywhere but rather grumbled along, with an outburst in a few widely scattered but important places every year.

The major trade routes in Europe during the Middle Ages. Along these came infected travellers bringing the plague to the important centres of commerce.

As the centuries went by, the plague seemed to become more virulent and, as transport steadily improved and national and international trade grew, it became more widespread. The populations of towns and cities steadily increased, in both number and density, making it easier for the establishment of an epidemic; consequently, the number of potential victims also rose.

Deadly persistence of plague

When the Black Death finally burnt itself out along its northern limits in the high latitudes of Europe, it might have disappeared forever. Had it done so, Europe would probably have soon recovered and the visitation would have been just a very bad dream. But somehow, somewhere, probably in the warmer climate of southern rural France, the plague hung on grimly. It must have continued at a low level in a handful of pockets in villages, with probably, on average, each victim infecting only one more person. It was biding its time. If an infectious traveller reached a small community where the population had been rebuilt to an adequate level, a small epidemic could start. This was the disease's chance: it could spread out locally, many more infected travellers would set out, and then there was always the possibility of establishing new epidemics, but it could never return on the scale of the Black Death, which conquered everything in its path.

What clues about this mysterious disease have we uncovered? It is quite clear that these plagues, which continued for over 300 years after the Black Death, were all epidemics of the same disease. Indeed, the Black Death had never departed; the plague continued with an identical pattern and the victims' awful symptoms were exactly the same.

The epidemics struck most commonly in the larger towns, particularly if they were sited on the main national and international trading routes. Trade was thus the engine of the plagues.

The French slowly learnt that the disease was brought to their cities by an apparently healthy travelling stranger, often some sort of trader, who was in fact infected (Andrew Hogson was such a traveller to Penrith). Only gradually were appropriate border control measures introduced – and they were not completely effective.

France never had a plague-free period and the disease was continuously present, somewhere, for over 300 years. The country formed a stronghold for the plague and was an effective reservoir for the infection. All the epidemics in the rest of Europe originated from here.

Northern Europe, the Iberian and Italian peninsulas and England were completely different: these areas suffered from sporadic, explosive major outbreaks, which were brought by infected people arriving from France. They were of relatively short duration and afterwards the disease would disappear completely – until another infected person arrived from France.

4

Tentacles of the Plague

Many of us have seen or read *Romeo and Juliet*, but probably few realize that the play turns on the restriction of movement that was imposed and rigidly enforced during a plague epidemic in Italy.

> FRIAR JOHN: Going to find a bare-foot brother out
> One of our order, to associate me,
> Here in this city visiting the sick,
> And finding him, the searchers of the town,
> Suspecting that we both were in a house
> Where the infectious pestilence did reign,
> Seal'd up the doors, and would not let us forth;
> So that my speed to Mantua there was stay'd.
> (William Shakespeare, *Romeo and Juliet*, V.ii)

We note the reference to the officially appointed searchers. Friar John's confinement in the house in Verona is crucial to the story, because he could not deliver a message to Romeo at Mantua explaining that Juliet had not died but merely taken a sleeping potion. So Romeo returned to Verona and the well-known tragedy followed.

The play is about the war between two noble families, the Montagues and Capulets (Mercutio says 'A plague o' both your houses') and the tragic consequences for two young innocents. It could serve as a metaphor for the warring states of Italy at that time, when close cooperation in combating the common enemy, the plague, was an urgent necessity.

Although Italy possessed a common language, local patriotism was too strong to permit the growth of a national unity and it consisted of three main groupings of states:

- The City States of the North: Venice, Milan (Lombardy), Genoa and Florence (Tuscany), immensely wealthy and jealous of one another.

- The Papal States, 'The Patrimony of St Peter'. The Popes were eager to increase their temporal power in Italy.

- The Two Sicilies to the south, the most backward and poorest of the states, consisting of two very different regions, Naples and Sicily, which had long been ruled by the King of Aragon in Spain.

Hostilities between these wealthy Italian states tempted the powerful rulers of Spain and France to interfere in their quarrels and try to gain control. Charles VIII and Louis XII of France both mounted invasions that were initially successful, but they were expelled by a coalition of the Italian states with Spain. As a result, the Spanish kings retained control of Naples. It was against this background of strife that they attempted to combat invasions of the pestilence.

Pioneers of public health

The plagues began in Italy with the arrival of the Black Death in Sicily in 1347. It was, as we have seen, immediately recognized as an infectious disease, and rudimentary public-health procedures were quickly introduced there. The city states of northern Italy led the rest of Europe in adopting measures for dealing with an epidemic, instituting quarantine, pest houses and health boards and, by 1400, they had devised official 'licences to travel' in times of plague. Physicians in Italy took great pains when carefully examining cases to determine whether a true plague had broken out; they were anxious to distinguish between what they called 'major' and 'minor' pests. The 'major' pests were true plague, whereas the 'minor' pests were probably outbreaks of a less serious disease and the health authorities did not bother much about them.

Italy was continuously threatened by infected people arriving by sea – maritime trading with all their known world was the life-blood of the Italian sophisticated civilization. Maritime quarantine was instituted in 1377 in the Venetian colony of Ragusa, the original purpose being to prevent the importation of the disease into northern Italy rather than to isolate individuals who were already ill. At first it was set at 30 days, but it was soon realized that this was too short a period: people continued to succumb to the dreaded disease and the progress of an epidemic was only little affected. However, if there had been no deaths in a community for 40 days, the surviving inhabitants knew that the danger was past and that they were safe – at least until the next epidemic. So 40 days became the decreed duration of the quarantine period.

People in Genoa in 1652 who had been in close and direct contact with infected people or merchandise were put in complete isolation for 40 days or more, plus a further period of isolation described as convalescence. The port followed strict quarantine procedures:

- Vessels from England, coming directly without touching an infected or suspected place and with clean bills, were allowed entry after a few days; however, goods and merchandise were sent first to the pest house where they were purified for 20 days, and if they touched any infected places complete quarantine had to be observed.

- Vessels coming from ports uninfected, but under suspicion, were subject to quarantine for 30 or 35 days. Nevertheless, the goods were sent immediately to the pest house.

- If any deaths occurred or if anyone fell sick during the voyage or during the quarantine, this period was extended for 50 or

60 days according to the danger and circumstances; the people and the goods were sent to the pest houses.

- Vessels from the Levant were quarantined for 30, 35, or 40 days if they came with a clean bill; the goods at the pest houses were purified for the same length of time.

When an epidemic was subsiding in Florence, as in 1630, it was usual for the health authorities to declare a general quarantine in which as many people as possible were locked up in their homes for a period of 40 days, so reducing human contact to a minimum. This was supposed to terminate an epidemic more quickly.

Thus the 40-day quarantine period gradually became accepted everywhere during the age of plagues. This standard was reached empirically by the various health authorities in medieval Europe, who were operating without our modern understanding of infectious diseases, and was a remarkable piece of work completed six centuries ago. It demonstrates the common sense of those early physicians and was the most important breakthrough in the attempts to control this strange disease.

England was slower to introduce these measures, but a quarantine period of 40 days was eventually established in London and the provinces during the reign of Henry VIII. At one point this period was reduced, but a 40-day quarantine was speedily reintroduced by law when the shorter period proved to be completely ineffective. We believed this to be another important piece of evidence. The successful operation of a properly established quarantine confirms what everyone believed: this was a 'simple' infectious disease, directly transmitted from one person to another. Furthermore, 40 days is an exceptionally long period for quarantine. It began to look as though this disease could have been infectious for a very long time – quite the opposite of the many accounts suggesting that people succumbed shortly after being in contact with a victim who was showing symptoms.

The vigilant health authorities in northern Italy were on the look-out for the certain symptoms of a 'major' pest – violet and black spots and blotches, small red spots on the chest, pustules and swellings in the groin and armpit. Onset was marked by a high temperature, vomiting, diarrhoea, cloudy urine and burning thirst. The acute fever in some was accompanied by madness and delirium, 'so much so that many hurled themselves out of windows'.

Sporadic but catastrophic plague epidemics in Italy

The Alps formed a useful barrier to the north of Italy and, in the early years after the Black Death, most visitations of the pestilence came from overseas via the ports. However, later on, infected people came over the mountain passes.

A careful year-by-year study of the plagues in the Italian peninsula revealed that there were only about 11 major epidemics over this 300-year period, probably thanks to the splendid work of the health authorities. Nevertheless, when the pestilence did come, the mortality was horrendous. We had stumbled on another clue: the behaviour of the plague was quite different in France and Italy. In France it was continuously persistent, whereas in Italy it was sporadic and died out completely after each outbreak. We wondered what was the cause of this significant difference.

We studied the sequence of events in epidemics that erupted after Italy had been free of plague for at least two years, so that we could be sure that these outbreaks were the result of a fresh introduction.

For instance, plague erupted in 1456 after a four-year break in Sicily, central Italy and the northern city states. Were these separate introductions by sea via the ports of Naples, Palmero and Venice (as seems most likely) or did the plague spread along the length of the country? In 1457, it was reported in the heel of Italy and moved from Velletri to Rome but disappeared from Naples; it was present in Venice and also appeared in

Bologna in the north. Evidently, it moved freely over long distances.

Again, Italy had been largely plague free for eight years when the disease was reported in southern Sardinia in 1476. In 1477 it appeared in Venice and exploded into a full-blown epidemic in 1478; 30 000 perished. Sicily was also hit at the same time. The disease was now widespread in the north, probably having spread radially outwards from Venice to the west and south, and there were 40 000 deaths. In Milan 22 000 died; some of the dying were so feverishly delirious that they threw themselves out of windows – a characteristic symptom of plague. Some 200 died each day for the first four months in Brescia in Lombardy, with a total of 34 000 and a mortality rate of 90 per cent. Many priests and friars refused to aid the sick, instead encouraging religious processions that merely exacerbated the spread of the disease. Piles of dead bodies were gnawed by stray dogs, and grave-diggers were accused of robbing and even sexually molesting the corpses.

A terrible epidemic erupted in the northern states in 1629 and the disease may have come from Venice (where 46 000 of the 140 000 inhabitants died), but it is more likely that, once again, it moved over the Alps; at the time plague was widespread in France, Germany and Switzerland and was present in Geneva and Basel. German and French troops were said to have carried it to Mantua in eastern Lombardy, where France was waging war against Austria and Spain. Eventually, the plague claimed an incredible 280 000 lives. Again, it all started with the arrival of strangers from a long distance away.

The importance of the quarantine regulations is clearly shown in this epidemic. Strict, but unpopular, preventive measures were instituted when the plague reached Milan in October 1629, including the isolation of all who had come in contact with those who had been infected, and it was believed that this practice contained the outbreak. But these regulations were unwisely relaxed in March 1630 during a carnival in Milan and the plague then broke out again. At its peak, 3500 were reportedly dying each day.

Victims suffered a sudden and high fever and developed large, foul-smelling boils; they were sometimes delirious and a severe headache was the usual prelude to death. A large percentage of those who died were artisans and Capuchin friars, or people who performed much of the custodial work during the epidemic. Nobody broke the standard 40-day quarantine and those appointed by the Office of Public Health dedicated themselves to their tasks of fumigation, burning mattresses and clothes, scrubbing floors and carrying away the dead for burial.

The plague was brought to Trespiano, a small village a few miles north of Florence, in July 1630 by a man who, violating the *cordon sanitaire*, had been on a business trip to the infected city of Bologna. It was a deadly transgression. In August suspicious deaths were recorded in the neighbouring village of Tavola and in Florence itself. The Florentines were told that the catastrophic infection was the result of God's anger and they responded by attempting to correct their behaviour. Masses were celebrated in the streets and special fasts were instituted and so Florence was transformed into an extremely moral city – at least for the duration of the outbreak. The public health regulations were scrupulously obeyed and the Grand Duke made a daily round to ensure that everyone was receiving food and was well cared for.

The mortality rates in these major epidemics in Italy were often very high, probably on average 40 per cent but sometimes reaching over 60 per cent, as in Verona in 1630–31. Naples, with about 300 000 inhabitants, suffered 150 000 deaths in 1656 and the mortality in the surrounding countryside has been estimated at 66 per cent. These epidemics lasted for two to three years in the big cities before burning out, perhaps because of the warmer climate in winter and early spring, although there was still a fall in the number of cases during the colder months.

The Iberian peninsula: the killer arrives by sea

Spain is separated from the rest of Europe by the Pyrenees and the story of the plagues there is quite different from what we have seen for France. While the mortality was still awesome, epidemics were much less frequent in Spain and Portugal and each eventually died out completely, the next outbreak being the result of a new introduction from overseas. The Spanish authorities always tried to determine the source of an epidemic and they usually identified the culprits (as we have seen before) as soldiers or travellers recently arrived from abroad. On some occasions they suspected a cargo of imported goods – probably it was really the ship's crew and passengers who were infected.

After the Black Death, there were many severe localized outbreaks in Spain and Portugal but from 1506 to 1652 there were only four major, widespread epidemics. The disease, it would seem, was not generally introduced by people travelling around the eastern edge of the Pyrenees from Narbonne, but rather by those arriving by boat. The Achilles heel of Spain lay in the seaports; it was vulnerable because Lisbon in Portugal and Seville in Andalusia in southern Spain were major centres of international trade and were common points of entry.

Seville is for most people the quintessence of the Spain of romance and art, home of Don Juan and Figaro, birthplace of Velazquez and Murillo. On one side of the Parque de Maria Luisa is the cigarette factory where Carmen, the eponymous heroine of the opera, worked.

Seville has acted for 2000 years as a port at the navigable head of the Guadalquivir River, as the great market-place of the Guadalquivir Valley and as the crossroads between the north-east and west of the Iberian Peninsula. The year 1492 was important in the history of Spain: it marked the final expulsion of the Moors, the unification of Spain under a single crown and the discovery of America. Columbus, returning from his first voyage, sailed into Seville on Palm Sunday in 1493 in triumph, bringing exotic birds and plants, and Indians 'the like of which had never before been seen in Europe'. Sevillans claim that the explorer planned his third and fourth voyages from the city and his magnificent tomb can be seen in its cathedral.

For 200 years after Columbus, Seville became the gateway to the New World, the Mecca of European commerce and the principal city of Spain. Were its geographic location and economic importance as well as its climate (little temperature variation through the year, with long, dry and hot summers and warm winters) ideal conditions for the plague to flourish?

Plague arrived at Seville in 1506 and was accompanied by a severe drought and food shortage. It spread widely in Andalusia, where 100 000 are said to have perished, and made a crucial leap northwards to Madrid, a distance of 250 miles (400 kilometres); another example of long-range transmission.

This exact pattern, with entry via Seville, was initially repeated in a long-lasting epidemic that began in 1596. Simultaneously, the pestilence was brought to the port of Santander on Spain's northern coast when the ship *Rodamundo* docked, carrying goods from the French port of Dunkirk. The epidemic exploded in 1599 and spread widely throughout the peninsula. The small city of Segovia lost 12 000 inhabitants over six months and responded vigorously to the plague: temporary hospitals were established, the city gates were guarded to prevent the arrival of infectives, victims were rapidly buried and bedclothes were burnt. The total death toll in this prolonged outbreak is estimated to have been over half a million.

The Holy Roman Empire

Present-day Germany, Austria, Bohemia, the Netherlands and Switzerland formed the major part of the Holy Roman Empire during the age of the plagues. For 200 years after the Black Death, a small number of cases of plague were reported sporadically throughout the region and these must have been brought by infected people travelling out from France. The exception was the three years between 1462 and 1465, when terrible outbreaks that killed thousands struck *in widely distant cities* in Germany. Here was further evidence showing that the pestilence was popping up all over the place. As in the rest of Europe, the explanation lay in the expansion of trade and the movement of infected traders going about their business.

For 100 years after the Black Death, a cluster of towns in the north heads the list of places where plague was most frequently reported: Hamburg was a large port on the River Elbe and was already a thriving trading town by the thirteenth century; the port of Lübeck was the major outlet for the Baltic trade.

After 1450, the places recording frequent epidemics spread southwards along the major trade route of the Middle Ages: Lübeck–Hamburg–Magdeburg–Nuremberg–Augsburg. These places were repeatedly and violently struck, so that there was 'dreadful death everywhere in towns and the countryside'. Carnivals were cancelled and the hardship was exacerbated by widespread famine. It was the same old story: misery, terror and death. The wealthy classes quickly learnt to move out of town, but this was not an option for the bulk of the population.

The situation changed after 1450 and persisted until 1670. The plague continued to erupt widely and epidemics still occurred in the towns in the north, but the major foci, with the highest number of outbreaks, were now in the south-west, with Basel and Geneva heading the lists of the locations most affected, together with Augsburg and other towns on the trade route to Milan, Innsbruck and Venice.

As we have seen, Geneva occupied a central position in Europe and was an ideal focus for plague outbreaks. Augsburg was an imperial city, the seat of a bishop, the home of princely merchants and bankers and a great centre of commerce and trade of Northern Europe with the Mediterranean and the East.

Basel was a large river port situated on the Rhine and was Switzerland's only outlet to the sea and the terminus of the Rhine navigation; for many centuries the Mittlere Brücke in Basel was the only bridge on the Rhine. The city was a busy trade centre. Basel suffered from a 15-month epidemic in 1610–11 when, out of a population of some 15 000 citizens, about 6000 contracted the disease and approximately 3600 died. Is this evidence that, as the decades passed, more people recovered from an infection of the plague?

The island of snowfields and glaciers

We were accustomed by now to the plague hopping across the Mediterranean and the English Channel, but it came as a great surprise to learn that Iceland suffered from two severe epidemics at the beginning and end of the fifteenth century. The story of these two devastating plagues in an isolated community has been told in detail and it provides the most convincing and important evidence so far concerning the nature of this disease.

The voyage from Scotland, where the boats with the infectious crew originated, would have been 1000 miles (1660 kilometres). Given the primitive boats available this journey must have taken quite a long time – perhaps a fortnight or more with normal winds.

These two plagues in Iceland have been rigorously researched and it is certain that the same disease that affected mainland Europe was responsible.

Since Iceland has few natural resources, it had relied heavily on Norway for a wide variety of imported goods. But when some 40 per cent of Norway's population died in the Black Death, its foreign trade ceased almost completely and Iceland's supply line was cut off. Volcanic eruptions, earthquakes and famines added to the woes of the Icelanders in the second half of the fourteenth century. Almost everyone lived on individual farms; there were hardly any villages and certainly no towns.

Most of what we know about the first epidemic, which struck in September 1402, is contained in the so-called *New Annal*, an ancient manuscript. The boat that brought the plague almost certainly arrived in the harbour at Hvalfjörður in the south-western part of the island and by Christmas the disease had reached the Bishop's See at Skálholt in the south and Skagafjörður in the north. Therefore it spread 200 miles (320 kilometres) in 16 weeks – a remarkably quick rate of movement in difficult circumstances. The *New Annal* calls 1403 the year of the great mortality and the epidemic did not begin to recede until Easter 1404. It is clear that even the exceptionally cold weather of an Icelandic winter did not halt its progress; the infection must have been spread inside the snug farmsteads.

The plague reached practically the whole of Iceland and the mortality was terrible, with 60–70 per cent of the population dying. The island's people, structure and economy were devastated and the long-term effects were far-reaching. Whole families were wiped out and the population did not recover for another 500 years. The traditional patterns of inheritance also changed. Farmland became concentrated in the hands of a few wealthy owners, the most important of which was the Catholic Church, to which many people had donated their property in the hope of staving off death from the plague.

In the early decades of the fifteenth century, English and German merchants began regular visits to Iceland, sometimes with dozens of boats each year. They brought grain, timber, sugar and other products much needed by the islanders. It is probably via this route that the second great Icelandic plague came in 1494, arriving in the south-west or south of the island. Contemporary documents confirm that the disease was active in the western and north-western areas during the winter of 1494–95. A well-known clergyman, Gottskálk Jónsson, wrote in the year 1495, 'Great disease and plague all over the country, except in Vestfirðir [a large peninsula], so that for the most part communes were devastated'.

Jón Egilsson, the author of *Bishops' Annals* gives a moving picture of the mortality:

> In this plague the mortality was so great, that no-one remembered or had heard of anything like it, because many farms were devastated, and on most farms only three or two survived, sometimes children, and some of them yearlings, and some sucking their dead mothers. Of these I saw one, who was called Tungufell's-Manga ... Where there had been nine children, two or three were left alive.

Probably 30–50 per cent of the population perished in the second plague.

We can see that this formidable disease could survive a long voyage and then strike with devastating ferocity in an island of snowfields and glaciers on the edge of the Arctic Circle. It survived and even flourished through an arctic winter when the average temperature in inland localities in northern Iceland was −3 °C. These conditions were very different from those enjoyed by the citizens of Seville, Sicily and the Mediterranean coastlands. Furthermore, the Icelanders were not concentrated in towns or cities but, in the main, lived in isolated farmsteads, which must have exacerbated the difficulties of spreading the infection. Evidently, this disease was very versatile.

While investigating these Icelandic plagues, we came across a remarkable piece of evidence that we shall return to later. One of the current theories of the Black Death is that the infection was carried by rats and fleas. It has been established with complete certainly that no species of rat existed in Iceland at the time of these plagues. Nor were rat fleas present in its cold and inhospitable terrain. This was a valuable clue that we filed away for future reference.

The big picture in Europe

Everything we learnt about the Black Death is confirmed by the study of the plague in the huge landmass of Europe over the following three centuries. There was always the same awesome ferocity and mortality; the victims displayed exactly the same symptoms and distress in their last hours; its spread was particularly effective in households and in crowded conditions; again and again we see that it was directly infectious, person to person; the response in each town was for the wealthy to flee and for civil unrest to break out among those who stayed behind; mass mortality invariably led to problems with disposal of the corpses. The disease was instantly recognized and it appears that the infectious agent remained remarkably stable throughout the 300 years of its reign of terror. In this respect it was unlike the influenza virus, which can mutate to give a new strain every year.

However, we have detected some subtle changes as the years slowly went by. After all, 300 years is a long time in human terms – about 12 generations. In the fourteenth century, the Black Death struck a population that had never experienced the disease before and it advanced at walking pace as an engulfing and deadly wave. In the years thereafter, the major epidemics spread sporadically, jumping from one focus to another. Transport and trade improved progressively and these greatly contributed to the wide spread of the epidemics.

In spite of the plague acting as a very effective culling agent, the population of Europe grew steadily, allowing the effective virulence apparently to increase. The disease killed more people simply because there were more potential victims. Outbreaks on the European continent became increasingly frequent over the centuries, culminating in the last terrible outbreak, which began in France and lasted from 1630 to 1637; thereafter the frequency of the epidemics there declined sharply.

While the plague was spread by travellers more and more widely across the continental landmass, was England safe in its island fortress?

5

England under Siege

Every plague epidemic in England was brought, perforce, by boats carrying infected seamen, traders and travellers. They came most frequently across the English Channel and the North Sea, although sometimes the disease was shuttled back and forth between Chester and Ireland. Consequently, the ports that were most commonly stricken were London and those of East Anglia, although Newcastle, York and Hull regularly received visitations. Once established in a port, the plague could travel outwards, spreading via the Thames or the river systems of East Anglia or by travellers on foot or horseback. In this way, the infection could be carried gradually to nearby villages and towns or it could leap along the roads and establish an outbreak many miles away. Once the new epidemic was up and running to the alarm of the citizens, it was ready to move onwards and to initiate more outbreaks further afield. A single boat carrying one or more infected persons could be responsible for 20 or more major epidemics and countless tiny, unreported outbreaks in any one year in England.

Nevertheless, we discovered a most important point when studying the pestilence in England: each outbreak of plague lasted at most two years. Thereafter, the epidemic was eliminated and England was completely free of the disease – until the next boat arrived carrying an infected crew.

For this reason, England was free from plague for 10 or 11 years after the Black Death before the disease erupted savagely in 1360 or 1361. It has been described as the second pestilence, 'great multitudes of people are suddenly smitten with the deadly plague now newly prevailing as well in the city of London as in neighbouring parts and the plague is daily increasing'. The epidemic spread to Leicestershire, Warwickshire and Lincolnshire, all of which suffered badly, and it moved thence to York and Lancashire. Several great personages died, including three bishops and Henry, Duke of Lancaster, at his castle in Leicester.

Although for the next 150 years plagues arrived only sporadically in England, by the sixteenth century transport had greatly improved and we gain the impression that the pestilence was rampant somewhere in most years. It is bewildering to study the various accounts and very difficult to sift out the evidence that provides us with clues about this disease.

Professor J. F. D. Shrewsbury, a medical microbiologist, ransacked virtually all published local histories and parish records and read very widely in contemporary chronicles and memoirs. He published *A History of Bubonic Plague in the British Isles*, a compendium of information about the epidemics. Inevitably it is a little dull and confusing in places, but it is occasionally illuminated by his dry humour.

Unfortunately, Shrewsbury interpreted all the accounts so as to fit with his belief that the plague was *not* a disease that spread from one person to another. We have, instead, relied on the original accounts and evidence wherever possible. As usual, it is perfectly clear that people at the time recognized that the pestilence was directly infectious.

The first 200 years of plagues in England

The English quite quickly came to accept that the plague was part of their way of life. John of Burgoyne was already complaining in the time of Richard II that the medical practitioner was a charlatan who made money out of the epidemics:

> And yet he was but easy of dispense;
> He kept that he wan in the pestilence.

For gold in physic is a cordial:
Therefore he loved gold in special.

Another manuscript that was circulating in England was probably produced about 1480 and was regarded as being so important that it was chosen among the first to be printed at an English press. It was reprinted in 1536 and became a standard textbook of its time for the avoidance, prevention and treatment of the pestilence. The author describes himself as the Bishop of Aarhus in Denmark and claims to have practised physic at Montpellier. He describes his preventive measures:

In the Mount of Pessulane I might not eschewe the company of people, for I went from house to house, because of my poverty, to cure sick folk. Therefore bread or a sponge sopped in vinegar I took with me, holding it to my mouth and nose, because all aigre [sour] things stop[ped] the ways of humours and suffereth no venomous thing to enter into a man's body; and so I escaped the pestilence, my fellows supposing that I should not live. These foresaid things I have proved by myself.

An interesting point here is that the sponge soaked in vinegar may have been an effective way of preventing a disease that was passed by droplet infection.

There were some features about the pestilence that puzzled him:

But about these things, two questions be mooted. The first is, wherefore one dieth and another dieth not, in a town when men be dead in one house and in another house there dieth none. [We have already noted this phenomenon.] The second question is, whether pestilence sores be contagious.

To the second question I say, that pestilence sores be contagious by cause of infectious humoures bodies, and the reek or smoke of such sores is venomous and corrupteth the air. And therefore it is to flee from such persons as be infectious.

He also seems to suggest that you could be standing close to an apparently healthy person in a crowd and be directly infected:

> In pestilence time nobody should stand in great press of people, because some man of them may be infectious. Therefore wise physicians, in visiting sick folk, stand far from the patient, holding their face toward the door or window. And so should the servants of sick folk stand.

The Bishop also believed that disease was carried by foul-smelling air:

> It is a good remedy to void and change the infectious place. But some may not profitably change their places. Therefore as much as to them is possible, it is to be eschewed every cause of putrefaction and stinking, and namely every fleshly lust with women is to be eschewed. Of the same cause, every foul stink is to be eschewed – of stable, stinking fields, ways or streets, and namely of stinking dead carrion; and most of stinking waters, where in many places water is kept two days or two nights, or else there be gutters of water under the earth which caused great stink and corruption. And of this cause some die in that house where such things happen, and in another house die none, as it is said afore. Therefore keep your house that infectious air enter not in. For an infectious air most causeth putrefaction in places and houses where folk sleep. Therefore let your house be clean, and make clear fire of wood flaming: let your house be made with fumigation of herbs.

He had grasped the basic idea of quarantine, which was not practised in England at that time: 'Also in the time of the pestilence it is better to abide within the house; for it is not wholesome to go into the city or town'.

He gives clear instructions for diagnosis and treatment:

> But some would understand how may a man feel when he is infectious. I say that a man which is infectious, that

day eateth not much meat for he is replenished with evil humours; and forthwith after dinner he hath lust to sleep, and feeleth great heat under cold. Also he hath great pain in the forehead ... He shall feel a swelling under the arm, or about the share, or about the ears ... When a man feeleth himself infectious, as soon as he may, let him be let blood plenteously till he swoon: then stop the vein. For a little letting of blood moveth or stirreth venom.

The idea that you should keep clear of other people when the plague was about was certainly followed. Parliament petitioned Henry IV in 1439 to cancel the ceremony of kissing the king in the performance of knightly service because 'a sickness called the Pestilence universally through [England] more commonly reignth than hath been usual before this time and is most infective'. Parliament adjourned to Winchester in 1449 to avoid 'the pestilential aire of Westminster'.

London was struck by a severe plague in 1499–1500 when some 20 000 died and the infection was still active as late as October 1501 during the reception of the young Princess Catharine of Aragon at Gravesend. She had come over for her marriage with Prince Arthur and became famous in history as the wife of his brother, Henry VIII. Henry VII gave the following instructions:

My lord Steward shall shew or cause to be shewed to the said Princess, that the King's Grace, tenderly considering her great and long pain and travel upon the sea, would full gladly that she landed and lodged for the night at Gravesend; but forasmuch as the plague was there of late, and that is not yet clean purged thereof, the King would not that she should be put in any such adventure or danger, and therefore his Grace hath commanded the bark to be prepared and arrayed for her lodging.

The pestilence certainly caused the Tudor royalty some anxieties: the Venetian ambassador wrote in 1511 that the queen-widow (the mother of Edward V) had died of plague and that Henry VIII was anxious. He moved his court regularly to Hampton Court, Greenwich or Gravesend, often travelling by water to avoid catching the disease. Erasmus wrote in 1514 that he was disgusted with London and 'deemed it unsafe to stay there' because of the plague. In going in procession to St Paul's Cathedral, the king preferred to be on horseback 'to avoid contact with the crowd by reason of the plague'.

In his diary for 1513, the Venetian envoy wrote:

> deaths from plague are occurring constantly; two of his servants sickened on the 22nd August, but did not recognize the disease; on the 25th they rose from bed, went to a tavern to drink a certain beverage called 'ale' and died the same day: their beds, sheets and other effects were thrown into the sea [probably the river Thames].

On 17th September he wrote to Venice that 'it is perilous to remain in London; the deaths were said to be 200 in a day, there was no business doing, all the Venetian merchants in London had taken houses in the country; the plague is also in the English fleet'. In October, the deaths were reported by the envoy at 300 to 400 a day; he had gone into the country. On 6th November and 6th December he wrote that plague was still doing much damage.

An epidemic was also violently active in London in autumn 1531, causing a weekly death toll of 300–400. Henry VIII paid expenses to the poor of Greenwich, who were summarily expelled as a precaution to prevent the infection being passed to him when he took refuge there.

Plague in the north

Most of the epidemics in the first half of the sixteenth century in the north of England appear to be confined to the eastern side of the country, from York to Berwick-upon-Tweed on the Scottish borders.

In 1538, as early as March, plague was killing the citizens of York, and by the beginning of April its activity was so fierce that the corporation of the city ordered that all the sick should be removed to houses outside the Lathrop Gate that had been set aside specially for their reception, that the Gate should be closed and that no infected person was to move in or out of the city. Later in the year, plague spread further and the Council of the North informed King Henry VIII that it was prevalent in Durham and Newcastle-upon-Tyne.

York was again affected by an epidemic that was officially recognized by January 1550, when the corporation ordered all the people 'dwelling in Laythrop' to evacuate their houses, which were required to accommodate the sick. These houses were the ones that had been built 12 years earlier for the same purpose and had been occupied by tenants and squatters in the intervening period. As this accommodation proved inadequate, two more buildings were erected in February on Hob Moor. Later in the month, the corporation levied a fund on the four wards of the city for the relief of the sick poor.

In the spring of 1551, plague appeared with renewed vigour in the city and, by the beginning of May, it was causing the authorities much trouble. Apparently the buildings at Laythrop and on Hob Moor were full of patients by this time, because on 7th May the corporation ordered all those sick of the plague to keep to their own houses and, as the disease continued to grow, it cancelled the Corpus Christi play on the 18th.

It was during this outbreak that the city council decreed that every infected house 'shall have Rede Crosse sat uppon the Dower [door]', which appears to be the first use of this colour as a sign of the plague in England. York probably lost at least half its population in this epidemic.

There was a great plague at Manchester in 1558, and the authorities at Liverpool were very concerned over the danger of its spreading to their town. Unfortunately it did so, and an unlucky Irishman, with the Welsh name of John Hughes, was held to be responsible. He was accused of having been ill when he arrived in the town from Manchester and of having taken his dirty clothes to be washed at the house of a certain Nicholas Braye. A child of Braye contracted the disease and died. Hughes was brought before the mayor and underwent severe questioning, but the accusations could not be proved. However, whether he had carried the plague or it had come by some other channel, several others in the same house died shortly after, 'and so after that it increased daily to a great number, that died between St Lawrence's day [10th August] and Martlemas [11th November] then next after, the whole number of 240 and odd persons'. The severity of this outbreak at Liverpool was such that the St Martin's fair was cancelled and no market was held during a period of three months.

The first plague order

An official proclamation was issued in 1543 and gave complete instructions for the public-health measures that were to be instituted in the plague.

A precept issued to the aldermen:

That they should cause their beadles to set the sign of the cross on every house which should be afflicted with the plague, and there continue for forty days [evidently the standard period of quarantine on the Continent was now being adopted in England]:

That no person who was able to live by himself, and should be afflicted with the plague, should go abroad or into any company for one month after his sickness, and that all others who could not live without their daily labour should as much as in them lay refrain from going abroad, and should for forty days after [illegible] and continually carry a white rod in their hand, two foot long:

That every person whose house had been infected should, after a visitation, carry all the straw and [illegible] in the night privately into the fields and burn; they should also carry clothes of the infected in the fields to be cured:

That no housekeeper should put any person diseased out of his house into the street or other place unless they provided housing for them in some other house:

That all persons having any dogs in their houses other than hounds, spaniels or mastiffs, necessary for the custody or safe keeping of their houses, should forthwith convey them out of the city, or cause them to be killed and carried out of the city and buried at the common laystall: [This order was based on the belief that dogs carried the infection in their hair. Later, in the great plagues of 1603, 1625 and 1665, thousands of dogs were killed, many of them having been left behind in the exodus of the well-to-do classes.]

That such as kept hounds, spaniels, or mastiffs should not suffer them to go abroad, but closely confine them:

That the churchwardens of every parish should employ somebody to keep out all common beggars out of churches on holy days, and to cause them to remain without doors:

That all the streets, lanes, etc. within the wards should be cleansed:

That the aldermen should cause this precept to be read in the churches.

The two-foot white rods that were required to be carried by those who must go abroad from plague-stricken houses described in the second paragraph were in use for much of the sixteenth century in England and France. Any offenders were to be 'committed to the cage'. The Venetian ambassador to France wrote from the neighbourhood of Paris in 1580:

This city, I hear, is in a very fair sanitary condition, notwithstanding that as I entered the city gate, which is close to where I reside, I met a man and a woman bearing the white plague wands in their hands and asking for alms; but some believe that this was merely an artifice on their part to gain money.

In the seventeenth-century plagues of London and provincial towns, the white wand was retained as the peculiar badge of the searchers of infected houses and of the bearers of the dead. The white rod or wand carried by inmates of infected houses had become a red rod by the plague of 1603.

Under Elizabeth I, the orders concerning scavenging, listed above, became much more severe; among other duties the 'scavengers' had the oversight of pavements, which were swept weekly, of slaughterhouses, dunghills and the like, of dangerous buildings and of encroachments on the streets, of chimneys and of precautions against fires (tubs of water to be in readiness at the doors to quench fires and cleanse the streets). In the plague of 1563, the Common Council appointed 'two poor men to burn and bury such straw, clothes, and bedding as they shall find in the fields near the city or within the city, whereon any person in the plague hath lyen or dyed'.

In April 1552, John Shakespeare, a glover and the playwright's father, a citizen of Stratford-on-Avon in good circumstances and afterwards mayor of the town, was fined twelve pence for not removing the heap of household dirt and refuse that had accumulated in front of his own door. When Queen Elizabeth visited Ipswich, she berated not only the clergy on the laxity of their behaviour, but also the civic authorities on the filthy condition of the streets.

These improved sanitation measures, while admirable, had no effect on the progress or severity of any plague, even when faithfully carried out. The infection was not borne on the stench of foul air.

The most rigorous measures in the plague of 1563 were those that Queen Elizabeth took for her own safety:

> a gallows was set up in the market-place at Windsor to hang all such as should come there from London. No wares to be brought to, or through, or by Windsor; nor any one on the river by Windsor to carry wood or other stuff to or from London, upon pain of hanging without any judgement; and

such people as received any wares out of London into Windsor were turned out of their houses, and their houses shut up.

People certainly recognized that the danger came with the arrival of travellers.

These plague orders were updated in 1568 and again in 1581. An essential part of the means for controlling plague was the institution of searchers. In the orders of 1543, the aldermen of the wards were directed to send their beadles to affix the sign of the cross to affected houses. However, in due course these duties of inspection, notification, isolation and registration in London passed into the hands of the Company of Parish Clerks. The original business of the Parish Clerks was with church music. Legacies and endowments fell to them for the performance of specific services or for their encouragement in general. The whole strength of the Company of Parish Clerks in those times would attend the funeral of some rich person and so they were readily able to adapt to their new role. Their duties included compiling, parish by parish, the weekly Bills of Mortality.

The orders of 1581 direct that 'two discreet matrons within every parish shall be sworn truly to search the body of every person as shall happen to die within the same parish and of their reporting to the clerk of the parish, who would report to the Wardens of the Parish Clerks'. The job of these discreet matrons was merely to say whether a death had been from plague or from some other cause, but they were sworn to discharge their duties faithfully, the swearing-in taking place at St Mary-le-Bow Church in Cheapside.

William Shakespeare escapes

Stratford-upon-Avon was struck by the pestilence quite frequently. The registers recorded on 11th July 1564 'Hic incepit first person to die was Oliver Gunne, an apprentice ⌐ₑge. The mistress of the house, Joanna Degge, was ⌐ᵤᵣᵢed nine days later. Oliver Gunne had carried the disease to five other households and a study of the registers suggests that he and Joanna Degge between them infected about 20 other people. And so the epidemic got under way, with deaths peaking in September before gradually fizzling out in the following January. A total of about 220 plague burials were recorded – a major epidemic, but not as severe as some.

William was the third child to be born to John Shakespeare and his wife Mary Arden, but the first to live beyond childhood. He was three months old when the epidemic began in 1564 and was lucky to avoid infection and to survive infancy. His mother may have fled to her family home at Wilmcote about 3 miles (5 kilometres) away, which was still occupied by her widowed stepmother. Otherwise, the writings of a genius might have been lost to us.

The real value of the parish registers and Bills of Mortality to the plague detective

As we have said previously, the practice of keeping parish registers of baptisms, marriages and burials dates back to about 1540. At first they were somewhat scrappy, but gradually they were regularized and provided more valuable information with each entry. Not only do they give hard data on localities affected, numbers afflicted and dates of burial, but also the names and other details of the victims. These detailed registers were maintained for over 400 years and are unique to England. A law was passed in the Elizabethan period that required the vicar or the clerk to record any plague burials in the parish register. We show later how these invaluable records can be analysed to uncover more important clues.

From about the middle of the sixteenth century other data lists such as the London Bills of Mortality were kept. These were weekly lists, and monthly and yearly digests of the number of burials, which later included the causes of death. Essentially, they were an early warning system for monitoring the arrival of a plague epidemic. Therefore there is an abundance of material for historians for the last 100 years of the age of plagues. Unfortunately, this is not the case for the period from 1350 to 1550.

The last 100 years of plague

As the years rolled by, the population of the towns and cities rose steadily, transport and shipping improved markedly, and trading and movement increased concomitantly. Troops were on the move. All this activity ensured that plague epidemics were widespread. They struck more frequently with increasing ferocity. The more people there were in the conurbations, the greater was the mortality. By the start of the seventeenth century, the pestilence was present somewhere in Britain in almost every year.

In June 1580, because plague was raging in Lisbon, Lord Burleigh, the Lord Treasurer, authorized that precautions should be taken on the arrival of ships from there to prevent the spread of the infection to London. Merchants or seamen were not allowed to lodge in the city or suburbs and goods were not allowed to be discharged 'until they had some time for airing'.

Later in that year, the Queen's Council commanded that all ships and merchandise in the port of Rye in Sussex on the south coast, where the plague was raging, should not proceed to London 'until they had been aired'. Furthermore, the inhabitants of Rye were not to come to the city, nor to send goods by land, as long as the plague remained there.

However, the Queen was informed in September 1581 that the increase of the plague 'was due to the fact that the orders passed with respect to the persons infected were not being carried out'. In consequence, she 'had been obliged to remove further off and to adjourn the law term' (that is, she had taken evasive action and fled).

In April 1582, the Lords of the Council gave orders 'to restrain burials in St Paul's churchyard' because the churchyard was so crowded that 'scarcely any grave could be made without corpses being laid open'.

In October 1582, the Queen issued orders prohibiting any merchants or other persons from the city whose houses had been infected from resorting to, or sending to Hertford, Ware or Hoddesdon, any sort of merchandise, food or such like.

By April 1583, the infection had much increased and the Queen commanded

> that infected houses should be shut up and provision made to feed sick persons and to prevent them from going out, that infected houses should be marked, and the streets thoroughly cleansed. Her Majesty expressed surprise that no hospital had been built outside the City to which infected people might be removed, although other cities of less great antiquity, fame, wealth, and reputation had provided themselves with such places.

Scotland

Meanwhile Scotland had not escaped and even as early as 1475, the island of Inchkeith in the Firth of Forth was being used as a quarantine station. Later, the islands of Inch Colm and Inch Garvie were also pressed into service for the same purpose.

Dr Gilbert Skene became physician to James VI in 1568, the year of the great plague of Edinburgh, and he wrote a treatise on the disease. He says that the pestilence entered the city on 8th September having been brought by 'one called James Dalgliesh, merchant'.

R. Chambers, who wrote the *Domestic Annals of Scotland*, gives the following account of the public-health practices that were put into practice during this epidemic:

> According to custom in Edinburgh the families which proved to be infected were compelled to remove, with all their goods and furniture, out to the Burgh-moor, where they lodged in wretched huts hastily erected for their accommodation. They were allowed to be visited by friends, in company with an officer, after eleven in the forenoon; anyone going earlier was liable to be punished with death [draconian measures, indeed] – as were those who concealed the pest in their houses. Their clothes were meanwhile purified by boiling in a large caldron erected in the open air, and their houses were cleansed by the proper officers. All these regulations were under the care of two citizens selected for the purpose, and called *Bailies of the Muir*; for each of whom, as for the cleansers and bearers of the dead, a gown of gray was made, with a white St Andrew's Cross before and behind.

The symptoms displayed by the victims were said to be:

> Sowning [swooning], cold sweats, vomiting; excrements corrupt, teuch [tough]; urine black, or colour of lead. Cramp, convulsion of limbs, imperfection of speech and stinking breath, colic, swelling of the body as in dropsy, visage of divers colours, red spots [God's tokens] quickly discovering and covering themselves.

This epidemic in Edinburgh lasted until February 1569, and 2500 citizens died.

Plagues at the turn of the century

Thomas Dekker, the dramatist, of whom it has been said that 'he knew London as well as Dickens', wrote *The Wonderful Yeare 1603, wherein is shewed the picture of London lying sicke of the*

Plague. He first described the condition of the 'sinfully polluted suburbs' of London by taking a

> walk through the still and melancholy streets in the dead hours of the night. He hears from every house the loud groans of raving sick men, the struggling pangs of souls departing, grief striking an alarum, servants crying out for masters, wives for husbands, parents for children, children for their mothers. Here, he meets some frantically running to knock up sextons; there, others fearfully sweating with coffins, to steal forth dead bodies lest the fatal handwriting of death should seal up their houses.
>
> When morning comes, a hundred hungry graves stand gaping, and everyone of them, as at a breakfast, hath swallowed down ten or eleven lifeless carcases; before dinner, in the same gulf are twice as many more devoured, and before the sun takes his rest these numbers are doubled – threescore bodies lying slovenly tumbled together in a muck-pit!

One gruesome story he told of the epidemic in 1603 was of a poor wretch in the Southwark parish of St Mary Overy, who was thrown for dead on a heap of bodies in the morning, and in the afternoon was found gasping for life. Others were thrust out of doors by cruel masters, to die in the fields and ditches, or in the common cages or under stalls. A boy sick of the plague was put on the water in a wherry to come ashore wherever he could, but landing was denied him by an army of brown-bill (a halberd painted brown, used by English foot-soldiers) men that guarded the shore, so that he had to be taken back where he had come from to die in a cellar.

While plague was raging in the poor outskirts of the City, 'paring them off by little and little', the well-to-do took alarm and fled, 'some riding, some on foot, some without boots, some in slippers, by water, by land, swarm they westwards. Hackneys, watermen and wagons were not so terribly employed many a year; so that within a short time there was not a good horse in

Smithfield, nor a coach to be set eyes on.' But they might just as well have remained as trust themselves to the 'unmerciful hands of the country hard-hearted hobbinolls. The sight of a Londoner's flat-cap was dreadful to a yokel: a treble ruff threw a whole village into a sweat.'

One Londoner set out for Bristol, thinking not to see his home again this side of Christmas. But when he had travelled 40 miles from town 'the plague came upon him' and he sought entrance to an inn. When his case was known, the doors of the inn 'had their wooden ribs crushed to pieces by being beaten together; the casements were shut more close than an usurer's greasy velvet pouch; the drawing windows were hanged, drawn and quartered; not a crevice but was stopt, not a mouse-hole left open'. The host and hostess tumbled over each other in their flight, the maids ran out into the orchard, the tapster into the cellar. The unhappy Londoner was helped by a fellow citizen who appeared on the scene and was carried to die on a truss of straw in the corner of a field; but the parson and the clerk refused him burial and he was laid in a hole where he had died.

Meanwhile, Dekker continued, the plague

had entered the gates of the City and marched through Cheapside; men, women and children dropped down before him, houses were rifled, streets ransacked, rich men's coffers broken open and shared amongst prodigal heirs and unworthy servants.

I could make your cheeks look pale and your hearts shake with telling how some have had eighteen sores at one time running upon them, others ten or twelve, many four and five; and how those that have been four times wounded by this year's infection have died of the last wound, while others, hurt as often, are now going about whole.

It sounds as though some victims recovered in the epidemic of 1603 in London.

Funerals followed so close after each other that 3000 mourners went as if trooping together, with rue and wormwood stuffed into their ears and nostrils, looking like so many boars' heads stuck with branches of rosemary. A dying man was visited by a friendly neighbour who promised to order the coffin, but he died himself an hour before his infected friend. A churchwarden in Thames Street, on being asked for space in the churchyard, answered mockingly that he wanted it for himself and 'he did occupy it in three days'.

John Davies, a schoolmaster from Hereford, described the plague of London in 1603 in a poem entitled 'The Triumph of Death; or the Picture of the Plague, according to the Life, as it was in A.D. 1603'.

> Cast out your dead, the carcass-carrier cries,
> Which he by heaps in groundless graves inters ...
> The London lanes, themselves thereby to save,
> Did vomit out their undigested dead,
> Who by cart-loads are carried to the grave,
> For all those lanes with folk were overfed.

He mentioned that the prisoners in the gaols were comparatively exempt from plague. One line suggests the great size that the plague buboes sometimes reached:

> Here swells a botch as high as hide can hold.

Both the universities, Davies commented, were forsaken.

> Each village free now stands upon her guard ...
> The haycocks in the meads were oft opprest
> With plaguy bodies, both alive and dead,
> Which being used confounded man and beast.

One macabre incident he vouched for (in a marginal note) as having occurred at Leominster in Herefordshire. A person with the plague was drowned to prevent infection, by the order of Sir Herbert Croft, a member of the Council of the Marches of Wales.

The pestilence visits London again

Charles I met his bride-to-be, Princess Henrietta of France, at Dover on 13th June 1625 and they entered London on the 18th, moving up the river in a state barge to Denmark House amid an immense concourse of people on the houses and shipping and in the wherries on the river, accompanied by salvoes of artillery and demonstrations of welcome to the Catholic princess. However, five days previously, the Lord Keeper had already written to Conway, Secretary of State, telling him that cases of plague had occurred in Westminster and that he wished his majesty had decided to come no nearer than Greenwich.

The nobility were kept in town to await the arrival of the new queen, some of them by the summons of Parliament. The Houses met on June 18th and were advised in the King's speech to expedite their business on account of the plague. Shortly after this, Francis, Lord Russell (afterwards Earl of Bedford) 'being to go to Parliament, had his shoemaker to pull on his boots, who fell down dead of the plague in his presence', so that his lordship avoided the House.

Salvetti, the envoy of the Grand Duke of Tuscany, kept a diary in which he wrote that on 1st July 1625, the plague had spread through all the streets and reached other parts of the kingdom. A general exodus took place to the country of everyone who had the means to do so (as usual). Once again, the magistrates, doctors, ministers and the rich men left the city to take care of itself. On August 9th Salvetti, who had himself escaped to Richmond, wrote:

> The magistrates in desperation have abandoned every care; everyone does what he pleases, and the houses of merchants who have left London are broken into and robbed.

On 1st September Dr Meddus, rector of St Gabriel's, Fenchurch Street, wrote:

> The want and misery is the greatest here that ever any man living knew; no trading at all; the rich all gone;

housekeepers and apprentices of manual trades begging in the streets, and that in such a lamentable manner as will make the strongest heart to yearn.

The scene was evoked in verse by Abraham Holland, the son of Philemon Holland, doctor of physic:

> A noon in Fleet Street now can hardly show
> That press which midnight could, not long ago
> Walk through the woeful streets (whoever dare
> Still venture on the sad infected air)
> So many marked houses you shall meet
> As if the city were one Red-Cross Street.

And by John Taylor, the water poet and Queen's bargeman:

> In some whole street, perhaps, a shop or twain
> Stands open for small takings and less gain.
> And every closed window, door and stall
> Makes every day seem a solemn festival.
> All trades are dead, or almost out of breath,
> But such as live by sickness and by death.

The circumstances were exactly the same as in 1603: the sextons, coffin makers, bearers, searchers, apothecaries and quacks were all profitably employed:

> And last to dog-killers great gain abounds,
> For braining brawling curs and foisting hounds.

Of the sick, Taylor said that there were

> Some franticke raving, some with anguish crying.

There were the same crowded common graves as in 1603, probably in the same graveyards:

> My multitude of graves that gaping wide
> Are hourly fed with carcases of men.
> Those hardly swallowed, they be fed again.

Or, as Taylor also put it:

> Dead coarses carried and recarried still
> Whilst fifty corpses scarce one grave doth fill.

It appears that the buboes and boils might come out in the same person more than once, and that the best chance was from their suppuration:

> Some with their carbuncles and sores new burst
> Are fed with hope they have escaped the worst.

The main hope was to flee. However, the people in their flight 'were driven back by men with bills and halberds, passing through village after village in disgrace until they end their journey; they sleep in stables, barns and outhouses, or even by the roadside in ditches and in the open fields'.

And that was the lot of comparatively wealthy men. Taylor said that when he was with the queen's barge at Hampton Court and up the river almost to Oxford, he had much grief and remorse to see and hear of the miserable and cold entertainment of many Londoners:

> The name of London now both far and near
> Strikes all the towns and villages with fear.
> And to be thought a Londoner is worse
> Than one that breaks a house, or take a purse ...
> Whilst hay-cock lodging with hard slender fare,
> Welcome, like dogs into a church, they are.
> For why the hob-nailed boors, inhuman blocks,
> Uncharitable hounds, hearts hard as rocks,
> Did suffer people in the field to sink
> Rather than give or sell a draught of drink.
> Milkmaids and farmers' wives are grown so nice
> They think a Citizen a cockatrice,
> And country dames are waxed so coy and brisk
> They shun him as they shun a basilisk.

He gave the following example:

> A man sick of an ague lying on the ground at Maidenhead in
> Berkshire, with his fit violently on him, had stones cast at
> him by two men of the towne (whom I could name), and
> when they could not cause him to rise, one of them tooke a
> hitcher, or long boat-hook, and hitched in the sick man's
> breeches, drawing him backward with his face grovelling
> on the ground, drawing him so under the bridge in a dry
> place, where he lay till his fit was gone, and having lost a
> new hat, went on his way.

One man at Richmond was drawn along naked in the night by
his own wife and boy and cast into the Thames, where the next
day the corpse was found. At Southampton on August 27th, a
stranger died in the fields. 'He came from London. He had good a
store of money about him, which was taken before he was cold.'

Dr Donne, the dean of St Paul's, confirmed these experiences in
a letter on November 25th from Chelsea:

> The citizens fled away as out of a house on fire, and stuffed
> their pockets with their best ware, and threw themselves
> into the highways, and were not received so much as into
> barns, and perished so: some of them with more money
> about them than would have bought the village where
> they died. A justice of the peace told me of one that died so
> with £1400 about him.

A story told of a woman who fled to Croydon 10 miles
(16 kilometres) to the south of London and, looking back on
Streatham Hill, said 'farewell plague', but soon after she was
taken sick and 'had God's tokens on her breast'.

A mini-epidemic at Malpas: an infective comes from London

Raffe Dawson returned from London, where the plague was
raging, to his father's house in Bradley, a hamlet in the parish

of Malpas in Cheshire, a journey of some 185 miles (300 kilometres). The parish registers specifically recorded that he had been infected while he was in London; another good example of the long-range transmission of the disease. Raffe Dawson displayed the characteristic symptoms and finally died on 25th July 1625. We later calculated that he must have been infected while in London on about 18th June. He had to be buried near the family house, because his infected body was not allowed in the churchyard.

All the members of the family, as well as the two servants, were then infected, one after another, and were also buried near the house. Raffe Dawson certainly infected five members of the household directly and probably two more, his uncle Richard Dawson and his young brother John. There was evidently a high household contact rate.

Thus, when Richard Dawson found the haemorrhagic spots, the dreaded tokens, on his chest, only his nephew John and a female servant were still left alive. The registers recorded the following poignant story of unsung heroism:

> Being sick of the plague and perceyving he must die at yt time, [he] arose out of his bed, and made his grave, and casuing [causing] his nefew, John Dawson, to cast some straw into the grave, w[h]ich was not far[re] from the house, and went and layed up[p]on, and so[e] dep'ted out of this world; this he did, because he was a strong man, and heavier then [than] his said nefew, and [the] other wench were able to bury[e].

The last person to die in the household was this maidservant, but she had already carried the infection to the nearby Clutton family, just as her symptoms were appearing. Two children and the mother, Maude Clutton, were the next to die, but they had infected a third child, who was the last to be infected in the localized epidemic in the little hamlet.

The story of this tiny epidemic at Malpas shows how the pestilence could jump a great distance from London, a journey that must have taken several days on horseback. At Malpas the outbreak was contained and there were only 13 deaths in total, because of the small size of the hamlet and the isolation techniques practised there.

John Handley lived in Shocklack, the parish adjacent to Malpas, which he visited during the mini-epidemic there. He also fell victim and was buried on 3rd September 1625. His children, John (15 years old) and Elizabeth (19 years old) became ill on 23rd September. John died two days later.

> And by reason he died so suddenly, and having Red-specks [the tokens] found upon him, he was supposed to have died of the Plague. And therefore was carried to the Church upon a Dragge by his Mother, Elleyn Handley and Randle Gylbert his half brother. And was buried in the Church Yard, at the Steeple end out of the alley; without Service, ringing or any other ceremonies of the Church.

Elizabeth Handley died two days later on 27th September.

> And because she had Red-specks found upon her and some sore under her arm, she was likewise suspected to have died of the Plague. And therefore she was buried in her Mother's Croft, near the Orchard upon Wed 28 Sep. And upon Monday the 3rd day of Oct., the aforesaid Eliz. Handley was taken up again out of her grave and brought to the Church, upon a Dragge by her half brother Randle Gylbert, aforesaid, which buried her near to her brother John Handley the younger without any ceremonies of the Church.

Elleyn Handley (the mother) was buried on 9th October 1625.

> And because her two children had died with Red-specks [God's tokens] upon them therefore she was suspected to die of the Plague. Wherefore she was carried to the Church upon a dragge by her son, Ran Gylbert, and laid by [the bodies of] her two children, John and Eliz. Handley.

Randle Gylbert (aged 28 years), who assisted with these family burials and who was 'supposed to have brought these troubles and sickness into the Parish of Shocklach, was confined to keep his Mother's house, and there kept in by watch and ward, night and day, himself alone a long time'. Eventually, he was stripped and viewed by certain neighbours and Parishioners, 'and then had no sign of any sore found upon him'. He escaped the plague and was married the following year.

A successful quarantine

There was a severe outbreak of plague in Lancashire and Yorkshire in 1631, which killed large numbers. Manchester, however, escaped completely, because the inn where the infection appeared was completely isolated:

> Anno 1631. The Lord sent his destroying angell into an inne in Manchester, on which died Richard Meriot and his wife, the master and dame of the house, and all that were in it, or went into it, for certaine weekes together, till, at the least, they burned or buried all the goods in the house ... No person else was that year touched with the infection.

This was an example of the successful application of public-health measures.

The record for infection?

In the town of Mirfield in West Yorkshire (where the Brontë sisters later went to school), 130 people died in this epidemic of 1631. The course of events there, and the lines of transmission of the infection, can be reconstructed from the parish registers. Again, the 'bringer of infection' was a stranger, Elizabeth Prince, who lodged with Janet France, a widow, whom she infected first. She then infected the five children in the house before she died; a typical story for the start of so many infections. Janet France then infected 33 other people in 19 families *during the first week of her infectious period* – something of a record for a small town during the cool month of April. She may have gone on to infect more. We wondered what sort of employment brought the widow into contact with so many families in such a short space of time. Was she a washerwoman or did she have a market stall?

A personal story

Leonard Gale wrote the following account in 1687 when he was 67 years old.

I was born in the parish of Sevenoaks, in Kent, my father, a blacksmith ... had, by a former wife, two sons, and by my mother three sons and one daughter; and when I was between sixteen and seventeen years of age, my father and mother going to visit a friend at Sensom, in the said county, took the plague, and quickly after they came home my mother fell sick and about six days after died, nobody thinking of such a disease. My father made a great burial for her, and abundance came to it, not fearing anything, and notwithstanding several women layd my mother forth, and no manner of clothes were taken out of the chamber when she died, yet not one person took the distemper; this I set down as a miracle.

After her burial, we were all one whole week, and a great many people frequented our house, and we our neighbours' houses, but at the week's end, in two days, fell sick my father, my eldest brother, my sister, and myself; and in three days after this my younger brothers, Edward and John, fell sick, and though I was very ill, my father sent me to market to buy provisions, but before I came home it was noysed abroad that it was the plague, and as soon as I was come in adoors, they charged me to keep in, and set a strong watch over us, yet all this while no one took the distemper of or from us, and about the sixth day after they were taken, three of them dyed in three hours, one after another, and were all buryed in one grave, and about two days after the two youngest both died together, and were buryed in one grave. All this while I lay sick in another bed, and the tender looked every hour for my death; but it pleased God most miraculously to preserve me, and without any sore breaking, only I had a swelling in my groin, which it was long ere it sunk away, and I have been the worse for it ever since, and when I was recovered, I was shut up with two women, one man, and one child for three months, and neither of them had the distemper.

This is an eye-witness account of the plague being confined to one household, probably partly because of the standard isolation techniques. We have included it particularly because Leonard Gale genuinely caught the disease but recovered. Was he partially resistant?

The key role of trade

The situation in England was fundamentally different from that of France – every epidemic in England had to be started by an infective arriving by a boat from continental Europe that docked at London or at one of the many ports on the south and east coasts. Once an epidemic had taken hold in the port, infected travellers would soon be setting out, carrying the pestilence all over the country. By the seventeenth century, one introduction might lead to 25 satellite epidemics.

As we have already seen, after about 18 months England would then be completely free of the plague – until everything started all over again when an infective next arrived by boat. The transmission of the disease was probably not entirely one way: infectious crews may well have carried the plague back from England to continental Europe, so helping to keep it going there.

In the fourteenth and fifteenth centuries, there were many years when England was completely plague free or when only one port was affected. But by the mid-sixteenth century, with increasing trade and travel, there were widespread and more ferocious epidemics starting in nearly every year from different ports.

After an introduction at a port, the plague was spread across England by infected people travelling on foot or horseback and, less commonly, by river or coastal traffic. It was carried to nearby towns by local traffic and then progressively along the main trade routes. Some of this spread was by normal commercial traffic. However, it quickly became recognized, particularly in London, that the safest response when an epidemic was discovered was to flee, an option available only to the rich and powerful. The poor had no alternative but to stick it out and they died in hundreds. It was for this reason that the plague was described as the disease of the poor. It became understood that, for safety, it was necessary to ride out of London for a day, a distance of about 20 miles. Inevitably, people fleeing – particularly those who had left it until the last minute – carried the infection with them radially outwards from the city.

The medieval wool trade made the greatest contribution to long-range movement in England. The handling and transportation of the fleeces proceeded throughout the year on a large scale and, consequently, this was a major factor in the dissemination of the plague. Private traders in wool and other commodities were travellers and individualists. These men travelled alone seeking livestock, corn or wool and were ready to forsake family and home in search of individual reward. They bought and sold in the inns and there they met other traders, which provided an ideal way for the onward transmission of the plague – talking at length indoors with the locals.

Sheep were usually washed and sheared in June, often by hired workmen who moved round the country. The wool was then packed and delivered to the buyer, either immediately or later. The clothiers often came with transport to collect the wool from a grower, sometimes in instalments, although carriers were also used. The clothiers and middlemen either stored their wool or sold it on immediately.

A very large volume of wool was sold in the sixteenth and seventeenth centuries through the special weekly public markets in manufacturing towns and wool-growing districts. The merchants sold much of their produce at Leaden Hall in London, which was not only a market but also the largest warehouse for wool in England. Thus, because London was the centre of commerce, it inevitably became the centre of plague mortality in England.

The Great Fairs

The annual Great Fairs were another major means of spreading the plague in England and were probably one source for bringing it into the country in the first place. The authorities recognized this and fairs were invariably cancelled at the first sign of plague. The most important fairs took place south and east of a line from Exeter to York and were on or near the navigable rivers or roads to seaports.

Professor J. F. D. Shrewsbury described the picture:

> The great fair at Sturbridge [in East Anglia], which opened on 18 September and lasted for three weeks, was the most important of the English fairs and was of sufficient repute to attract merchants from many European trade centres. You can be present at the great Sturbridge fair and there see Venetian glass, Bruges linen, Spanish iron, Norwegian tar, Hanse fur, Cornish tin and Cretan wine, all for sale in the

half of a square mile which was occupied for three whole weeks. During Sturbridge Fair, Blakeney, Colchester, King's Lynn, and perhaps Norwich, were filled with foreign vessels. The ships brought the merchandise of the Levant from Venice, and other commodities from overseas.

The ports, and London in particular, were the focus; as in the rest of Europe, trade was the engine of the dissemination of the plague through England.

For more than 200 years people throughout Europe had battled against the heavy mortality of the plague and had more than held their own – the population numbers continued to grow, albeit very slowly. But gradually the enemy was gaining the upper hand; as we have seen, because of ever-increasing trade, it spread more widely, more places were attacked and mortality rose sharply. From the end of the sixteenth century for some 80 years, the population of Europe (and particularly in England where more detailed statistics are available) was static and even fell slightly. The plague was winning – if this were to continue our civilization could have disappeared.

6

Portrait of an Epidemic

W e were learning more and more about the plague and the evidence was piling up. A much clearer picture of its characteristics was gradually emerging, but this came from a great variety of scattered and fragmented sources from across Europe, coupled with various eye-witness accounts. We decided to return to our detailed analysis of the Penrith records to provide a portrait of an epidemic that was completely typical of provincial towns in the UK, and probably throughout Europe also, in the sixteenth to seventeenth centuries. This pattern of events and the story of terror, agony and heroism were repeated again and again.

The plague that broke out at Penrith in 1597, which we described in the Introduction, was not an isolated event: it was one of a series of epidemics that ravaged the north of England and were transmitted sequentially from one market town to the next. We decided to study this major outbreak, far from London, in detail to discover exactly how it spread and from whence it came. By the end of the sixteenth century, all the countries of Europe had lived with the plague for 250 years and they were in continual fear that one day an infected traveller would come into their midst, or one of their own would return from a place where the plague was raging. If the worst happened, they grimly responded in a much more organized fashion than the blind panic that had greeted the Black Death.

We remembered that the Penrith parish register had recorded that there was a 'sore plague' in Newcastle, Durham and

Darlington in 1597. Evidently, our next step was to examine the registers and records of the places mentioned to see how they had fared during the epidemic.

The start of the terror

The end of the sixteenth century was a period of great hardship and famine in the north of England and there were excessive mortalities recorded in many of the parishes. In January 1597, the Dean of Durham wrote,

> the effect of want and waste had crept into Northumberland, Westmorland and Cumberland; and ... the scarcity of food was such that people travelled from Carlisle to Durham, a distance of 60 miles [100 kilometres] over some of the worst country in the kingdom, to buy bread.

The disease was first reported at the seaport of Newcastle in north-east England, suggesting that it was brought across the North Sea from continental Europe. During the summer of 1597 Newcastle was ravaged, although there are no figures for the total mortality.

On 26th May 1597 the Dean of Durham again complained that there was great scarcity in Durham: on some days, 500 horses were in Newcastle for foreign corn, although that town and Gateshead were dangerously infected. On 17th September Lord Burghley, minister of state, was informed that the plague increased at Newcastle, so that the Commissioners 'cannot yet come thither' (in fact the Assizes were not held at all, on account of the plague at Newcastle and Durham). Foreign traders were selling corn at a high price until some members of the town council produced a stock for sale at a shilling a bushel less.

Moving south along the Great North Road (later the A1), which ran to the east of the Pennines, the disease had arrived in the city of Durham by about midsummer 1597 and over 1000

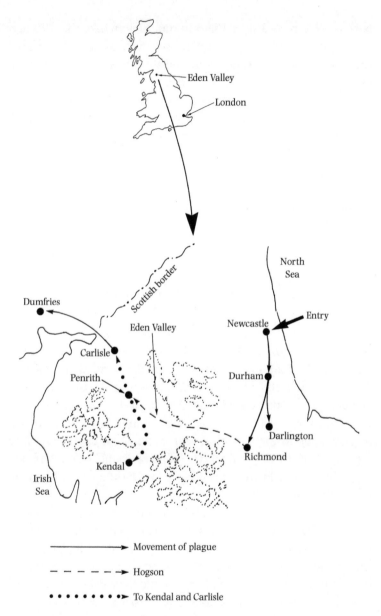

Geographic spread of the plague from north-east to north-west England via the gap over the Pennines, 1597–98. Dotted line encloses land over 500 metres. Dashed line shows probable route taken by Hogson.

burials were recorded by the autumn. Meanwhile, the infection was on the move again, travelling southwards, and it appeared simultaneously in Darlington in County Durham and Richmond in August 1597.

Richmond was a market town in the North Riding of Yorkshire and its people suffered for 16 long months. The eventual death toll was so huge that the churchyard was inadequate and many of the dead had to be buried in emergency grounds in the Castle Yard and in Clarke's Green. The epidemic died down in the autumn, limped along through the winter and reemerged in the following spring, with deaths peaking in summer 1598. It was finally gone by December.

The pestilence arrives at Penrith

In the meantime the disease had not been stationary, but had travelled along the trade route across the Pennines from east to west, via the Stainmore–Bowes Moor gap, striking at Penrith. The town had suffered a terrible famine in 1596 when 153 persons were buried and had not recovered when the little community was dealt a second, devastating blow by the arrival of the plague in the following year. It was brought, as we have seen, by Andrew Hogson, who presumably came from Richmond or perhaps from further afield, such as Darlington or Durham, where the epidemic was raging.

The entry in the register after Hogson's burial shows clearly that the vicar and the inhabitants recognized at once from the signs of the dying man that they had a visitation of the plague on their hands. They were right. Alarm and terror must have spread quickly through the town and they would have waited with bated breath to see whether there were any further cases. Perhaps they were going to be lucky and escape a full-blown epidemic.

Nothing happened for three weeks and they were beginning to hope, but then Elizabeth Railton died and the community faced up to the inevitable. The members of her family had been infected in quick succession, indicating a high contact rate within the household.

The epidemic rose to a small peak in November–December, although a total of only nine families were infected. Thereafter the plague all but disappeared during the cold of a northern winter and there were no plague deaths in January and only one in February 1598.

Nevertheless, the outbreak exploded again in the warmer weather of April and the daily death toll rose steadily, peaking in July before gradually fizzling out. An emergency burial ground had to be opened on the fell during the chaos of the summer and 213 bodies were interred there. Some were also buried in the grammar school yard and some in their own gardens. The final death toll was at least 640, over half of the population.

Furness, in *The History of Penrith from the Earliest Record to the Present Time*, gave the following account of events in the plague, although it was probably anecdotal.

During this dreadful time the actual state of Penrith can scarcely be imagined. Not a solitary marriage was registered for the whole summer. Houses supposed to contain the infection were shunned, and their inmates suffered to die unaided. People almost feared each other's looks. Evening, the time when the attacks of this disease generally came on, had peculiar terrors during the visitation of the plague. The first paroxysm or period, which included the evening to the following night, was frequently fatal. The third and fifth days were considered, on the whole, those of greatest danger, and if they survived over the fifth day and the bubo was fully formed, then the patients were considered almost out of danger. All these circumstances were only too well known where the plague had been for some time raging. The wild and furious look accompanying the disease in its incipient state, which ought to bespeak pity for the sufferer, dispelled all feelings of humanity from the breast of those whom circumstances brought in their way. The staggering occasioned by an extreme prostration of strength was a warning to his neighbour to flee. The poor sufferer sought his home – perhaps he was the last of his household – and the indifference to recovery, which was considered a most unfavourable symptom, alone relieved the horrors of his despairing and forlorn condition.

Public-health measures

A policy of partial isolation was put into practice during the epidemic at Penrith. The farmers from outside the town (understandably) would not enter while the plague raged, all regular markets were suspended and temporary markets were set up on the outskirts. Furness reported that 'the inhabitants of the dales, who were doubtless especially timorous, came no nearer than Pooley' (about four miles away). The townsfolk paid for their supplies by tossing coins into hollowed-out plague stones containing some crude, supposedly disinfectant fluid, possibly vinegar. The use of plague stones during an epidemic had become widespread in England and one is still preserved in a field in Penrith. Certainly, from this evidence everybody believed that the pestilence was directly infectious.

The victims speak

It was back to the Record Office at Carlisle again to obtain another view of the events during the crisis at Penrith. On this occasion, Sue was using first-hand information gained by studying the wills of the people who had died in the epidemic.

Reading the wills of those who died in the plague allows an insight into the devastating rapidity of the progress of the disease and, more particularly, reveals the tragedy in those stricken families who faced the inevitable with dignity and resignation.

Throughout all this misery, fear and suffering, the citizens continued with their daily lives as far as they could. In spite of the fact that they were about to face an agonizing death, these men and women carefully made their wills, paying particular attention to the guardianship of their children – if they should survive (although they rarely did).

They remembered the poor of the parish, often leaving them a quantity of bigg, a poor form of barley, and a number of them left money for the building and repair of the bridges in the town. Several bequeathed belongings that had been left to them by their father who had already died in the plague, but which they had not yet inherited.

The only people who made wills during the plague were those with substantial possessions to leave, and these prosperous members of the town, mostly successful tradesmen, were all interconnected and interrelated with one another and with their witnesses. They were a separate group from the gentry, of whom only three died in the outbreak; most had fled once the epidemic started up again in the spring. Here are extracts from some of the wills made by those who died of the plague.

Michael Dobson, 20 years old, was married on 20th July 1598 but did not long enjoy matrimony. He made his will a month later on 27th August 1598 and was buried five days after that, on 1st September. He left to his wife Isabell (who survived the plague) all his 'tenements barnes and yeards with the appurtenance and my tythe estait and tenament right during her wydowehood'.

John Steinson made his will on 30th August 1598 and was buried three days later on 2nd September. He left 'all that tenement with appurtances which was my fathers' to his eldest son Thomas (who probably survived the plague) and 'all the rest of goode[s] movable and umovable I do maike and ordaine to my son Richard and Margaret my daughter'. Tragically, Richard was to be buried two days after his father, whereas Margaret survived a little longer, dying of the plague some six weeks later. A minor bequest was 'to the poore of the parish 6 peck[e] of ote [oat] meale'.

The family of Arthur Gibson was badly hit. He lost his daughter Elizabeth on 10th July 1598, some 10 weeks before the plague struck his family again; she was buried on the fell. A child of his was buried on 19th September 1598 and Arthur made his will two days later on 21st September. His wife died on the next day and he and another child (Ann, aged 9 years) died on 24th September. In his will, he wished:

> my bodie to be with the bodies of my wyffe and children so manye of us as shall die at this tyme be buried within the parishe church yard of Penreth ... I give and bequest all my lande tacke and tenements to John my eldest son [who survived the plague; he may have been living away from home on his own land] ... I give to Jane my eldest daughter hawked [hawkey, a black-and-white cow] cow[e] and also if all my children dye but her I give her twenty sheep[e].

Jane is described as a servant and may have been living away from home. She died in 1606 aged 26 years.

Robte Holme wrote his will on 25th September 1598 and was buried on 3rd October. The following are extracts:

> I give and bequeath to the building of Sandgate Bridge 6s 8d and 4s 3d which Willm Bowman of Kirkoswald oweth me, and to the repairing of Midlegaet [Middlegate] Bridge 3s 4d.
>
> I give to Margaret and Frances my two daughters all my lande, houses, tackes and tenements ... [They survived the plague but were 23 and 25 years of age and may have left home.]
>
> I give to Agnes my wieff two of my best kyne [cows]. [She was his second wife and probably survived the plague].

Stephen Jackson made his will on 3rd July 1598 but did not die until 1st August. Evidently, he set out his wishes as soon as the plague appeared in his family and not when he first displayed any symptoms: his son aged 13 years was buried on the 3rd or

5th July and his wife Dorothy was buried on 15th July, 17 days before Stephen. Their son John survived. Stephen makes no mention of his wife in the will and he seems to assume that she was doomed. If she was showing the characteristic symptoms by 3rd July, her suffering lasted 12 days.

Isabell Nelson, spinster, made her will on 23rd July 1598 and was buried on the following day. She gave 'and bequeath all that my child's portion dewe to me by the last will and testament of Stephen Nelson my lait [late] father'. (Evidently she had not yet received her bequest.)

Robert Gibbon made his will on 1st October 1598 and was buried four days later. He made the following requests:

> Item ... the tuition and government of my sonne Anthonie [aged 3 years] and my tenement Heath and yard in the head of Penreth with the appurtenances together with his portion to Gilbert Gibbon and William Gibbon my bretheringe [bretheren] during his none age [i.e. until he attains his majority]. Item I maike Anthonie my sonne my whole executore of this my last will and testament. And if I and my wyffe dye I gyve all my goods to Willm and Gilbert my bretheringe.

Robert Gibbon, his wife and their young son Anthonie were all buried on the same day, 5th October 1598. There were no survivors in the family.

Jefferaye Stephenson made his will on 20th October, the same day that his daughter Isobel was buried, and he died two days later. He gave 'all his lands meddowes and heridaments ... all my goods movable and ummovable' to Elizabeth, his daughter. He made her 'my whole executrix' and 'I comytt [commit] the tuition and government of my daughter Elizabeth to Agnes Stephenson and John Stephenson my brother during her non aige.' He gave further directions 'if my daughter Elizabeth dye' and made other minor bequests as follows: 'Item I give to Sussan Emerson my wief's best cott [coat] and sle..es [?shoes]. Item I give to Margaret Todd my wief's best hatt.'

Elizabeth Stephenson was buried on 23rd October, the day following her father. Jefferaye made no mention of his wife Janet in the will and even bequeathed some of her best clothing, although she was not buried until 24th October. (Was she already showing symptoms whereas the daughter Elizabeth was not, although she died very quickly?)

Elizabeth Browne, widow, made her will on 29th May 1598 and was evidently suffering from the plague and was being cared for by the Crosbie family, because she wrote that 'the said Thomas Crosbie and his weife shall maintain ... me in my visitation'. She left the bulk of her possessions to the Crosbie family, but gave to 'Elioner Crosse, one chadgoe [an item of clothing?] and my daughter Jane's clothes' and 'unto Elizabeth Crosbie ... my lynen web [listed in the inventory at 8s 4d]'. All the members of the Crosbie family who had cared for her survived the plague.

Thomas Sutton, tailor, made his will on an unknown date and was buried on 22nd July 1598. Evidently he was aware that his wife might be affected by the pestilence although, in fact, she was not buried until a month later, on 22nd August. He made the following bequests:

> to the poore of the Parish 10s and to the building of the Sandgait bridge whensoever 5s.
>
> to Thomas Sutton my sonne ... my tenement in Penreth after the death of my wyffe Mabell and I give to her my lease I gave ... of one other halfe wood land.
>
> to John Sutton my brother John elder son[ne] my steall [steel] cape sword and arrowes I used for service of the Prince.
>
> my other bowes I gyve the one to John of John Turner with 12 shafte and to ... my quyver and all the arrowes in the same. And to Richard Cel ... my brother in law my good blewe [blue] cott [coat] and my wedding dublett and to ... brother my suit of leather apperell.
>
> to Robert Wilson my gymmer bowe with c ... arrowes and butt ... shafte. And if God doe call me to his mercie and my wyffe I do gyve to the said Robert one chest[e].

to my wyffe the great chest and meale in the same, and if God do call on her, then the chest and meale to be sold to paye my debts.

will that if it please God to call me and my wyffe of this visitation that her ... friends and myne shall devide the remaine of my goode equallie amongst them.

I appoint Mabell my wyffe to be myne executrice.

I gyve to Henrie Ewrie if we both[e] dye a peck[e] of bigg and five cartfull of peet[e].

Why did some people escape infection?

Not everyone who must have been in contact with an infected person died. We have seen that Elizabeth Browne, a widow, was cared for in her last days by the Crosbie family, all of whom survived. There are many cases where one or more in the family, often a young child, escaped death and survived the plague. We found that many people who witnessed the will of a dying plague victim also survived, even if there was plague in their own families too. There does not appear to have been any difficulty about finding someone prepared to be exposed to the infection when witnessing the will, and some had over six witnesses. This indicates that some people in this epidemic were resistant to infection, a point that we had noted in the accounts of the Black Death and other plagues.

Although we found examples of people who must have been infected by a person on their death-bed, we suspected that usually a person was *less* infectious once the symptoms had appeared. This would account for so many witnesses surviving.

And what of the survivors at Penrith? Rather like the survivors of the first Black Death, the little community got back on its feet quite quickly; the market opened again and people moved in from the surrounding districts, taking up the vacant lands and houses and exploiting all the job opportunities. Sue Scott's historical researches showed that the community became like a frontier town and the illegitimacy rates rose sharply. Who would blame them for throwing caution to the wind as they struggled to rebuild their lives?

Today, the emergency burial ground on the fell at Penrith is marked on the Ordnance Survey map but it is now covered by a housing estate – and it is easy to imagine that the ghosts of those who died in the visitation of the pestilence might still linger there.

The epidemic spreads through north-west England

As we have seen, the disease spread remarkably quickly from Penrith to Carlisle, where more stringent public-health measures were introduced by the civic authorities. Evidently, by 1597 even remote rural towns knew what should be done when the plague struck their community. At a City Council meeting, it was recorded:

> necessary[e] observations thought meate to be kept in this Cittye, the third day of November 1597: for the avoiding[e] of further infection of the disease of the plague then suspected there to be, if so it pleace God to blesse there carefull indeavours therein.

Infected houses were sealed off, the provisioning of their inhabitants was arranged and orderly arrangements were made for the removal and disposal of the dead. Daily visits were to be made by honest experienced men to discover cases of sickness.

One of the resolutions laid down was that a weekly collection must be taken in each street for the better relief of every poor person visited. Of the total of £209 9s 10d, the amount raised by the citizens themselves was only £14 4s 10d; the largest amount came from the Common Chest and donations were received from several county gentry. The poor were attended without fee or charge for medicine, but those who were in a position to pay were expected to do so.

The city gates were placed in the charge of honest men whose orders were to prevent the admission of anyone known or suspected of infection or who came from any place where the infection was thought to be. 'Foreigners' and wandering beggars were expelled from the city and during the visitations none was admitted without a permit from the city bailiff. Movement within the city itself was also restricted.

The infectious nature of the disease was fully appreciated and infected houses were marked, as usual, with a red cross, 'there to continue until lawfull opening of the same house'. The period of quarantine was considered to be 40 days (as usual) – the citizens of Carlisle knew all about the plague. They recognized the dangers associated with the arrival of strangers and they adopted sensible preventive measures to minimize the spread of the disease, such as the isolation of infected people in their houses.

Arrangements were made to pay the stipends of the officers and ministers, of the corpse bearers and the corpse viewers, the latter apparently receiving a flat rate of 10 shillings per week. A similar sum was paid to those who cleansed houses where all the inhabitants had died, or had fled to the fields for safety. Help was also given to those of the poor who survived, although they had been in daily contact with the sick, and to such as had recovered from the plague.

This account supports our conclusion above that not all those who came into intimate contact with the infection succumbed. Were they resistant? It also suggests that recovery from this infection was possible.

It is not known when the practice of removing sufferers to pest houses (which were primitive isolation centres) began at Carlisle, but properties were commandeered to deal with the emergency and several isolation hospitals were speedily built outside the city walls. Strict orders were enforced regarding the burial of the dead: special biers were to be provided for carrying the corpses, which had to be buried between 10 a.m. and 4 p.m.; no corpse was to be lifted until the bellman gave the word that the grave had been prepared; and the beadle had to walk before those carrying the body to give people warning as he came.

Kendal was first struck on the same day as the plague appeared in Carlisle. There are few details of the epidemic there because the parish registers are not complete, but it is evident that the outbreak at Kendal was severe. During this time, the baptisms, weddings and burial sections of the records stop in the summer and are not resumed until Christmas, a gap of five months. For some months before this gap, there are some burial entries with the marginal notation 'p' or 'pla'.

During the plague provisions were brought to Coneybeds, a fort situated on Hay Fell, by the country people and left for the inhabitants of Kendal 'which was their only intercourse during that destructive period'.

We have not traced any records of the plague striking at Keswick in the north of the Lake District, but Barnes, a local historian, recounted in 1891:

> In Keswick there is a tradition that when the plague raged, as no markets were held for fear of the infection, the people of the dales carried their webs and yarns to a large stone, which is very conspicuous on one of the lower elevations of Armboth Fell, and there periodically met and did business with the trades. The stone still goes by the name of the 'web stone'. Mr. J. Fisher of Crosthwaite informs me that he has heard old people say that when the plague was in Keswick the country people came to 'Cuddy Beck', but did not cross the little stream. The money was placed in the water and then taken, and the produce was laid on the ground for the Keswickians to take back.

Major epidemics were experienced only in the large market towns and cities. Analysis of the available registers for the smaller parishes of the Eden Valley showed that plague burials were recorded in only a handful of places and, in some cases, the total burials number fewer than 12. This confirmed our suspicion that a full-blown outbreak of this disease occurred only in communities above a certain minimum size, like market towns and cities, which were a centre for local trade and were regularly visited by drovers and wool traders. Wool, admittedly of poor quality, was an important export produced in the Eden Valley.

At Warcop (a village 15 miles, 23 kilometres, south-east of Penrith), the disease appeared to be confined to one part of the parish and to only two families. Adam Mosse and his two children died of the plague 'as it was thought' on 19th October 1597. On 4th November, Margaret Mosse and Agnes Lancaster were buried in a garth (a courtyard within a cloister) at Blatarne. The next burials occurred on 25th May 1598 (presumably a fresh outbreak), when Richard Lancaster and his wife 'died both so daynelyne upon the plague as it was thought and were buried in their own yeard at Blatarne'. Another entry on 6th June 1598 stated: 'Dyed Thomas son of Richard Lancaster of Bletarne and the barne wherein he died burned and the corps afterwards interred.' Although plague was not given as the cause of death, the fact that purging by fire was deemed necessary would imply a highly infectious and much-feared illness.

The parish registers at Penrith record that the plague also struck at Appleby at the head of the Eden Valley and the inference is that it was a severe attack to merit inclusion with Kendal and Carlisle. The outbreak apparently occurred late in the pandemic and probably the infection again arrived from Richmond.

The illness eventually moved northwards from Carlisle, reaching Dumfries in Scotland by the winter of 1598. The epidemic caused problems for trade and even a scarcity of food; two men sent from Dumfries to Galloway were stopped at Wigton with 38 head of cattle and compensation was sought because the impounded cattle became lean.

The suffering of the victims

We have not traced any accounts of the symptoms of plague victims at Penrith or Carlisle, but Richard Leake, 'preacher of the word of God at Killington within the Baronie of Kendall, and in the Countie of Westmerland', delivered his so-called plague sermons either in 1598 or in 1599, when he said:

> It pleased God by the space of two yeares together, to give our country (in the North parts of this land) a taste of his power in iudgement, being provoked thereunto by our manifold enorm[I]ous sinnes: he visited us with many and grieuous sicknesses, as first with the hot feuer, after, with the bloodie issue, and lastly, most fear[e]fully with the extre[a]me disease of the pestilence, inflicted upon many, and shaken at all in our whole countrie. And albeit neither I, nor any of the people under my charge, were infected therewith, yet had we all of us, the cause thereof within our sinfull hearts, as well as any others.

The victims suffered from the usual hot fever that was followed by the 'bloodie issue', although from which source is not clear. We were confident that the same infectious disease was responsible for this outbreak as for all the other plagues of Europe.

Emerging profile of the serial killer

This, then, was the picture of a typical, voracious epidemic in the provinces. The pestilence had struck before at some of the larger towns in the east, such as Newcastle and Durham, but the smaller, market towns had probably only rarely encountered the horror of a visitation.

We studied scores of the epidemics in the provinces, using the contemporary parish registers, and gradually learnt more and more about the plague. We assembled the evidence:

- Often an outbreak is recorded in the burial register as being started by a traveller or stranger or by an inhabitant who had returned from a place where the plague was known to be raging. Clearly, these people had been infected elsewhere. For instance, the registers of Oundle in Northants record that the epidemic that began in 1625 was started by the daughter of William Abels, 'who came downe from London' (where the plague was raging) to visit her father and died on 14th July. She was accompanied by her daughter, who died nine days later.

- The plague was opportunistic and basically it behaved in exactly the same way in each outbreak.
- However, we recognized two completely different types of epidemic in England, governed by the size and density of the population:
  - First, the epidemic never took off in the villages and scattered parishes. The infection never spread far, although whole families were wiped out if it got a toe-hold in a house. While the pestilence may have grumbled on for several months, mortality was always low. Probably about 1000 inhabitants were necessary for a critical mass.
  - Second, in the larger towns where there were a sufficient number of people congregated together, the epidemic exploded in the summer months. It always spread slowly at first but gradually gathered momentum.
- These full-blown, typical epidemics lasted for eight or nine months – from spring to December.
- The mortality was terrible – often about 40 per cent of the people, although we had no measure of how many people had fled at the first signs of trouble.
- The disease struggled through the winter with difficulty. An epidemic that started in the autumn limped along and often fizzled out completely in the winter, doubtless to the relief of the population.
- Once an epidemic had established itself, the citizens put the plague orders in force, although this made little difference to the outcome.

- The infection had a prodigious rate of movement – for example, it moved over 150 miles (240 kilometres) in about six weeks in the epidemic in the north-west of England. It pressed forwards remorselessly, striking opportunistically wherever it could get a footing.

- The time between the appearance of the dreaded symptoms and death was quite short, perhaps an average of five days.

What was the pattern of events in an enormous conurbation like London when the plague struck at the height of its powers?

7

The Great Plague of London

Of all the visitations of the pestilence in Europe, we know more about the Great Plague of London, which began in 1665, than any other. Samuel Pepys gave an eye-witness chronicle in his famous diary. Daniel Defoe, who was only six years old at the time, reconstructed the story in 1722; while this is undoubtedly a lively and readable account, some historians have criticized its authenticity. However, W. G. Bell, who wrote the definitive *The Great Plague in London*, defended Defoe, saying that these comments 'do less than justice to the pains taken by Defoe in using such historical sources as were at his hand'.

The weekly Bills of Mortality were maintained (although probably not quite as accurately as might be hoped, because the figures were underplayed to improve morale), which means that detailed statistics are available. The mortality was horrendous – the plague was at the height of its powers in England. But paradoxically, this was its swansong. Within five years it would have disappeared forever.

Where did it come from?

Plague was rampant in Holland in 1664 and the Commissioners of Customs had earlier been warned to ensure that no infected refugee was allowed to land in Britain. To no avail: two

Frenchmen were reported to have died of the plague in Long Acre in London at the very end of the year.

The winter of 1664 was severe: the earth was held in an almost continual black frost from November, which did not abate until March 1665. The dry cold continued after the frost broke, producing, it was said, 'an unusual number of cases of pleurisy, pneumonia and angina', the result of the 'direst winter spring and summer that ever man alive knew ... the grounds were burnt like highways, the meadow ground ... having but four loads of hay which before bare forty'.

This cold winter put a severe damper on the progress of the epidemic, as Harvey says in *The City Remembrancer* published in 1769:

> And being restrained to a house or two, the seeds of it confined themselves to a hard frosty winter of near three months continuance: it lay asleep from Christmas to the middle of February, and then broke out again in the same parish; and after another long rest till April, put forth the malignant quality as soon as the warmth of spring gave sufficient force, and the distemper showed itself again.

Weekly registered plague deaths reached a total of 43 at the start of June 1665 and the first official notice was a proclamation on 14th June cancelling Barnwell fair 'for fear of spreading the plague'. That was a wise precaution, but nothing would stop the outbreak now.

At the end of June, the official Orders Conceived and Published by the Lord Mayor and Aldermen of the City of London were promulgated and this lengthy document included:

> The master of every house, as soon as any one in his house complaineth, either of blotch or purple, or swelling in any part of his body, or falleth otherwise dangerously sick, without apparent cause of some other disease, shall give knowledge thereof to the examiner of health within two hours after the said sign shall appear.

Defoe pointed out:

> In this interval, between their being taken sick and the examiners coming, the master of the house had leisure and liberty to remove himself or all his family, if he knew whither to go, and many did so. But the great disaster was, that many did thus after they were really infected themselves, and so carried the disease into the houses of those who were so hospitable as to receive them, which, it must be confessed, was very cruel and ungrateful.

London was now put on full alert and all the tried-and-tested health regulations were rigorously put into practice.

Diary of a terrible summer

Samuel Pepys stayed in the city through the plague and went about his daily business. From his famous diary, we get a glimpse of what it must have been like to live through those dreadful days:

June 7th – The hottest day that ever I felt in my life. This day, much against my will, I did in Drury Lane see two or three houses marked with a red cross upon the doors, and 'Lord, have mercy upon us,' write there; which was a sad sight to me, being the first of the kind that to my remembrance I ever saw.

June 15th – The town grows very sickly, and people to be afraid of it.

June 17th – going with a hackney coach, the Coachman I found to drive easily and, at last stood still, and came down hardly able to stand, and told me that he was suddenly struck very sick, and almost blind, he could not see; so I [a]light and went into another coach, with a sad heart for the poor man, and for myself also, lest he should have been struck with the Plague.

June 21ˢᵗ – I find all the town going out of town, the coaches and carriages being all full of people going into the country [i.e. they were fleeing].

[*June 22ⁿᵈ* – Pepys sent his mother, Margaret Pepys, away. She was late at the posting-house and lost her place on the crowded coach and 'was fain to ride in the wagon part'.]

June 25ᵗʰ – The Plague increases mightily.

June 29ᵗʰ – To Whitehall, where the court was full of wagons and people ready to go out of town. This end of the town every day grows very bad of the Plague. The Mortality Bill is come to 267; which is about ninety more than the [last week's total].

July 22ⁿᵈ – I by coach home, not meeting with two coaches, but with two carts, and the streets mighty thin of people.

August 30ᵗʰ I went forth and walked towards Moorfields to see (God forgive my presumption!) whether I could see any dead corpse going to the grave; but, as God would have it, did not. But Lord! How everybody looks, and discourses in the street of death that the town is like a place distressed and forsaken.

September 3ʳᵈ – donned my new periwig, bought a good while since, but durst not wear, because the plague was in Westminster when I bought it; and it is a wonder what will be the fashion after the plague is done, as to periwigs, for nobody will dare to buy any hair[e] for fear of the infection, that it had been cut off people dead of the plague.

September 6ᵗʰ – To London, and there I saw fires burning in the streets, through the whole city, by the Lord Mayor's order.

September 14ᵗʰ – To hear that poor Payne, my waiter, hath buried a child, and is dying himself. To hear that a labourer I sent but the other day to Dagenham's, to know how they did there, is dead of the plague; and that one of my own watermen, that carried me daily, fell sick as soon as he had landed me on Friday morning last, when I had been all night upon the water, and is now dead of the plague. To hear that Captain Lambert and Cuttle are killed in the taking these ships; and that Mr. Sidney Montague is sick of a desperate fever at my Lady Carteret's, at Scott's-hall. To hear that Mr. Lewes hath another daughter sick. And, lastly, that both my servants, W. Hewer and Tom Edwards, have lost their fathers of the plague this week, do put me into great apprehensions of melancholy, and with good reason.

September 20th – To Lambeth. What a sad time it is to see no boats upon the river; and grass grows all up and down Whitehall Court, and nobody but wretches in the streets!

October 16th – Walked to the Tower; how empty the streets are and melancholy, so many poor sick people in the streets full of sores. And they tell me that in Westminster, there is never a physician, and but one apothecary left, all being dead.

Thomas Vincent, formerly minister of St Magdalen's, Milk Street, also stayed in London at this time. He wrote *God's Terrible Voice in the City*, which again described the scene graphically:

In August how dreadful is the increase! Now the cloud is very black, and the storm comes down upon us very sharp. Now Death rides triumphantly on his pale horse through our streets, and breaks into every house almost where any inhabitants are to be found, when they are shaken by a mighty wind. Now there is a dismal solitude in London streets; every day looks with the face of a Sabbath-day, observed with greater solemnity than it used to be in the city. Now shops are shut in, people rare and very few that walk about, insomuch that the grass begins to spring up in some places, and a deep silence almost in every place, especially within the walls; no prancing horses, no rattling coaches, no calling in customers, nor offering wares, no London cries sounding in the ears. If any voice be heard, it is the groans of dying persons, breathing forth their last, and the funeral knells of them that are ready to be carried to their graves ... it would be endless to speak what we have seen and heard of: – some in their frenzy rising out of their beds and leaping about their rooms; others crying and roaring at their windows; some coming forth almost naked into the streets.

Spectres of death: the dreaded plague-nurses and watchmen

Pepys' diary shows that, as in previous plagues, all who could afford it fled from London, but the poorer classes in the populous suburbs on both sides of the Thames could not do so and it was they who suffered most. Employment and hence wages mostly ceased when the wealthy left, so that malnutrition and starvation were added to the vicissitudes with which people were afflicted.

So desperate was their situation that many were forced to undertake the dangerous work of the day- and night-watchmen of the shut-up houses, the buriers and the dreaded plague-nurses who were appointed by the authorities and who were said to contribute to the early demise of their patients. Vincent declared 'that the plague stricken were more afraid of the official plague-nurses than of the disease itself'. This is not surprising: these plague-nurses had no skill or experience in nursing and in most cases were of dubious character. Their wages were paid by the parish and were insufficient for their subsistence, so that they were forced to rely for a livelihood on the opportunities that came their way for peculation and theft.

Defoe was more forthright:

A great many frightful stories told us of nurses and watchmen who looked after the dying people; that is to say, hired nurses, who attended infected people, using them barbarously, starving them, smothering them, or by other wicked means hastening their end, that is to say, murdering of them; and watchmen, being set to guard houses that were shut up when there has been but one person left, and perhaps that one lying sick, that they have broke in and murdered that body, and immediately thrown them out into the death-cart! and so they have gone scarce cold to the grave.

There was likewise violence used with the watchmen, as was reported, in abundance of places; and I believe that from the beginning of the visitation to the end, there was not less than eighteen or twenty of them killed, or so wounded as to be taken up for dead, which was supposed to be done by the people in the infected houses which were shut up, and where they attempted to come out, and were opposed ... Not far from the same place they blew up a watchman with gun powder, and burned the poor fellow dreadfully; and while he made hideous cries, and nobody would venture to come near to help him, the whole family that were able to stir got out of the windows one storey high [and so escaped], two that were left sick calling out for help.

Stories of heroes

Not all the physicians and apothecaries fled at the start of the epidemic: some stayed valiantly at their posts and gave such succour as they could. The result was that most died with their patients. Dr Boghurst, who practised in St Giles-in-the-Fields and who survived, gave the following account of his ministrations:

Though at first I was much baffled in giving judgment, yet afterwards by use and long observation of the particulars I arrived at a greater skill; for I rendered myself familiar with the disease, knowing that the means to do any good must be not to be fearful; wherefore I commonly dressed forty sores in a day, held the pulse of patients sweating in their beds half a quarter of an hour together, let blood, administered clysters [enemas] to the sick, held them up in their beds to keep them from strangling and choking, half an house together commonly, and *suffered their breathing in my face several times when they were dying* [our italics]; eat and drank with them, especially those that had sores; sat down by their bedsides and upon their beds, discoursing with them an hour together. If I had time I stayed by them to see them die, and see the manner of their death, and closed up their mouth and eyes; for they died with their mouth and eyes very much open and staring. Then if people had nobody to help them, I helped to lay them forth out of the bed, and afterwards into the coffin; and, last of all, accompanied them to the ground.

What is so striking about this account is how this man escaped infection. He was continuously in close contact with a multitude of victims and yet he did not succumb.

Defoe also related the following touching story:

One man, a master of a family in my neighbourhood, having had the distemper, he thought he had it given him by a poor workman whom he employed, and whom he went to his house to see, and he had some apprehensions even while he was at the poor workman's door, but did not discover it fully; but the next day it discovered itself, and he was taken very ill, upon which he immediately caused himself to be carried into an outbuilding which he had in his yard, and where there was a chamber over a workhouse, the man being a brazier. Here he lay, and here he died, and would be tended by none of his neighbours, but by a nurse from abroad; and would not suffer his wife, nor children, nor servants to come up into the room, lest they should be infected, but sent them his blessing and prayers for them by the nurse, who spoke it to them at a distance, and all this for fear of giving them the distemper, and without which he knew, as they were kept up, they could not have it.

Perhaps the most moving story in Defoe's book is that of a poor waterman, who was able to work for his plague-stricken family by keeping himself isolated from them and who thanked God that he was able to preserve them from want: 'Oh, sir! ... it is infinite mercy if any of us are spared; and who am I, to repine?'

A catalogue of death

Mortality in London was almost beyond belief. The epidemic followed the standard pattern for the pestilence with deaths rising dramatically at first to a crescendo in mid-September and then falling during the autumn and winter. The official total was that 68 595 died, but there is general agreement that this was an underestimate. W. G. Bell was certain that many plague deaths were either deliberately hidden from the women 'searchers' or that those officials were bribed, or intimated, to refrain from reporting fully. These views are confirmed by the entry in Pepys' diary for 30th August 1665:

> Abroad and met with Hadley, our clerk, who, upon my asking how the plague goes, told me it encreases much in our parish; for, says he, there died nine this week, though I have returned but six: which is a very ill practice, and makes me think it is so in other places; and therefore the plague much greater than people take it to be.

In addition, because the Quakers, Jews and Anabaptists refused to allow the plague deaths among their members to be included in the church returns, these mostly escaped the bills. Pepys wrote on 31st August 1665:

> In the City died this week 7,496, and of them 6,102 of the plague. But it is feared that the true number of the dead this

week is near 10,000 [a staggering total]; partly from the poor that cannot be taken notice of, through the greatness of the number, and partly from the Quakers and others that will not have any bell rung for them.

Defoe recorded:

The confusion among the people, especially within the city at that time, was inexpressible. The terror was so great at last that the courage of the people appointed to carry away the dead began to fail them; nay, several of them died, although they had the distemper before and were recovered, and some of them dropped down when they have been carrying the bodies even at the pit side, and just ready to throw them in; and this confusion was greater in the city, because they had flattered themselves with hopes of escaping, and thought the bitterness of death was past.

Although more people in London died in this outbreak than in any other visitation, this should be seen against the sharp rise in the population to about 460 000, giving a plague mortality, according to the official figures, of 15 per cent, which compares to a corresponding value of 13 per cent for the earlier epidemic of 1625.

Death: a blessed release

The medical reports suggest that some lucky few succumbed quite quickly after the tokens appeared, but for most the end was the usual drawn-out, agonizing affair. Defoe told the following stories, which show poignantly what the poor victims suffered.

It would be endless to speak of what we have seen and heard of some in their frenzy rising out of their beds and leaping about their rooms; others crying and roaring at their windows; some coming forth almost naked, and running into the streets. Strange things have others spoken and done when the disease was upon them; but it was very sad to hear of one who, being sick and alone, and, it is like, frantic, burnt himself in his bed. ...

The swellings, when they would not break, grew so painful that it was equal to the most exquisite torture; and some, not able to bear the torment, threw themselves out at windows or shot themselves, or otherwise made themselves away, and I saw several dismal objects of that kind. Others, unable to contain themselves, vented their pain by incessant roarings, and such loud and lamentable cries were to be heard as we walked along the streets that would pierce the very heart to think of, especially when it was to be considered that the same dreadful scourge might be expected every moment to seize upon ourselves. ...

I heard of one infected creature who, running out of his bed in his shirt in the anguish and agony of his swellings, of which he had three upon him, got his shoes on and went to put on his coat; but the nurse resisting, and snatching the coat from him, he threw her down, ran over her, ran downstairs and into the street, directly to the Thames in his shirt, the nurse running after him, and calling to the watch to stop him; but the watchman, frighted at the man, and afraid to touch him, let him go on; upon which he ran down to the Stillyard stairs, threw away his shirt, and plunged into the Thames, and, being a good swimmer, swam quite over the river; he reached the land not till be came about the Falcon stairs, where landing, and finding no people there, it being in the night, he ran about the streets there, naked as he was, for a good while when ... he takes the river again and swam back to the Stillyard. ...

People in the rage of the distemper, or in the torment of their swellings, which was indeed intolerable, running out of their own government, raving and distracted, and oftentimes laying violent hands upon themselves, throwing themselves out at their windows, shooting themselves, &c.;

mothers murdering their own children in their lunacy, some dying of mere grief as a passion, some of mere fright and surprise without any infection at all, others frighted into idiotism and foolish distractions, some into despair and lunacy, others into melancholy madness ... In some those swellings were so hard that no instrument could cut them, and then they burnt them with caustics, so that many died raving mad with the torment, and some in the very operation. In these distresses, some, for want of help to hold them down in their beds, or to look to them, laid hands upon themselves, as above. Some broke out into the streets, perhaps naked, and would run directly down to the river, if they were not stopped by the watchmen, and plunge themselves into the water wherever they found it.

The horrors of the pit

The plague pits were 'held in horror by the poor who strove to prevent burial of their dead therein'. Apparently, the bodies of victims were committed at night without any rites nor with a minister of religion in attendance, and W. G. Bell said that anyone who by mischance was nearby when the dead carts emptied their ghastly loads 'fled precipitately from a sight that must have strained the strongest nerves. The flares lit up a scene that is best left to the imagination.'

Defoe tells us that

when they dug the great pit in the churchyard of our parish of Aldgate. A terrible pit it was, and I could not resist my curiosity to go and see it. As near as I may judge, it was about forty feet in length, and about fifteen or sixteen feet broad, and at the time I first looked at it, about nine feet deep; but it was said they dug it near twenty feet deep afterwards in one part of it, till they could go no deeper for the water; for they had, it seems, dug several large pits before this ... in another ground, when the distemper began to spread in our parish, and especially when the dead-carts began to go about. Into these pits they had put perhaps fifty or sixty bodies each; then they made larger holes, wherein they buried all that the cart brought in a week, which, by the middle to the end of August, came to from 200 to 400 a week; and they could not well dig them larger, because of the order of the magistrates confining them to leave no bodies within six feet of the surface; and the water coming on at about seventeen or eighteen feet, they could not well, I say, put more in one pit.

One cart, going up Shoreditch was forsaken of the drivers, or being left to one man to drive, he died in the street, and the horses going on, overthrew the cart, and left the bodies, some thrown out here, some there, in a dismal manner. Another cart was, it seems, found in the great pit in Finsbury Fields, the driver being dead, or having been gone and abandoned it, and the horses running too near it, the cart fell in and drew the horses in also. It was suggested that the driver was thrown in with it, and that cart fell upon him, by reason his whip was seen to be in the pit among the bodies.

Apprentices and maidservants: the naïve immigrants

We were greatly surprised to discover how frequently the first victims in each parish were apprentices or maidservants and also that their deaths formed a high proportion of victims. But in fact, the vulnerability of this particular section of the community simply confirmed our analyses of the previous terrible epidemics in London in 1603, 1625 and 1636. Defoe also noticed this:

Infection generally came into the houses of the citizens by means of their servants ... whom they were obliged to send up and down the streets for necessaries; that is to say, for food or physic, to bakehouses, brew-houses, shops, etc.; and who going necessarily through the streets into shops, markets, and the like, it was impossible but that they should, one way or other, meet with distempered people, who *conveyed the fatal breath* [our italics] into them, and they brought it home to the families to which they belonged.

Defoe obviously understood the implications of droplet infection and his suggestion that the servants were responsible for carrying round the infection in the course of their work may have had some truth in it. This had occurred to us, but it is difficult to account for the preponderance of deaths among the apprentices as well as the servants and we suggest an alternative scenario. Since London was bombarded by the pestilence from the end of the sixteenth century, the families who had lived there for a long time seem to have been developing some form of resistance. The percentage mortality in the epidemics was actually falling steadily through the seventeenth century.

London was an extraordinarily unhealthy place: not only the pestilence but many other diseases were rife. Mortality was high and life expectancy was low. Consequently, there was an insatiable demand for labour. Immigrants, like Dick Whittington, poured into the metropolis seeking their fortune. They came from far and wide, sometimes as far afield as York, and in great numbers: there were between 32 000 and 40 000 apprentices in 1600 alone. This movement, particularly of younger people, speedily filled the gaps left by the excessive mortality.

Of course, these young, naive immigrants had none of the resistance to the pestilence shown by hardened London families and they died in their thousands. Even as early as the mid-sixteenth century, about 15 per cent of indentured apprentice carpenters died before they could complete their service.

In the first strike of the Black Death, we saw evidence of a few people who were apparently resistant to infection. And 300 years later, that resistance was probably quite widespread in places like

London that had been under almost continuous bombardment by the pestilence for decades. What can be the explanation for this? Since the plague normally killed its victims, there is no question of an acquired immunity. This resistance was more deep-seated and these lucky individuals must have inherited it from their parents. The plot thickens, as they say, and evidently we had much more to learn about this devastating disease.

Aftermath

Unfortunately for Londoners, the epidemic lingered on through the winter of 1665, reemerging in the following spring, although the worst was over. The people who had fled began to creep back and everyone tried to pick up the threads of their lives once more. Nevertheless, the plague hung on and deaths continued at a low level throughout the following year, causing a further 2000 burials. Apart from some stray and sporadic outbreaks, this was the end of the pestilence. Having reigned supreme, rampaging unhindered through Europe for 300 years, it now disappeared when it was at the height of its powers, as suddenly and inexplicably as it had appeared on the scene.

The people of Europe must have continued to hold their breath for many years, wondering whether their old enemy had gone for good or was merely hiding somewhere, waiting for the opportunity to reemerge. What was stopping it from appearing on the scene once more? However, soon they had other worries: a more virulent form of smallpox came to the fore in the 1630s and before long this disease took over the role of the most feared killer, although it never reached the status of the pestilence.

We have uncovered an accurate historical picture of the plague's long reign of terror and assembled a great deal of evidence. But we are left with many unanswered questions. Among them, where on earth (quite literally) had the disease come from in 1347? And why did it disappear in 1670?

Before we can even begin to answer such questions, we have to admit that we do not, as yet, understand the true nature of this mysterious killer disease. In technical parlance, what was the infectious agent?

Can we bring the full force of the modern science of infectious diseases to bear on our historical evidence and so assemble an identikit of the medieval killer?

8

How Bugs and Germs Operate

We have learnt a great deal about this strange disease that terrorized Europe from its first strike in the Black Death in 1347 until the Great Plague of London in 1665. It is absolutely clear from the contemporary accounts that, right from the word go, the people at the time realized that it was a directly infectious disease spread from one person to another. The success of the 40-day quarantine rule confirms that they were correct. But what was the infectious agent and why was it so hideously effective? First, we need to learn more about the basis of bugs and germs.

Ever since they first walked on the planet, humans have been engaged in a war with infectious diseases. Until relatively recently with our growing knowledge of the underlying causes and the advent of antibiotics and vaccines, it had been a very heavily one-sided battle. Our mothers and grandmothers simply referred to 'germs' and they greatly feared their effects on the safety and health of their children. Rightly so, because they had been brought up on the stories of the terrible childhood mortality caused by infectious diseases in earlier eras. Some had seen first-hand the devastating effect of the 1918 influenza pandemic, and they had witnessed the terrible paralysis and often fatalities caused by polio before the development of Salk's vaccine in 1954. The risks of childhood were many and varied: diphtheria, whooping cough, measles, chickenpox, influenza, colds, bronchitis, pneumonia, pleurisy, gastroenteritis, Dhobi's itch, round worms, thrush, impetigo and even the indignity, after a visit to the swimming baths, of athlete's foot and veruccas. In the Duncan family, we suffered from them all in the days before antibiotics and vaccination, although we avoided trench fever. And around us we could see people suffering and in some cases dying from tuberculosis, polio and meningitis.

Our earlier ancestors, of course, had witnessed many of these diseases, although for centuries the major killer of young children had been smallpox. Following a worldwide vaccination campaign in 1977 this disease was effectively wiped out, except for stocks kept for research purposes, but it is not surprising that smallpox and plague are the two diseases that have the greatest power to invoke fear and widespread panic should they be used in a terrorist attack.

Smallpox is a disease that we, the authors, know well. Since the early 1990s we have studied it rigorously, not working with the actual virus but from the safety of our offices, where we used the data contained in the London Bills of Mortality, the parish burials registers and the Ministry of Health records. These wonderful sources gave us information about those who had died of the disease from the earliest recorded outbreak in the sixteenth century to the last major epidemic in Europe in 1870. We had been successful in modelling the various outbreaks in rural and urban areas and had elucidated the factors that were important in triggering epidemics. We published our work in a number of scientific journals and our reputation must have spread because, following the terrorist attack on the USA on 11th September 2001, our expertise was suddenly in great demand and we found ourselves assisting in attempts to analyse the possible effects of the release of the virus by terrorists.

In a sense, humans today have learnt to live with infectious diseases, and measles and whooping cough cause serious mortality only among inadequately nourished children in developing countries. Much more serious in the tropics are other lethal infectious diseases such as malaria, sleeping sickness, bilharzia and cholera, which are the really big killers today. And everybody knows about the pandemic of HIV and AIDS. Our arsenal of weapons to combat infectious diseases continues to grow and we do win some battles, but undoubtedly the war still goes on.

A similar analogy can be used to describe the conflict that occurs when the human body becomes infected. Germs, or infectious agents, are parasites and they all have one feature in common, namely that humans are their niche where they have shelter and food and can reproduce prodigiously. Every infection is a race between the infectious agent and the host: the parasite strives to survive and reproduce, while the host's immune system mounts a warlike defence that is designed to find, destroy and eliminate the microbe.

Another factor that is of crucial importance to infectious agents is that they have to achieve transmission from one human to another. This is fundamental to the survival strategy of all infectious diseases, because eventually a host will either clear the infection or die. Spread of the disease may be direct, from person to person (as with measles and smallpox), or indirect, involving an intermediate animal (as with the mosquito that transmits malaria). Over thousands of years, evolution has been at work to favour those germs that can most effectively achieve this transmission from one victim to the next.

Studying epidemics

An important branch of medicine is epidemiology, the science of epidemics, and an example of its routine application is the annual international study to determine the strain of influenza virus that is most likely to strike during the coming winter. Once this is known, sufficient quantities of the appropriate vaccine can be made available. Today, when a new disease such as Lassa fever, Ebola, SARS or AIDS emerges, the epidemiologist has a battery of techniques available to determine the nature of the infectious agent. These include on-the-spot examination of the victims, looking at samples of blood and other tissues, tracing the lines of infection, determining the course of the disease and its characteristics, and estimating its lethality and infectiousness. Gradually, from all these sources, a picture of the disease can be built up and supplemented by techniques drawn from mathematical statistics and model building, microbiology, serology and molecular biology, including DNA sequencing.

The historical epidemiologist, however, has a much more difficult task, particularly when working with epidemics of infectious diseases prevalent in the Middle Ages, because there is often very little hard evidence at all, other than some anecdotal accounts that have survived the passage of time. A typical example is the baffling and lethal English 'sweating sickness' of the fifteenth and sixteenth centuries (discussed at length with other afflictions in Chapter 18). Furthermore, it is difficult to be sure what is reliable and what has been invented in the intervening centuries to fit the prevailing ideas of the time. However, in spite of these problems, we can rely on the fact that every disease does leave its fingerprints. Any serious attempt to understand the infectious agent responsible for the plague must begin with a scientific study of its biology and characteristics, so far as we can discover them.

Reading the fingerprints

Before we can proceed further in our investigation, we must state one important fact, which is that every infectious disease is characterized by two important constants: the *incubation period* and the *infectious period*. The incubation period is the time from when a person is infected to when the first symptoms show. During this stage, the invading germ is multiplying rapidly inside its victim, generally without their being aware of it. The infectious period is the time during which the person can transmit the infection to other people.

The sequence of events for a simple, directly transmitted disease (such as measles or chickenpox) is shown in the diagram below.

Infection is followed by a latent period, during which the germs multiply prodigiously until the victim becomes infectious. The germs continue multiplying until there are enough to produce symptoms – at which point the person realizes that they have been infected and are suffering from the disease. Thus, the incubation period is characteristic for each infectious disease because it is largely dependent on the rate of growth of the invading organism.

If the latent period of a disease is shorter than the incubation period, an infected person will be infectious before the symptoms appear and so may unwittingly transmit the disease to others – a highly effective way for the infectious agent to enable transmission to another host. The victim may or may not still be infectious after the symptoms have appeared, depending on the disease, and transmission, while still possible, becomes less likely.

Eventually the disease runs its course in the body, and for the infection to persist it *must* have infected at least one other person. At some point, the infected person passes to the noninfectious stage, often before the symptoms disappear, and onward transmission then becomes impossible.

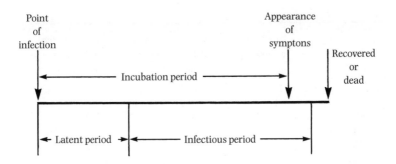

The sequence of events during a simple disease directly transmitted from one person to another. The time after infection before the appearance of symptoms is termed the incubation period. During the latent period the victim is not infectious.

Thus, the time courses of the incubation, latent and infectious periods and their relationship to one another are specific for each infectious disease and are shown in the table below.

The duration of the infectious period is the most important of these parameters, because this is the maximum length of time during which the disease can be transmitted to another person. We have all wondered, when suffering from a streaming cold and feeling sorry for ourselves, just how long we are infectious. The table reveals that the story of how infectious diseases operate is more complicated than we had hitherto supposed: the length of the infectious period varies greatly between diseases. Influenza is a particularly interesting example: there is only a maximum of three days during which this disease can be passed on – and for part of this time the victim will be too ill to get out of bed. Therefore, an epidemic of influenza would not have spread far in the days when most people were limited to travelling on foot. The situation is completely different today with air travel.

In many of the common diseases of childhood – such as measles, rubella and chickenpox – the latent period is shorter than the incubation period, and so the victim becomes infectious before the symptoms appear. These diseases are particularly difficult to control, because an apparently healthy child can

Disease	Incubation period (days)	Latent period (days)	Infectious period (days)	Is the patient infectious before symptoms appear?
Measles	8–13	6–9	6–7	Yes
Mumps	12–26	12–18	4–8	Yes
Whooping cough	6–10	21–23	7–10	No
Rubella	14–21	7–14	11–12	Yes
Diphtheria	2–5	14–21	2–5	No
Chickenpox	13–17	8–12	10–11	Yes
Poliomyelitis	7–12	1–3	14–20	Yes
Influenza	1–3	1–3	2–3	Sometimes
Smallpox	10–15	8–11	about 6	Yes

infect many other children at school, and isolation in quarantine, when the symptoms have already appeared, is of limited value.

In contrast, diphtheria and whooping cough both have a very short incubation period: the symptoms appear soon after infection, but the victim does not become infectious until a further two weeks have elapsed. These potentially lethal diseases should be easy to control – provided they are diagnosed early and the patient is then isolated. This may have saved the life of one of the authors, Chris Duncan, when, as a small boy during the Second World War, he and his younger brother Colin were both unwell and confined to bed in the same room. Colin had a severe sore throat and the family doctor came every day to paint his throat with some antiseptic – a most unpleasant experience for a small boy. Eventually, after some days of this treatment (which was completely ineffective), the doctor realized that Colin had diphtheria and he was quickly taken away to the isolation hospital. To the surprise of the family Chris did not catch diphtheria, despite having been in close contact with Colin while he was showing symptoms of the disease. Thanks to the early diagnosis by the doctor, who isolated his patient *before* he became infectious, Colin did not transmit the disease to anyone else.

HIV is an example of a disease with a long incubation period, making it very difficult to control. The latent period is of the order of days to weeks, whereas its incubation period, before any symptoms appear, is about 10 years, during which time a great many people may be infected – much of its success can be attributed to this very long period of time when a victim is infectious. Even more striking is new variant CJD (popularly called human 'mad cow' disease), which has killed 100 people since 1996 – this has an incubation period of up to 40 years.

From the foregoing, it is apparent that every disease has its own characteristic latent and infectious periods and these determine the course of events during an epidemic. Would it be possible to determine these parameters for the plague, even when there is so little information now available on which to work? First, we needed some further information on the behaviour and epidemiology of directly infectious diseases.

How does a disease spread?

Not all diseases are equally infectious. A wise friend told us that he taught his students this basic fact by a simple example: if you go to a party with smallpox, the people you dance with will catch the disease; however, if you go with measles, everyone in the room will catch it.

This leads us to the question: can you measure infectiousness? One useful measure is the average number of people to whom an infected person transmits the disease during the period of the illness. This can be illustrated with a story. Imagine a man who travels to London during one of the many plagues there in the seventeenth century and becomes infected. After he has completed his business, he returns slowly to his home village, 185 miles (300 kilometres) away, unwittingly bringing the infection with him. On arrival home, he is apparently perfectly healthy because the disease is still in its incubation period. Since he is the infected person who first arrives in the little community, he is called the *primary* case and his story is illustrated in the following diagram.

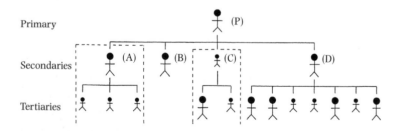

The story of the man, the primary case (P), who brought the plague to his village and infected four people (secondary cases A, B, C and D).

Suppose that he directly infects four other people (called *secondaries*). First, he infects his wife (*A*) who, in turn, transmits the disease to three of their children. The last one of these dies 11 weeks after their father was infected in London.

Second, he infects his labourer (*B*), who dies alone in his little cottage and does not infect anyone else.

Then, he infects the daughter (*C*) of the family living in a nearby cottage when she comes to play with his children. She subsequently carries the disease to other members of her family.

Finally, he goes to the tavern with an old friend (*D*), who becomes infected. A fortnight later *D* goes to a nearby fair, where he transmits the disease to many others who were enjoying the fun and games there. He certainly sets the ball rolling.

In this story the primary case, returning from a journey outside the community, infects four people and thereby initiates four lines of infection. One secondary case (man *B*) does not infect anyone else, so this line of infection dies out. Two secondary cases (wife *A* and child *C*) infect members of their family – who, in turn, may subsequently infect other people in the village with whom they come in contact. The epidemic would now be gradually gathering momentum. Man *D*, who goes to the fair in late summer during his infectious period, jostles with the crowd there and transmits the plague to seven people.

The four secondary cases between them infect twelve people (called *tertiaries*) and on average, therefore, each secondary case infects three further people.

By following all the lines of infection in an epidemic much further, it is possible to get a general measure of the infectiousness of the plague in terms of the *overall average* number of people to whom an infected person transmits the disease.

Of course, human behaviour will ensure that there will be wide variation in the rate of transmission of the disease. For example, one man shut up alone in his house will infect nobody, whereas a man going to church may infect three people during the service. A man spending an evening in the tavern with his friends may transmit the disease to four others in a single visit, but a man going to the market, mingling with the crowd and chatting with his acquaintances, may infect ten people.

This story shows how the rates of transmission along the lines of infection could vary considerably. From what we have learnt, it was relatively easy to spread the plague within the family, but more difficult to transfer it to another household. Furthermore, the disease was propagated much more readily where people were crowded together. As we have seen, the authorities in England had learnt this hard fact of life by the sixteenth century: the big annual fairs were always cancelled at the first sign of a plague epidemic.

Profile of an epidemic

The average number of people who catch the disease from an infected person is called the *transmission rate*. A great deal can be learnt about a disease by following the actual transmission lines that we have described above:

- If *on average* each infected person transmits the disease to only one other susceptible person, the disease will continue to chunter along at exactly the same level. Under these conditions, the disease is said to be endemic.

- If *on average* each infected person transmits the disease to more than one person, an epidemic will explode. The greater the transmission rate, the bigger and more rapid the explosion.

- However, if *on average* each infected person transmits the disease to fewer than one other person (for example, four infectives transmit to only two people in total), the epidemic will, inevitably, disappear. The turning point in an epidemic is when the transmission rate falls below one.

We can now put together all these details about the theory of epidemics of infectious diseases. In the next diagram we show

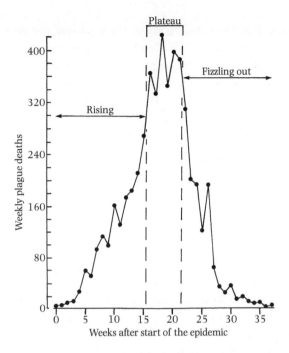

Weekly plague burials at Newcastle-upon-Tyne after the start of the epidemic, 14th May 1636. Typically, the death toll rises sharply to a peak at 16 weeks before levelling off for a plateau, which lasts for six weeks. Thereafter the epidemic fizzles out.

the time course of a plague epidemic at Newcastle-upon-Tyne, England, in the summer of 1636.

The magnitude of the mortality impresses us immediately: 350 deaths per week at the height of the epidemic translates into a death toll of over 4000. The next point that is apparent is that the community suffered from this epidemic for over nine months – a very long time for an outbreak of an infectious disease.

We can divide this epidemic at Newcastle into three stages. First, an initial, rising phase when the epidemic gets under way. Mortality rises slowly but then gathers an ever-increasing momentum. Obviously, each infective is transmitting the disease to more than one other person during this phase.

147

Second, a plateau lasting some six weeks at the peak of the epidemic, when the weekly death rate remains approximately steady. At this point, each infective *on average* will be transmitting the disease to only one other person. Although the weekly mortality is at its height and things look black for the people of Newcastle, in fact the end is in sight.

Finally, a falling phase during which the epidemic fizzles out. The average transmission rate is falling steadily now, and throughout these last stages an infected individual is *on average* spreading the disease to fewer than one other person.

This bell-shaped curve is typical of all infectious epidemics, but diseases differ markedly in the details, particularly in the rate of rise during the first stage and the duration of the epidemic. Why is this?

When a plague arrives in a community, courtesy of the primary case, the whole population of susceptible people is ready to be invaded. Transmission is relatively easy at first. If, say, each infected person transmits the disease, on average, to four other people, the number of victims *in each successive wave* will quickly mount up: 4, 16, 64, 256 ... and so the epidemic explodes at an ever-increasing rate. This is the start of the first phase of the epidemic.

But this cannot go on for ever, because more and more people are being killed and the infectious agent is encountering increasing difficulty in finding fresh victims. And so, inevitably, the transmission rate begins to fall and the epidemic reaches the plateau phase, when *on average* each infective transmits the disease to only one other person. Although the suffering community would think otherwise, an epidemiologist would realize that the worst was over – it was the beginning of the end.

The plateau phase may be quite short because the transmission rate will inevitably continue to fall and, once it is below one, the epidemic starts to fizzle out during the final phase. The mopping-up operation may take some time because, with a long incubation period, the opportunistic infection has time to seek out odd remaining victims.

Of course, human behaviour can modify the progress of an epidemic. If the community is quick off the mark in establishing quarantine measures, isolating early victims and their contacts, and if some members immure themselves safely in their houses, the rate of transmission of the disease will be significantly reduced.

The time course of a plague epidemic, such as that illustrated in the example above, is the kind of evidence that a historical epidemiologist can use. These graphs are like the fingerprints left by a criminal 400 years ago.

Interpreting the bell curve

We have seen that the exact shape of the bell curve describing the epidemic is determined by two factors that are specific and characteristic of the disease. First, the length of the incubation period, which determines the time between any two successive infections in a line of transmission; the longer the incubation period, the more slowly the epidemic develops and the longer it lasts. Second, the infectiousness of the disease, in terms of the average number of people to whom an infected person transmits the disease; the outbreak develops more rapidly when infectiousness is high.

Since we understand the factors that determine the bell shape of the graph, it is possible to write an equation that describes it and then to construct a computer program that would model an epidemic. All we have to do is to feed in the variables, such as the incubation period, the transmission rate at the start of the epidemic and the size of the population, and the computer program produces the graph of the predicted time course of the disease.

This point is illustrated by looking at computer modelling of the epidemics in the same community of two very different diseases: influenza (which has a short incubation period of three days)

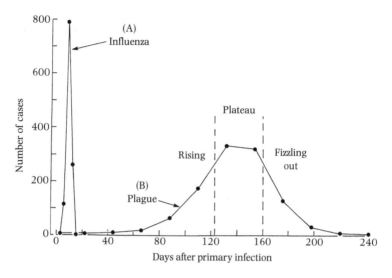

Computer modelling showing the big difference between influenza and plague epidemics.

and a hypothetical plague (with a much longer incubation period). The same initial transmission rate is assumed in both epidemics.

There is a striking difference between the two curves. Influenza races up to its peak and the epidemic is finished in about a fortnight, whereas the plague epidemic gets up steam only very slowly and persists in the population for about eight months.

We ran the computer program many times, varying the length of the incubation period, and found that the duration of the epidemic was increased as the incubation period was lengthened. With the benefit of hindsight the result is obvious, but now we had concrete facts to work on.

Since it obeyed the rules of epidemiology, there was a strong probability, as we suspected already, that the plague epidemic at Newcastle was the result of an outbreak of an infectious disease that was directly transmitted from one person to another. Because this outbreak and many of the plagues in England lasted some eight months, the computer modelling strongly suggested that this disease had a long incubation period, probably about a month – quite unlike the quick explosion of an influenza epidemic. We are now all set to use this information in the next chapter.

9

Building an Identikit of the Killer

There is one invaluable source from which it is possible to extract, with a great deal of work, all the necessary information we need. These are the registers of the English parishes; surprisingly, no historian has made detailed use of this wonderful source of information for studying the epidemiology of lethal infectious diseases. Unlike a modern detective, we cannot visit the actual scene of the crime, so it is essential to reconstruct all the details of the events of an epidemic that struck 400 years ago. For this, we need to know who was living in each household at the time and the interrelationships between the families. Sorting this out is a time-consuming job, but Sue Scott, in her historical studies of Penrith, had already established the make-up of all the families in the parish – a tremendous task given that there were 40 000 entries over a 300-year period – and she had determined the family groupings and the ages of a large number of people who were living when the plague struck. We felt that we had a vivid picture of the community there and that we knew them almost as well as we know our neighbours today.

So we returned for the third time to her findings: the nearest we could come to witnessing the scene of the crime. It was in this way that we made the breakthrough.

Historical detectives at work

The first job working with the burial registers is straightforward: count up the number of plague deaths in each month and plot them.

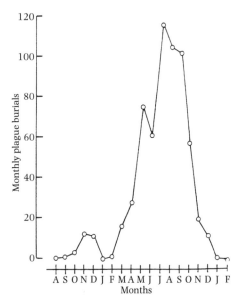

Monthly plague burials at Penrith during the epidemic that began in September 1597. There were a small number of deaths during the autumn and the outbreak almost vanished in the winter, but it reappeared in the spring and rose to a peak in summer 1598.

The first plague burial was on 22nd September 1597 and the last was recorded on 6th January 1599. The visitation at Penrith lasted for 15 months, a remarkably long time for an infectious epidemic. Once again, the villain has left his mark.

What becomes immediately apparent is that the epidemic appears to be in two separate parts that were only tenuously connected during the winter. We therefore divided the outbreak into three stages.

The first phase occurred during the autumn of 1597, when there was a mini-epidemic. After the first burial on 22nd September, there was a surprisingly long break with no further deaths until 14th October, over three weeks later. This is the next clue to the epidemiology of the plague. Evidently there was a slow start to the epidemic, with the death toll rising gently thereafter to a small peak in November–December.

As we saw before, the onset of winter in the second phase put a dampener on the plague. At the end of the sixteenth century, during the Little Ice Age, winters were very cold and unusually long. Conditions in the Eden Valley would have been particularly severe, since their dwellings (like those of most of the population of England) were cold, draughty and poorly insulated, fuel was in short supply and clothing lacked the sophistication of outdoor wear today. This disease found it very difficult to achieve transmission to its next victim and the epidemic appeared to fizzle out; there were no plague deaths in January 1598 and only a single burial in February. The plague survived through the winter only by the skin of its teeth, and there were remarkably long intervals between successive deaths at this time. If only the line of infection had been completely broken, the community would have escaped the worst that was yet to come.

The epidemic got going again in March for its third phase and fatalities started to rise steadily, with an explosion in May. This was the most devastating phase of the outbreak and deaths were at a peak in July and August.

Eventually, the third phase faded out and, after the last burial on 6th January 1599, 'HERE ENDETH THE VISITATION' was written in the registers; words that somehow seem inadequate to announce the end of what had undoubtedly been the worst period in the whole history of this little town.

The pattern of deaths from March to December 1598 in phase three corresponds exactly with the sequence of events of every epidemic of an infectious disease: an initial rising curve of infections, followed by a brief plateau before the outbreak fizzles out. Furthermore, the third phase corresponds exactly with the epidemic at Newcastle, both lasting nine months.

The real value of the parish registers

So far we have merely used the burial registers to list the monthly plague deaths. By analysing these bald statistics we have learnt a great deal about the plague, but the registers conceal much more, very valuable information about the disease. They contain information about the critical events in the lives of real people.

Below is an excerpt from the Penrith register beginning on the fateful day of 22nd September, covering the first phase of the plague. This list of names provides a little glimpse of our history – and we wonder about the story of the 'poor boyes unknown' who were buried on 15th October and 8th November.

Penrith Burial Registers, 1597

September

22	Andrew Hogson, a stranger

HERE BEGONNE THE PLAGE (GOD PUNISMET) IN PENRTH

Those that are noted with thys letter P dyed of the infirmity and that those that are noted with F are buried out on the fell.

24	Grace Walker, a poor wensh
25	Thomas Herd of Muray Gaitt
27	John Steel of Carleton
27	a poor child

October

3	*the same day beginneth plague at Carliell* [Carlisle]	
5	Thomas s. of Edmund Blaickburne	
10	Elizabeth Stell, wydowe	
11	Elizabeth d. of Thomas	
13	a poor child called Robt. Wilson	
14	Elizabeth d. of John Railton	P
15	a poor boye unknown	
15	Steve Nelson de Kill	
15	Lancelot Musegrave, gent	

15	Annes Cartmell of bridg	
20	a sonne of John Railton	P
22	Thomas Bunting, waller	
24	John Railton, culter [cutler]	P
24	Xpofer [= Christopher] s. of John Steel	
25	Margaret d. of Willm Blysse	
26	John s. of Steven Nelson	
27	Janett d. of Steven Nelson	
28	Mr. Richard Drewrie dyed at Penreth	
28	Richard s. of Mr. Willm Hutton	
28	Isabell d. of Thomas Winder	

November

1	Anthonie Railton, a boye	P
1	Xpofer s. of John Stell	
4	Mabell, wyffe of John Railton	P
4	Sussane Railton, wydowe	P
6	Katheren wyffe of Robt. Jackson	
6	Elizabeth Railton	P
8	Helen wyffe of James Emetson	
8	a poor boye unknowne	
10	Mabell d. of John Gibson	
10	Anthonie s. of Thomas Hewer	P
12	Margaret d. of Thomas Hewer	P
13	Thomas Hewer	P
15	Isabell wyffe of Roland Wood	
16	John Gibson of Dockray	
16	Ambrose Pope	
20	John Haskew, clenser	P
20	Jane d. of Thomas Sklater	
22	Marion d. of Thomas Barne	
23	Katheren d. of Thomas Hewer	P
23	Barbara wyffe of Myles Turner	
24	John s. of Robert Symson	
24	Gilbert s. of John Watson	P

24	Jane d. of Thomas Hyne	
24	Marie d. of John Watson	P
24	Thomas s. of Willm Haskew	P
26	John s. of Thomas Hewer	

December

3	Katheren wyffe of John Cooke	P
3	Annes Clerke	
3	Michaell s. of John Walker	P
3	Elizabeth d. of John Watson	
3	Gilbert s. of John Cook	P
6	John s. of Robert Richardbie	
9	Janet wyffe of Robt. Ladiman	P
12	John Lyvocke, joyner	P
16	a dau. of Richard Blysse	P
22	Alice d. of John Walker	P
22	Elizabeth wyffe of John Smalman	
24	Annes d. of Richard Blysse	P
24	Marion wyffe of Thomas Hornsbie	P
25	John s. of Richard Blysse	P
26	Jane Walker, wydowe	

We again checked the dates of the original wills of the people who died in the plague and from these, we surmised that the time from the appearance of the symptoms, when the victim knew he or she was doomed, to death was about five days.

From our earlier computer modelling, we suspected that the disease may have had a long incubation period. But would this fit with the actual events at Penrith? After reworking our computer model, we calculated that the incubation period was about 32 days and so, as a working hypothesis, we began with $32 + 5$ days, equalling 37 days, for the time from infection to death.

To work out the sequence of infections requires some careful and detailed work and we need to set out our information in a special tabular form. Anybody can try it for themselves if they obtain a copy of one of the many wonderful printed parish registers that list the burials during an outbreak of plague; these can be found in many local reference libraries. Here's how you go about it.

The start of an outbreak is of critical importance in this work. Events develop slowly at this point and analysis is possible; at the height of the epidemic the multiple burials on any one day and the total confusion that was reigning make it very difficult, if not impossible, to sort out the many lines of infection.

We first grouped the victims into families, which were then set out sequentially in the order in which they were struck by the plague. The first few months of the epidemic, starting on 16th August 1597, are shown in the diagram below.

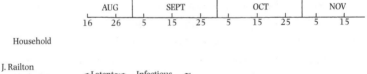

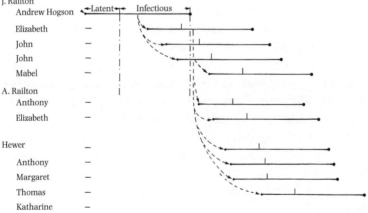

The start of the plague at Penrith in autumn 1597. The line against each victim is divided into latent and infectious periods; death is indicated by the large dot. Andrew Hogson, the stranger, who was lodging with John Railton, infected only three members of the family before he died. Mabel Railton must have caught the disease from one of her children.

159

The first victim, the stranger Andrew Hogson, died on 22nd September, and his burial can be marked on the diagram with a dot. Because we believe that he was infected 37 days earlier, a line extending back to 16th August can be drawn against his name, indicating the period from infection to death.

Hogson arrived between 23rd August and 6th September 1597 and lodged with John Railton, a cutler, who lived in a little stone-roofed, white-washed cottage that once stood at Nether End, which was part of the great north-west road that ran through the centre of the town. Hogson infected three of the family when they were all cooped up indoors, but did not pass the disease on to anyone else. Presumably he did not spend a great deal of time in the inn, nor did he move around the town much.

The family of John Railton is listed next on the diagram. The burials of the daughter Elizabeth (age 22), son John (age 20) and John Railton himself are indicated by dots, with each of the lines carried back 37 days to show when they were infected. It becomes clear from the diagram that Hogson transmitted the disease to each of them before he died during the period when he was infectious. The register shows that Mabel, the wife of John Railton, died on 4th November, but it can be seen from the diagram that she was infected *after* Hogson died, so the disease must have been passed to her by one of her family, probably her daughter Elizabeth. Thus, the man who brought the plague to Penrith directly infected only three people there.

The epidemic spread next to the family of Anthony Railton, brother of John. Elizabeth and John Railton carried the plague first to their Railton cousins, Anthony (age 14) and Elizabeth (age 22), infecting them indoors when they were visiting their home.

The plague had surmounted its first hurdle: it had made the jump to another household. Continuing an infection within a family was relatively easy, but if the disease were not to die out completely it was essential that it transferred to another household. Mission was now accomplished.

The members of the Hewer family were infected next, with the father Thomas and three children dying between 10th November and 23rd November. The diagram shows that John Railton and his two children must have been responsible for transmitting the disease to them. Anthony Railton senior had married Isabel Hewer, who was the sister of Thomas Hewer. So it was quite natural for Elizabeth Railton to visit her relative Elizabeth Hewer, who was of the same age. Unfortunately, while there, she infected three members of the Hewer family.

In this way the epidemic slowly got up steam in the autumn of 1597. From our analysis, we believed that the disease was mainly spread by the teenagers and young people visiting their relatives. For example, the register shows that Mary (age 17) and Gilbert (age 8) Watson were buried on 24th November – they were also cousins of the Railton families.

The course of the epidemic can easily be followed and illustrated in this way – at least in its early stages – and we continued the analysis through until the following May. By this time our diagram was huge and covered the desk: it extended for over 220 days and the deaths of over 75 plague victims were recorded.

Once we stood back and examined this graphical description of the plague, everything became clear. There was no doubt that this was a 'simple' infectious disease spread directly from one person to another; it was caught from an infected person in exactly the same way that we catch chickenpox today. A person was infectious for a long time before the symptoms appeared. The disease also spread easily within the family during the autumn, but it was more difficult at this time of year to make the jump to another household. In contrast, the disease hopped readily between households in the following summer, when the epidemic spread widely and rapidly.

Even more importantly, we could determine the vital statistics of the plague:

- Latent period = 10 to 12 days
- Infectious period before appearance of symptoms = 20 to 22 days

- Therefore incubation period = approximately 32 days

- Average period displaying symptoms before death = 5 days

- Total infectious period = about 27 days, assuming that the victim remained infectious until death, although we believe that infectiousness probably decreased once the symptoms had appeared. (The analysis suggests that people were probably most infectious soon after the start of the infectious period.)

- Average time from the point of infection to death = 37 days.

We could now divide the horizontal line against each victim on the diagram into the latent and infectious periods.

We were astounded when we worked out the duration of these critical periods that characterized the epidemic at Penrith, and we believed that our conclusions were probably correct for all the other plagues of Europe. The correspondence with the universal 40-day quarantine period confirmed that we were correct. This was the photofit of a dangerous serial killer, the vital statistics of the most wanted medieval criminal. This was the breakthrough.

Subsequently, we studied more than 50 different plague outbreaks in England and verified the length of the latent and infectious periods many times. There were no exceptions to this rule.

Here, before our eyes, was the explanation for the persistence of these epidemics. It was evident that the key to the success of the plague in the Middle Ages lay in its exceptionally long incubation period. By this means the plague could jump very long distances, even in the days of primitive transport; it could appear apparently from nowhere; it could mysteriously reappear many days after the last victim had died. Since the incubation period of the plague was 32 days, a person once infected had over a month in which he could travel a considerable distance before the dreaded symptoms appeared, when he began to feel seriously unwell and people knew that he must be isolated. During this unusually long incubation period, he was fully infectious for about three weeks – plenty of time to infect unwittingly all and sundry. An epidemic would be up and running before anyone knew about it.

We had discovered the plague's secret weapon.

10

Debunking History

All we had uncovered so far was in complete contrast to the traditional teaching for the whole of the twentieth century, which was that all the plagues were not the result of a normal infectious disease. Everybody believed that the plague was caught from rats and fleas. But as we have seen, everyone in Europe in the fourteenth century assumed instantly that you could catch this terrible infection from somebody you met and this belief continued throughout the age of plagues (with good reason – the evidence was before them) and then persisted for over 200 years until the end of the nineteenth century.

Daniel Defoe had perspicaciously noted that, in the Great Plague of London in 1665,

> because of its infectious nature, the disease may be spread by apparently healthy people who harbour the disease but have not yet exhibited the symptoms. Such a person was in fact a poisoner, a walking destroyer perhaps for a week or a fortnight before his death, who might have ruined those that he would have hazarded his life to save ... breathing death upon them, even perhaps his tender kissing and embracings of his own children.

It is obvious from this that, at least by the seventeenth century, people understood the basic biology of plague: in particular, the time span during which an infected person could spread the disease and the specific danger of droplet infection. That they understood this without our modern medical knowledge speaks volumes for their capacity for objective observation. And yet for the whole of the twentieth century, going completely against common sense, it was universally and unequivocally believed that all the plagues were caused by a disease of rodents called bubonic plague, and that the infection was transmitted to people from rats by fleas. Rats and fleas are the established dogma of all history books today. What a pity that little attention has been paid to Defoe's observation.

This chapter explains how this muddled thinking came about and describes the fierce scientific debate that is now raging.

Bubonic plague

Unbeknown to most people, a completely different disease had been grumbling quietly along in India and elsewhere in Asia for centuries. It was usually fatal when it appeared in humans and was characterized by swellings of the 'glands' or lymph nodes in the armpits and groin, which were termed buboes. Hence this disease was named bubonic plague.

Towards the end of the nineteenth century, bubonic plague erupted and became a serious medical problem in India and also spread widely into south-east Asia. Research teams were sent out and a debt of gratitude is certainly owed to Alexandre Yersin, a French microbiologist who was born in Switzerland, and to the Plague Commission of India for a splendid piece of scientific detective work in which they meticulously unravelled the complex biology and epidemiology of bubonic plague.

Yersin trained under Pasteur in Paris and arrived in Hong Kong in 1894 when he answered an appeal for help from the plague-stricken colony, which was resigned to a major pandemic. Working with very little assistance in a hut made of straw that he built himself, because the Hong Kong administrators refused to provide him with a laboratory, he was reduced to bribing mortuary guards for access to plague corpses. Yersin demonstrated conclusively that bubonic plague is a disease of rodents, spread from one rodent to another by fleas. He showed that the course of an epidemic in humans is dependent on many factors because of the multiple hosts involved, and that it is completely different from an epidemic of a simple infection, which is spread directly from person to person. Yersin demonstrated that the infectious agent that is transmitted from rat to flea to human is a bacterium, which was named *Yersinia pestis* – *Yersinia* after the man who discovered it and *pestis* after the disease (the pestilence) that it was thought to have caused.

To avoid confusion and misunderstanding, we now name the epidemics of the Black Death and all subsequent plagues haemorrhagic plague (because extensive haemorrhaging is an important symptom) to distinguish them clearly from bubonic plague.

The characteristic (but not specific) symptom of bubonic plague is the appearance of the bubo. Once Yersin had announced his seminal results, it was realized that victims of haemorrhagic plague also sometimes presented with swollen lymph glands. It was, apparently, immediately assumed that the Black Death was caused by bubonic plague. Nobody compared the two diseases objectively and for the whole of the twentieth century this view, based solely on the appearance of one symptom, was written on tablets of stone and universally accepted without question.

No scientist should base conclusions or develop a hypothesis on the basis of a single observation or experiment. No doctor would make a diagnosis on the basis of a single symptom; instead he would examine his patient carefully, checking all the signs and symptoms; he would probably await the results of further laboratory tests and he would make a decision when he could see the whole picture. Scientists and medical practitioners should also be ready to change their minds if subsequent experiments fail to confirm their initial conclusions, or if the patient does not respond to the prescribed treatment.

Of course, this universal and unquestioning acceptance in about 1900 of the view that haemorrhagic plague was no more than a series of epidemics of bubonic plague was a complete reversal of the opinion that had previously been held for over 500 years, and the history books had to be rewritten. Various tales about the plagues had to be embroidered or even adapted to fit with the new story of bubonic plague.

Even distinguished scholars contributed to the obfuscation, such as the microbiologist Professor Shrewsbury, whom we have already encountered. In 1970, in his retirement, he published a wonderful piece of scholarship entitled *A History of Bubonic Plague in the British Isles*. He had meticulously researched and assembled every piece of information relating to the plagues in Britain, although he did not extend his studies to continental Europe. The result is a bible for all serious students of the plague.

As you would guess from the title, Shrewsbury, along with everybody else, firmly believed that bubonic plague was responsible for the plagues in Britain, and yet he was a trained scientist as well as a qualified medical practitioner. He saw clearly that in many of the outbreaks it was biologically impossible that bubonic plague was the cause. He, above everyone else, knew what he was talking about and he was probably the first to point out possible cracks in the foundations of the accepted story.

He began by discounting (correctly, as we shall see) many of the epidemics as being bubonic plague, usually suggesting (incorrectly) that typhus was responsible. When epidemics were reported in cold weather (inimical to bubonic plague), he suggested that it was probably a mild winter. When he found that the records indicated that about 50 per cent of the population had died in the Black Death (far too high for bubonic plague), he was forced to suggest that the records might have been wildly exaggerated and that the true mortality may have been nearer 5 per cent (an impossibly low value, as we have seen).

However, Shrewsbury remained a stalwart defender of the view that many of the epidemics in Britain were outbreaks of bubonic plague, and he would have been flabbergasted by the criticism that greeted his honest appraisal. His crime, apparently, was not that of accepting the impossible but of suggesting that there were any loopholes at all in the working hypothesis and that not all epidemics were outbreaks of bubonic plague.

The Black Death: A Biological Reappraisal

Dr Graham Twigg is a distinguished zoologist who has specialized all his professional life in the biology of rodents in general and rats in particular. He is one of the leading experts in the world today on the biology of bubonic plague. He published *The Black Death: A Biological Reappraisal* in 1984, in which he carefully assembled all the evidence. This book is exactly what it purports to be, a critical and authoritative appraisal of the Black Death (he does not consider the later plagues) by an expert, and he concludes that this pandemic was *not* caused by bubonic plague. Twigg was the first person to recognize this and to state it publicly. It was a path-finding piece of work.

Alas, it was completely ignored, and books and television programmes describing the behaviour of rats and fleas in plague epidemics continued to pour out. The historian R. S. Bray simply said, 'There are many objections to Twigg's thesis and it would be wearisome to list them all.'

Happily, Graham Twigg has continued to work on plagues, concentrating now on the later epidemics in England. He carries on the fight for acceptance of his seminal views and regularly contributes papers in which his common sense and all-round expertise shine through his elegant prose.

The next step

If what everybody believes were true, that bubonic plague and *Yersinia pestis* were responsible for the multitude of the terrible epidemics of haemorrhagic plague, there would be no question of whether the Black Death will return. Bubonic plague has never gone away; indeed, since Yersin's discovery it has spread far and wide through the world and we have learnt to live with it. There are many individual cases and some mini-epidemics each year, but there is no reason to fear an outbreak: it is readily treatable if diagnosed in time and is no threat to humans.

We have already seen that haemorrhagic plague, the cause of the Black Death and other plagues, was a directly infectious disease. In the next chapter, we explain the nature of bubonic plague and examine how the facts do not match.

11

The Biology of Bubonic Plague: A Myth Revisited

Ladies and gentlemen of the jury, the somewhat seedy prisoner in the dock that you see before you, with his attendant fleas, is Mr Rat. He stands universally accused for the whole of the twentieth century of being indirectly responsible for the Black Death, the most horrible disease ever to strike mankind. I shall bring evidence to show unequivocally that my client has been seriously maligned and is completely innocent of the charge on which he was wrongly found guilty 100 years ago. I ask that he be released without a stain on his character.

Humans have been afflicted by bubonic plague for hundreds of years, particularly in the central Asiatic plateau, which is considered to be the home of the disease, and there are said to have been 232 outbreaks in China between AD 37 and 1718. It had become established in Yum-nan and, in 1855, troops were sent to suppress a rebellion there, whereupon bubonic plague spread further, probably as a consequence of the movement of refugees. It reached the provincial capital Kunming in 1866 and Canton and Hong Kong eight years later, a fairly slow rate of spread. The infection then moved back to India via Calcutta in 1895 and Bombay in the following year. The great pandemic of the twentieth century had begun. Bubonic plague spread to the African and American continents and has persisted there and in

Asia to this day, although the plagues of Europe disappeared by about 1670, over 300 years ago.

Resistant rodents: the key to understanding bubonic plague

Bubonic plague is a disease of rodents that is only occasionally and accidentally spread to humans. The key to understanding the disease lies in the very marked differences among rodents in their susceptibility to an infection by the bacterium. Rats are highly vulnerable and die of *Yersinia pestis*, whereas other rodents, such as gerbils and voles, are resistant and can survive an infection, apparently without much harm. This difference is of great importance in determining the persistence of an outbreak of bubonic plague in a population of rodents, because the disease will die out if they are all highly susceptible, whereas it persists in areas where there is a balance between susceptible and resistant hosts. For example, in central Colorado an isolated colony of prairie dogs was completely wiped out by the disease when it was introduced there because they were highly susceptible and all died. The take-home message is that bubonic plague can persist in local rodents only if a reservoir of resistant species is present.

Hotbeds of bubonic plague

Bubonic plague is usually transported around the world's ports by infected rats carried by boat. On arrival at a port in a suitable locality, the disease is transferred from the rats, via their fleas, to the local resistant rodent species, such as gerbils or ground squirrels, and in this way it can then persist for long periods of time. Occasionally the disease then spreads widely and rapidly to susceptible rodents, causing spectacular mortality. In some of these outbreaks dead rats have been collected by the barrowful, and their bodies are often the first indications that bubonic plague is present in a locality.

The geographic distribution of rodents (excluding rats) that have been reported with an infection of *Yersinia pestis* is very revealing:

North America	51
South America	42
Asia (excluding India)	44
Africa	44
India	11
Europe	0

During the twentieth century, the development and use of faster steamships meant that bubonic plague could be transported more easily to ports around the globe before all the rats on board had died. The disease thus spread from Asia and became established in North America, South America and southern Africa.

The crucial point here is that, despite this readiness to spread, *Yersinia pestis* has never persisted in any European rodents (which are not resistant). Therefore bubonic plague could not have been established there during the age of plagues – nor, most significantly, in the twentieth century when the disease was being spread elsewhere throughout the world. The conclusion is inescapable: it was impossible that *Yersinia pestis* was responsible for the haemorrhagic plagues in England and continental Europe.

The dreaded rats

In Europe today there are only two species of rat: the brown rat and the black rat. The brown rat is a hardy animal and is the one that is commonly seen today. Most importantly from our point of view, this species came from Russia in the early eighteenth century, not arriving in Britain until some 400 years after the arrival of the Black Death and some 60 years after the last plague. So it could not have had anything to do with the spread of the plague and it may be dismissed as having any possible role in our story.

The black rat, on the other hand, is a descendant of an animal that probably originated in India and established itself in the tropics, in both towns and rural areas. Although the precise date is uncertain, it is believed that it arrived in England some time in the Middle Ages.

If this rodent is introduced to a port in the tropics where there are no competitors, it spreads rapidly. In temperate latitudes, however, it is confined to buildings because for most of the year the outdoor temperatures are too low for its liking. Unlike the brown rat, it is a good climber and can readily gain access to ships, which have carried it over much of the world, and it lives in the roofs and ceilings of buildings but rarely inhabits burrows or tunnels in the ground.

In the Middle Ages, the black rat could have survived in the warmer areas of southern France, Spain and Italy, and it may have existed in the grain ports of northern France and southern Britain, although only in small numbers. The population of black rats in a town would have disappeared after a few years without recurrent introductions.

Today, this rodent is a native of the Mediterranean area, and in England it is sometimes found in the ports, but does not usually spread more than a few kilometres inland. Populations in England in the twentieth century depended for their survival on frequent topping-up by the importation in cargoes. With canal traffic ceasing and containers replacing loose cargo, the animal has begun to disappear even from the ports so that now it is a rare mammal in Britain. Small populations still exist on Lundy Island in the Bristol Channel and on the Shiant Islands in the Outer Hebrides.

The black rat was the only rodent present that could possibly have carried bubonic plague in Europe in the Middle Ages. However, it needs the warmth of human habitations and does not spread far from them. Even when bubonic plague appears in humans in warm countries, its spread is governed by the climate. It is inconceivable that the black rat could have transmitted bubonic plague rapidly and widely in winter.

No rats in rural England

Dr Twigg has continued with his careful study of the black rat in England during the age of the plagues and has collated overwhelming unpublished evidence that it did not spread to rural areas. We are grateful to him for telling us of two examples. The design of dovecotes in England was completely unchanged until the 1720s, 50 years after the plague had disappeared, because there were no problems with predation by rats. However, when the brown rat arrived and dispersed through the countryside, it quickly discovered how to plunder the nests, eating both the birds and their eggs, and the dovecotes had to be redesigned to make them rat proof.

Farmers also had no problems with damage to stored grain until the brown rat appeared. Corn ricks were built on the ground. After 1730, for the first time, grain had to be stored on special mushroom-shaped, rat-proof structures called staddles on which the date of construction was carved. The spread of the brown rat can be plotted by the dates on these stones.

These are splendid pieces of scholarship that confirm that the black rat could not have transmitted bubonic plague through rural England during the three centuries when haemorrhagic plague rampaged freely.

The plagues in Iceland

We have seen that haemorrhagic plague was carried across the sea to Iceland and that there were two severe and well-authenticated epidemics in the fifteenth century. Yet it is known for certain that no rats were present on the island during the three centuries of the plagues. Rats did not appear until hundreds of years later.

Human mortality was high and 60 per cent of the scattered population died in the first outbreak. Infections continued through the winter when the average temperature was below $-3\ °C$; transmission by human fleas was therefore not possible. This one piece of evidence alone is unequivocal and conclusive: it is completely impossible that bubonic plague caused the epidemics in Iceland.

Absence of dead rats

It has been regularly reported that the start of an outbreak of bubonic plague spreading to humans is presaged by rats dying in the streets: in a small village perhaps just a few; in a large South African township perhaps many barrowloads. And yet it is generally agreed that there is no mention in any of the accounts of rat mortality during the epidemics in the age of plagues in Europe. One comment was that 'Historians have noted that contemporary accounts omit any mention of rat mortality', but they have chosen to ignore this important point.

Speed of spread

In England and particularly in France the pestilence leapt over large distances, sometimes 100 miles (150 kilometres) in a few days, with no intermediate outbreaks. As we have seen at Malpas in Cheshire in 1625, it was carried 185 miles (300 kilometres) by someone returning from a visit to London. The Black Death spread from southern Italy to the Arctic Circle in three years.

This rapid movement is completely inconsistent with the spread of bubonic plague, which is dependent on the limited activity of rodents. The Plague Research Commission of India gave an example where in 1907, it took six weeks to travel 100 yards (160 metres). In South Africa in 1899–1925, it moved only about 8 to 12 miles (13 to 20 kilometres) per year.

Flea-bitten

We have seen that bubonic plague can potentially circulate between a flea, a rat, humans and resistant rodents. Clearly, this disease is much more complex than we had thought. Now we look at the role of the flea.

Adult fleas are small, wingless insects that are suited to clinging by means of hooks and their legs are adapted for impressive jumping – it is in this way that they transfer to their different hosts. Their mouthparts are designed for piercing the skin of suitable, warm-blooded mammals, whereupon blood is sucked from a tiny vein into the flea's stomach. A flea takes in a large number of bacteria in a blood meal from an infected rodent, which then form a solid mass by dividing rapidly. When the infected flea attacks another rodent, the *Yersinia* are driven straight into the bloodstream of the bitten host, and in this way the bacteria are transferred from mammal to mammal.

In the wild, the survival of the flea depends critically on its ability to reproduce and raise more fleas, which in turn depends on environmental and other factors. The rat flea can lay about 300 to 400 eggs (the adult is a veritable reproductive machine), but the temperature and humidity of the environment greatly affect both egg laying and the development of the larvae. A temperature of between 18 °C and 27 °C and relative humidity of 70 per cent are ideal for egg laying, whereas temperatures below 18 °C inhibit it.

Graham Twigg has collected all the available climatological data for central England between AD 900 and 1900, and has shown that at no time was the average July–August temperature above 18.5 °C and suitable for flea hatching. Britain did not have a climate capable of sustaining regular seasonal outbreaks of flea-borne bubonic plague, even in the summer months, and certainly not in the winter. Indeed, in Europe it is only in the south-west, in the Mediterranean coastal region and in the Italian and Iberian peninsulas, that conditions may possibly have been suitable.

It is inconceivable that fleas could have been breeding and that black rats could have been active during the epidemics in England and Scotland, nor in Iceland and Norway close to the Arctic

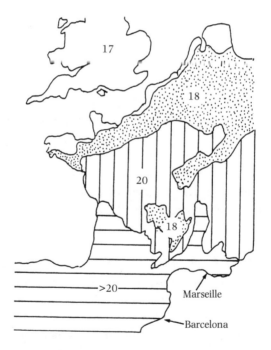

Mean July temperature in °C in western Europe in the twentieth century. It is only in Spain and the Mediterranean coast of France that summer temperatures are suitable for sustaining seasonal outbreaks of flea-borne bubonic plague.

Circle. It is important to remember that during the Little Ice Age, when the plague was rampaging most fiercely, the conditions would have ensured that flea breeding was absolutely impossible.

Bubonic plague in humans

The important point established above is that bubonic plague is a natural disease of rodents, and that humans are only occasionally and accidentally infected through the bites of rat fleas, *which have deserted their normal host after its death*. Consequently, the appearance of bubonic plague in humans is completely unpredictable. If an infected wild rodent strays near human habitations and then shares its fleas with rats living around the settlement, *Yersinia* can spread from rodent to rat, and from rat to human. The rat is just an intermediary and is not a reservoir of bubonic plague: its role is to die and then pass on the infection.

There are several other ways in which humans can be infected. When they go out – for example when hunting or picnicking – they may catch bubonic plague directly from the fleas living on wild rodents. This mode of infection usually occurs on a small scale, from trapping, skinning or eating wild rodents, although in Manchuria between 1910 and 1911, 60 000 hunters caught bubonic plague from marmots, which they were hunting for their skins. Occasionally someone gets plague from eating a domestic animal (such as a goat or camel) that has ranged over an area inhabited by infected wild rodents.

The flea is central to the spread of bubonic plague between its different hosts. Not surprisingly, human mortality in outbreaks of bubonic plague is always relatively low because it is a disease of rodents and it is spread randomly by fleas, whereas the death toll when haemorrhagic plague struck a native population in England or continental Europe was probably about 30–40 per cent, although it could be as high as 60 per cent.

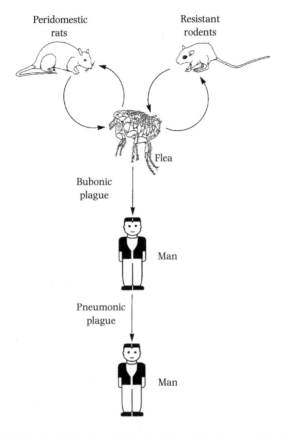

The central role of the flea in cycling *Yersinia pestis* between resistant rodents and susceptible rats and in transmitting bubonic plague to humans. Direct transmission between humans is possible only with pneumonic plague.

There are two forms of bubonic plague in humans: bubonic and pneumonic (which we describe in more detail below). In any outbreak in humans today, patients with bubonic plague are found in open wards. They have been infected by fleas and *they are not normally infectious to other people*.

The bubo is the characteristic symptom of bubonic (but not pneumonic) plague and gives the disease its name. It is a lump of variable size formed by a swollen lymph gland that is found most commonly in the groin, but its location depends on where the flea bites and this, in turn, depends on how the victim is clothed. Dr A. B. Christie, who wrote an authoritative account of infectious diseases, says that an Indonesian peasant wearing only pants and a hat can be bitten anywhere, most easily on the legs. A Libyan farmer wears boots, breeches and flouncing robes, and the flea needs all its wits to get to his skin: the arm or the neck may be easier than the leg. When a patient gets plague from skinning an animal, the infection will be through his hands and the bubo will develop in his armpit. If he eats the flesh, the bacterium may settle on his tonsils and the bubo will be in his neck. Infection of humans with *Yersinia pestis* is obviously a haphazard business.

The bubo appears early in the illness, on the first or second day, and is usually very painful and tender. In patients who live long enough or survive, it breaks down and discharges pus.

There is wide variation in the onset and course of the disease: it may be mild enough to be overlooked or it may be overwhelming. Most significantly, the incubation period is typically only two to six days after exposure, notably different from the value that we have derived for haemorrhagic plague.

We looked up an autopsy report of a seaman who had died of authentic bubonic plague in 1900 and noted that the internal organs showed only limited signs of necrosis. The importance of this point will become apparent later when we describe the reports of primitive dissections of the bodies of people who had died of the haemorrhagic plague in the seventeenth century.

Pneumonic plague: a deadly variant

In about 5 per cent of cases of bubonic plague, before the victim dies, the bacterium reaches his lungs and if the patient lives long enough he coughs out the bacterium in his sputum. Anyone who is in close contact may inhale it and get pneumonic plague. From then on, one patient can directly infect another with pneumonic plague in the same way without the intervention of a flea. The onset is abrupt and severe and, most significantly, the victim is rapidly prostrated and dies on about the third and never later than the sixth day. Without modern medical treatment, pneumonic plague is invariably fatal.

A full understanding of pneumonic plague is of particular importance when we look at the plagues in Europe. Bubonic plague could not suddenly jump long distances in a cold climate where there were no resistant species of rodents, no active fleas and only the sedentary black rat to carry the disease around. It is for this reason that many people have claimed that the person-to-person transmission of pneumonic plague was responsible for the plague epidemics of Europe.

However, they ignore three important points. First, it has been clearly demonstrated that pneumonic plague cannot occur in the absence of the bubonic form and that it cannot persist independently. Therefore, all the objections to the presence of bubonic plague still stand. Pneumonic infection probably markedly exacerbated the mortality of many outbreaks of bubonic plague, but its main effect was confined within the household and the family who nursed the patient and such neighbours who came to visit.

Secondly, there is general agreement that the time from infection to death in pneumonic plague is short, probably about five days, and a patient will be infectious for an even shorter period. It is completely impossible that a mortally sick person who was rapidly prostrated when infected with the pneumonic form and who was only three days away from death could have spread the disease over long distances, either by land or sea. Consequently, an outbreak of pneumonic plague would be short-lived and the epidemic would soon be finished off. This is the exact opposite of what we saw in the bell-shaped curve of a long-lasting epidemic of haemorrhagic plague.

Thirdly, the presentation of buboes during the plagues of Europe rules out pneumonic plague because these do not appear in this form of the disease.

Was the human flea responsible?

Other historians who reluctantly came to accept that the plague was directly transmitted from one person to another came up with a fresh idea: they claimed that bubonic plague was spread via the human flea. Although transmission via this route is possible and does occur, it is considerably less effective than the rat flea, so that all the objections to the involvement of fleas that we have listed above still apply, only more so.

In any case, proponents of this far-fetched suggestion, which does seem to be an example of clutching at straws, do not say how the human fleas came to be infected with *Yersinia pestis* in the first place. If it was from an initial epidemic of standard bubonic plague with resistant rodents, rats and fleas, then all the arguments presented above apply, with an unnecessary additional complication that makes this scenario even more unlikely.

Persistence of a myth

We can be quite certain that bubonic plague has been wrongly identified as the culprit and Mr Rat is completely innocent:

- Absence of resistant rodents in Europe.
- No rats in rural England.
- Bubonic plague spreads too slowly.
- Temperatures too cold for fleas.
- Mortality of bubonic plague is too low.
- Spread of bubonic plague was impossible in the conditions of Iceland.

Why, then, has the bubonic plague theory persisted? Most historians lack detailed knowledge of the complex biology of bubonic plague and it is for this reason that we have devoted a whole chapter to explaining the interactions between fleas, resistant rodents, rats, humans and the environment that are necessary for an epidemic of this disease to occur.

Few have studied the outbreaks in continental Europe alongside those that occurred in England. For example, if Professor Shrewsbury had studied the plagues in Europe, he would never have described some of them as typhus, nor would he ever have estimated the mortality in the Black Death at only 5 per cent, to which extreme he was forced so as to justify his belief that bubonic plague was the infectious agent.

It was just too easy, when Yersin announced the results of his outstanding research, to jump to the conclusion that *Yersinia pestis* was also responsible for all the plagues of Europe without bothering to examine the evidence and facts objectively. Once historians had made up their mind, they obdurately clung to their opinion and it was accepted without question by everybody for the whole of the twentieth century.

With all the evidence before us, it is impossible to escape the conclusion that haemorrhagic plague was unrelated to bubonic plague. Indeed, apart from the fact that the victims of both diseases presented with enlarged glands and subcutaneous swellings, it is difficult to suggest a more unlikely candidate than *Yersinia pestis* as the infectious agent of haemorrhagic plague.

We have categorically dismissed bubonic plague as having a role in our story. Nevertheless, did the disease ever break out sporadically, albeit briefly, in favourable areas of Europe?

12

DNA Analysis: A Red Herring

Haemorrhagic plague, from 1347 to about 1670, was confined to Europe and occasionally to the North African coastlands. Bubonic plague, on the other hand, was widespread and rampant throughout Asia and the Middle East during the three centuries when the mysterious pestilence dominated Europe. Indeed, it penetrated right up to the doorstep of Europe. We now know that bubonic plague could never have become firmly established there because there were no resistant rodents present that could have formed a permanent reservoir for the disease. In addition, as we have seen, the climatic conditions were completely unsuitable over much of this vast area. And so effectively, the two plagues held separate strongholds.

There is an exception, however: Graham Twigg was the first to show that the climate and temperature of the Mediterranean coastlands would have been suitable for flea breeding during the summer. Shipping from the eastern Mediterranean and North Africa must have been regularly bringing black rats infected with bubonic plague into the ports of Italy, Spain and southern France during the age of plagues. Did any of these rats come ashore and establish a brief epidemic among the local black rats and other susceptible rodents?

We decided to examine the records of likely ports and discovered that, indeed, there was evidence of minor outbreaks of bubonic plague along the Mediterranean coastlands.

In Italy, the health authorities of the northern states called such outbreaks of bubonic plague 'minor pests', to distinguish them from the 'major pests' (which they took much more seriously). The epidemics began in the ports and sometimes spread a little way inland, but they did not persist and the disease never became established.

The Mediterranean port of Barcelona in Spain was struck by at least 11 outbreaks of bubonic plague between 1370 and 1590, but these caused very few deaths and occurred sporadically. In the fifteenth century, Barcelona was a thriving city of merchants, navigators, traders and professionals and it had traffic with the whole of the Mediterranean, and so would have received a regular supply of infected black rats and fleas. The epidemics did not spread far inland or to any other city and, most importantly, mortality did not rise to a peak and then fall again, as we saw earlier in a typical epidemic of an infectious disease. The outbreak in Barcelona in 1497, for example, showed single deaths daily from July to September, and this is quite unlike the course of events in haemorrhagic plague.

The situation is more complicated than we had first thought. While haemorrhagic plague rampaged throughout Europe, there were undoubtedly occasional epidemics of bubonic plague in the Mediterranean ports. They were necessarily brief because they were extinguished once all the local rodents had died. These localized, sporadic and short-lasting epidemics of bubonic plague were of no significance in comparison with the terrible mortality and suffering that the people had to endure from haemorrhagic plague, but they have added to the confusion of present-day historians.

Genuine bubonic plague at Marseille in 1720

Fifty years after haemorrhagic plague had completely disappeared, the Mediterranean port of Marseille in France suffered from a major plague epidemic that has been well documented. We have fully analysed the sequence of events and there is no doubt: this was a genuine epidemic of bubonic plague. The pattern and details of the outbreak are completely different from haemorrhagic plague. So Graham Twigg's suggestion that the climate and conditions in the Mediterranean ports were suitable for *Yersinia pestis* was certainly correct.

Even though the health authorities had not seen a major plague epidemic for 50 years, they knew what they must do. They put the old, well-established 40-day quarantine measures and *cordons sanitaires* into practice. Eventually, ring fences were set up over distances of many miles. Of course, these precautions were completely ineffective because they were dealing with a disease that was new to them. Rats and their attendant fleas are not contained by a *cordon sanitaire*, nor are they subject to any sort of quarantine. The people of Marseille were doomed from the start; everything that had been learnt during 300 years of suffering from haemorrhagic plague was worthless in the face of this new enemy.

By 1720 the brown rat had probably arrived in the port and multiplied prodigiously. In 1966 Raymond Roberts related at a meeting of the Royal Society of Medicine that the fishermen netted 10 000 dead rats in the harbour and dragged the corpses out to sea. This does show the absolutely devastating mortality in the rat population when it was hit by an infection of *Yersinia pestis*.

Eventually, bubonic plague spread outwards into the country-side of Provence, creeping along to villages and hamlets and to some towns in the area.

The debate rages on today

'We believe that we can end the controversy: medieval Black Death was [bubonic] plague'. So wrote Didier Raoult, Michel Drancourt and their colleagues at the University of the Mediterranean in Marseille in October 2000. They had dug up skeletons from graves in Provence in the French Mediterranean coastlands. These purported to have come from plague victims in the Black Death and in the sixteenth and eighteenth centuries. They had made DNA extracts from the dental pulp of the teeth and, using the tools of molecular biology, claimed to have identified the presence of *Yersinia pestis*.

This news is somewhat disconcerting at first sight – it goes against everything we have established. However, there are a number of reasons why their premature and sweeping assertion can be confidently discounted.

Identification of the excavated graves

The graveyard of Saint Côme and Saint-Damien in Montpellier, southern France, had been used as an extramural cemetery from the ninth to the seventeenth centuries. Raoult and his colleagues concluded that

> of the 800 graves excavated at this site, it seems likely that four were catastrophe graves because they contained multiple skeletons without shrouds. These four graves have been dated as having been dug between the thirteenth and late fourteenth centuries, because of their position on the top of a thirteenth century remblai [embankment], behind a wall dated from the second half of the fourteenth century ... Therefore we hypothesized that these grave skeletons were those of Black Death victims.

There is no reason to suppose from this slack archaeological investigation that the skeletons were victims of the Black Death in Provence in 1348. All we can conclude is that the bodies were buried some time between the ninth and seventeenth centuries.

The second mass grave was excavated at Lambesc in Provence. It contained 133 skeletons and 'historical data indicate ... that they were victims from ancient bubonic plague quarantine hospitals and were buried between May and September 1590.' Again, the historical and archaeological evidence is sketchy.

The third grave contained some 200 skeletons buried in May 1722 in Marseille. This was more than 50 years after haemorrhagic plague had disappeared and, as we have seen, was the scene of a genuine outbreak of bubonic plague. It is not surprising that traces of *Yersinia pestis* have been found in these victims.

Is the DNA-testing technique valid?

At a meeting of the British Society for Microbiology in Manchester in September 2003, Alan Cooper, head of the Ancient Biomolecules Centre at Oxford University, suggested that the DNA-analysis technique used by Raoult and Drancourt was flawed. Furthermore, he believes that splitting the teeth and scraping out the inside, as the French team did, contaminated them with bacteria. Suspiciously, nearly all the French samples tested positive – a high survival rate for DNA in the warm climate of Montpellier.

The field of DNA analysis is a bourgeoning one today, but its history has been plagued by problems of contamination from the DNA that is ever-present on human hands, bacteria and other sources. For example, a Viking tooth recently tested at Oxford yielded genetic material from at least 20 different people. To compound the problem, even relatively recent bones contain vanishingly small quantities of DNA that are difficult to extract.

Alan Cooper remains convinced that the *Yersinia* DNA found by Raoult and his colleagues in teeth from bodies buried at Marseille and Provence is a case of mistaken identification because of accidental contamination of the samples.

Have traces of *Yersinia pestis* been found in plague victims elsewhere in Europe?

Alan Cooper and his colleagues, using molecular biology techniques that they believe are specific for *Yersinia*, have analysed 121 teeth from 66 skeletons found in five mass graves, including one in East Smithfield in London dug for Black Death victims in 1349. They also looked at suspected plague pits at Spitalfields in London, Vodroffsgaard in Copenhagen, and Angers and Verdun in France. Not one tooth harboured identifiable *Yersinia* DNA.

As Cooper points out, his negative findings do not prove that these victims did not die of bubonic plague because the bacterium might not have penetrated the teeth, or the *Yersinia* DNA might not have survived.

These latest findings come as no surprise to us. We believe that these victims died from a viral disease, haemorrhagic plague.

We are not qualified to judge the validity of the DNA analyses. However, even if eventually the results of Raoult, Drancourt and their colleagues were to be replicated and proved genuine, they would in no way prove that 'the Black Death was bubonic plague'. This disease of rats, as we have seen, was occasionally present in Marseille and the surrounding area, so that traces of *Yersinia pestis* could have persisted.

The True Story of a Historic Village

With our newly acquired knowledge of haemorrhagic plagues, we returned to one of the most famous visitations of the pestilence to re-examine its course. It gives a vivid picture of the horrors of an outbreak.

We also came up with a surprising discovery. Even in the first strike of the plague, the Black Death, we saw signs that some people who must have been exposed to the infection were apparently protected against this new disease. And as the plague rampaged on for the next 300 years and our story unfolded, we gathered more and more hints and evidence of this.

We examine in this chapter the epidemic at Eyam (where the idea of bubonic plague as the responsible agent has been laid down on tablets of stone) and discover another important clue about the nature of the resistance to haemorrhagic plague, which had gradually developed in the people of Europe during the age of plagues.

The making of a myth

The story of Eyam in Derbyshire, the most famous plague village of all, was first told in 1855. It is quite clear from this account that everyone, including the villagers, believed that it was an infectious disease spread directly from person to person. The rector, William Mompesson, persuaded the villagers that it was their duty to draw a *cordon sanitaire* around the outskirts of Eyam and to prohibit anyone from coming in (not that anyone would be likely to want to do so) or, more importantly, from leaving. Nobody was allowed to flee; by so doing they would have taken the infection to other villages or towns (although some did escape in the early stages of the outbreak). The inhabitants stayed there, cooped up, and watched each other die one by one. This heroic sacrifice was completely successful and the plague was contained within the village.

After Yersin had elucidated the nature of bubonic plague at the end of the nineteenth century and the idea that the disease was the cause of the plagues took root, the story of Eyam was adapted and modified, and a mythical folklore developed. This has been carefully and lovingly preserved by the local historians. The traditional story now became (with some variations) that Alexander Hadfield received a box of damp cloth, from which jumped an infected flea (or in some versions, an infected rat) which bit his assistant, George Viccars, when he hung the contents out to dry. Viccars was then seized with a violent sickness; he became delirious and large swellings appeared on his neck and groin. On the third day, the fatal plague spot appeared on his breast and he died of bubonic plague.

It is particularly important that we sort out, once and for all, the truth about the plague at Eyam, because everyone still obdurately clings to this 100-year-old story of an outbreak of bubonic plague in spite of all the contradictory evidence. For instance, on 24th February 2002, Channel 4 television in the UK broadcast a *Secrets of the Dead* programme that aimed to tell the story of Eyam. It showed a man shaking out a cloth containing infected fleas. Nevertheless, having thus depicted the arrival of bubonic plague, the remainder of the programme apparently described the spread of a simple, directly transmitted infectious disease through the village.

Sue Scott decided to do the fieldwork properly and drove over the Pennines on a wintry day to explore Eyam. Map in hand, she walked around the scene of the crime and saw what remains of

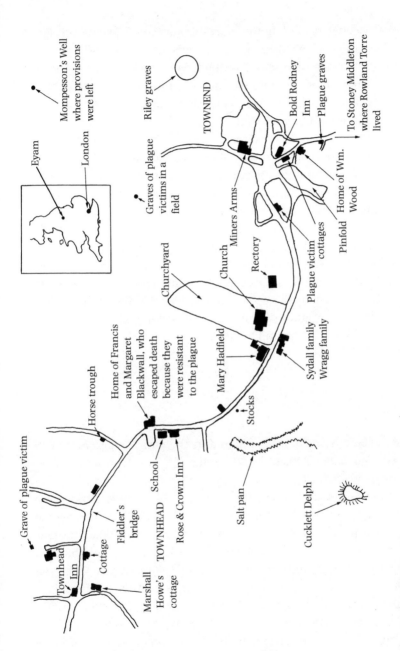

Map of Eyam in Derbyshire.

the evidence, including the much-photographed plague cottages where the epidemic began, and a cupboard in the north aisle of the church that was said to be made from the box that contained the famous cloth. She visited the local museum and learnt that lead mining, shoe making and silk weaving were once the occupations of the inhabitants.

Nobody has questioned the heroism of the people of Eyam, but commentators usually point out that a *cordon sanitaire* was a futile means of containing rats and bubonic plague – in other words, that the villagers had made their sacrifice in vain. This goes against common sense because in fact, the tactic of ring-fencing the township was completely successful and the plague did not escape to attack any other community in the vicinity. This, as we have seen, is in complete contrast to the behaviour of authentic bubonic plague in the hinterland at Marseille in 1720–22, where the *cordons sanitaires* were totally ineffective and bubonic plague crept along and disseminated to many of the surrounding villages and hamlets.

Historical detective work again

As ever, the truth is to be found in the parish registers, which were meticulously kept by the rector of Eyam. They form a day-to-day log of the plague.

We began by plotting the total monthly plague burials and found a remarkable similarity to events at Penrith. The plague began in early September 1665 and there was a small autumn peak in October, with the epidemic then decaying and limping along through the winter. The third phase exploded in the following May and rose rapidly to a peak in August. Thereafter, the epidemic fizzled out and had disappeared by December 1666.

We were encouraged and excited by the results so far and proceeded to construct a table of the spread of the infection within and between families. The results were unequivocal. The

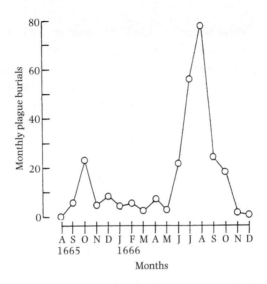

Monthly plague burials at Eyam. Like at Penrith, there was a small outbreak in autumn 1665 followed by a quiescent period in winter, before the disease reappeared in the spring with the usual summer peak.

infection was again brought into the village by a travelling stranger and the pattern of secondary and tertiary infections was identical to that at Penrith. The latent period of the disease was 12 days and the time from infection to death was 37 days. There was no doubt that the same infectious disease was responsible for the epidemics at Penrith and, nearly 70 years later, at Eyam.

To unravel the true story of the plague at Eyam, we must return to the original evidence, including the wills of the villagers and the parish registers. The account we give below is based on facts that have been derived as accurately as possible from the primary sources. In particular, we have reconstructed the families of Eyam and traced the lines of infection within and between them.

Eyam is one of a cluster of ancient villages tucked away on the eastern edge of the Peak District in Derbyshire, lying on the slopes above the Derwent valley. A remote and isolated place in 1665, lying 245 metres above sea level, the approaches to the village were by rough and narrow tracks. Even today, the signpost pointing up the steep and wooded valley of Eyam Dale is easily missed. It is sited on the road out of Stoney Middleton, the nearby village that gave such stalwart support to the people of Eyam by bringing food to the plague stone during the months of the crisis. The nearest towns, Matlock, Chesterfield, Buxton and Sheffield, lie about 12 miles (19 kilometres) away and the local market town, Bakewell, is 7 miles (11 kilometres) to the south.

Most of the cottages were built of stone, with stone-slab roofs and often with stone floors. Eyam is still a working village and, although it attracts huge numbers of tourists each year, it is neither a picture-postcard scene nor a museum.

The itinerant tailor

Mary Cooper had been married to a lead miner and had two sons by him: Jonathan, then aged twelve, and Edward, three. When her husband died, she was left with no means of support. But Mary was a survivor. She married Alexander Hadfield on 27th March 1665 and the family lived together in one of the two-storey cottages to the west of the churchyard at Eyam.

Five months later, on 9th August 1665, Mary was living temporarily alone with her younger son because Alexander and the older boy were away, hiring out their services to help with the harvest. George Viccars, a travelling tailor, knocked at the door and asked if Mary could give him temporary lodging while he plied his trade in the village. She would have welcomed him warmly, there was never enough money to buy bread and a few extra pennies would come in very handy.

Mary installed Viccars in a tiny room in the cottage, where he slept and did his work. He was to have his meals at the table with the rest of the family. The next morning he was drumming up business in the neighbouring cottages and in the little houses across the road. Viccars was soon accepted into the little community, and when the neighbours popped in to see Mary they found time to have a word with him, cooped up in his tiny room.

On the morning of 2nd September, Viccars did not appear for breakfast and Mary found him with a malignant fever. He was desperately thirsty and gulped down one cup of water after another.

The next morning, he was obviously very much worse and was sinking fast. He had been ill through the night and was screaming with pain. As Mary watched, he vomited blood and started to bleed from the nose.

Mary eventually went for help and advice from the rectory, which was nearby. The Reverend William Mompesson was an active man, aged 28, who took his duties as parish priest of Eyam conscientiously and seriously. He had seen the plague before and immediately recognized the angry haemorrhagic spots, God's tokens, on Viccars's chest.

George Viccars died on 7th September; it was a merciful release. William Mompesson took the funeral service, which was attended only by Alexander (who had been hastily recalled) and Mary Hadfield. A dark silence now hung over the village – had the dreaded disease infected anyone else?

The epidemic breaks out

As time went by, some of the villagers would have begun to hope against hope. But on 17th September, ten days after Viccars had died, little Edward Hadfield complained of feeling unwell, the bottom dropped out of Mary's world, and everyone knew that the epidemic was up and running. This break corresponds exactly with the pause after Andrew Hogson's death at Penrith. Thereafter the infection spread in the same predictable way that the plague always spread. It was remorseless.

First, Mary's near neighbours, who had been on friendly terms with Viccars, succumbed and it was soon apparent that the travelling tailor had transmitted the plague to five other families, all living close to the Hadfields and on visiting terms with Mary. The disease ripped progressively through these families like wildfire. Opposite Mary lived the Sydalls; their 12-year-old daughter, Sarah, was buried on 30th September. She had by then infected four of her brothers and sisters, as well as her father John. Only her mother Elizabeth and her sister Emmott survived – they are important people in our unfolding story.

Mary Hadfield suffered a second tragedy when her elder son Jonathan died on 28th October. He had been infected by his brother Edward just before the latter died.

The epidemic continued through the autumn of 1665. Rector Mompesson continued to visit and care for the sick and dying, and he also helped them draw up their wills; he conducted all the burial services and carefully recorded all the deaths in the parish register.

As winter approached, Mompesson noticed that the epidemic seemed to be abating. Could a really cold Eyam winter finish it off? But it was not to be, because the teenagers kept it going. Elizabeth Warrington was infected by Hugh Stubbs on 23rd October; they were both aged 18 and perhaps they were sweethearts. Elizabeth was a crucial link in the chain: the few plague deaths that occurred in November and December all originated from her.

The disease survived the winter at Eyam only by the skin of its teeth – the infection line was tenuously maintained all through the long period of December 1665 to May 1666, during which time there were few plague deaths.

Mompesson prepared for the worst when he found that the plague was still alive and kicking, albeit feebly, in the early spring. He asked his wife Katharin to take their children to stay with friends in Yorkshire, but she returned to be at her husband's side after she had taken them to safety. This decision was to cost her her life.

Now comes the poignant story of Emmott Sydall who, as we have seen, had survived the outbreak in her family in October. She was betrothed to Rowland Torre, who lived in Stoney Middleton, a hamlet about a mile away, and he came to see her every day during the winter. But when the plague broke out again in the spring they agreed that they would come every night to opposite sides of the Cucklett Delph, a natural amphitheatre, and communicate by shouting and signalling. Emmott attended the wedding of her mother Elizabeth, who had also survived the first wave of the epidemic, when she remarried on 24th April 1666. On the night following the wedding, Emmott failed to keep her tryst because she had already been infected and was seriously unwell. Rowland feared the worst but nevertheless continued to come to the Cucklett Delph every night. When finally the plague had gone and the *cordon sanitaire* was lifted, he was the first to come running into the village. Heartbroken, he found that Emmott had perished and her home was empty.

Elizabeth Sydall's wedding was a critical event because it was here that Isaac Thornley, aged 13, was infected by Emmott Sydall. After Emmott died, Isaac was the only surviving link in the chain of infection and if it had stopped with him there would have been no epidemic, but he infected between 15 and 18 others and the summer epidemic exploded with a terrible mortality. The epidemic peaked in August and then slowly died down.

What happened to Mary Hadfield? She survived the epidemic, in spite of nursing and losing all her family, and married for the third time six years later on 5th June 1672. Her husband was Marshall Hole (or Howe).

The parish registers record in graphic detail the awful months of 1665 and 1666 when heroic men, women and children died agonizing deaths. Not only do we marvel at their fortitude and courage, but they also speak to us across the centuries, sending an invaluable message about the nature of the resistance to haemorrhagic plague.

The famous cordon sanitaire

The rector acted positively in late May 1666 and, although his measures were completely successful in containing the epidemic within the village, he was too late to prevent the plague devastating his flock.

First, he persuaded his parishioners to draw the famous *cordon sanitaire*. A few villagers had already fled and a number of children had been sent away. Some villagers were living rough in shacks built on the hillside, outside the *cordon*.

The second decision, taken by the villagers in June 1666, was that there were to be no further organized funerals or burials in the churchyard. People were advised to bury their own dead in gardens, orchards or the fields.

The third decision taken by the rector was to close the church and hold services in the open air, thereby avoiding crowding people together indoors. The services were held in the natural amphitheatre of the Cucklett Delph where everyone kept in their family groups, which were separated by some distance (at least four metres) from one another while Mompesson preached from a prominent rock.

All these measures were sensible precautions against an infectious disease and would have helped to confine infections within families, and they probably helped to restrict the scale of the outbreak. They were ultimately defeated and the epidemic ran its course (albeit probably attenuated by the public-health measures) for three main reasons.

First, the isolation practices were not begun in autumn 1665. Second, people did not properly understand the significance of the long incubation period, concentrating instead on the victims when the symptoms had appeared. By this time they were already less infectious – most of the damage had already been done. Finally, the disease spread much more readily *out-of-doors* in the warm weather of summer and it was more difficult to control at that time.

Stories of the Eyam epidemic

Marshall Howe, a lead miner, lived in a cottage on the west side of Eyam and is said to have contracted the disease but recovered – although he subsequently lost his wife and son. Since he believed himself to be safe, he volunteered to dispose of the bodies where the families were unable to perform this task. He then claimed a burial fee and frequently appropriated their chattels. He seems to have been a rather unpleasant character who profited from the misfortunes of others: it is recorded that when he was dragging out the body of a man called Unwin, whom he believed to be dead, his victim regained consciousness, called out for a drink and survived the plague. We have a suspicion that there may have been a small error in the records somewhere and that this man Marshall Howe was the same man Mary Hadfield married; after all, they had both lost their spouses in the plague. Not quite such a romantic ending for Mary.

Elizabeth Hancocke saw her family wiped out in a single week. Two children died on 3rd August, followed by two more and her husband John on the 7th. Two more daughters died on the 9th and 10th. The people of Stoney Middleton, as they climbed to the boundary stone to bring the supplies of food to the stricken community, saw Elizabeth dragging out the bodies for burial in a field near her home. When the epidemic was over, she went to live with her one remaining son in Sheffield. One of his descendants returned to Eyam and collected the scattered headstones of the children and grouped them round their father's grave, where they are now protected by a surrounding wall, the so-called Riley graves.

Mompesson and his wife continued conscientiously to visit their parishioners. One evening, about 19th August 1666, when they were returning from paying one of these calls, she is said to have exclaimed, 'How sweet the air smells.' The rector must have been transfixed; he could not smell anything unusual, but he knew that this was one of the characteristic signs of the plague.

His wife died in his arms on 25th August and her much-photographed grave can be seen in the churchyard.

It appears that this sweet smell was detected by victims just before the painful symptoms appeared. Another example is recorded from the hamlet of Curbar, two miles south-east of Eyam, which had suffered from an epidemic 30 years before in 1632. Here a woman was visiting the house of a victim and on leaving, said to her husband, 'Oh! My dear, how sweet the air smells.' The major symptoms appeared that night and she died five days later. This sickly sweet smell is probably an early sign of the necrosis of the internal organs. The story is also of interest because it shows that plague had been present earlier in this remote area of Derbyshire.

Margaret Blackwall (whose house still stands in Eyam) was living with her brother Francis, the other members of their family having died earlier. She eventually contracted the disease and appeared to be in the terminal stages when her brother, who had cooked his breakfast, poured the excess fat into a jug, which he left in the kitchen. When he went out he was certain that she would not be alive when he returned. Shortly after his departure Margaret, who was delirious, was overcome with a great thirst (a typical symptom of the plague); she left her bed and, finding the warm fat that she assumed to be milk, drank it greedily, probably causing her to vomit. When Francis returned, not only was Margaret still alive, but she was clearly much stronger; she recovered and remained convinced that the bacon fat had cured her.

It will be surprising to learn that Francis and Margaret Blackwall are probably, from our point of view, the most important historical characters in this chronicle of the plague at Eyam. One of the descendants of Francis Blackwall is alive and living in Eyam today. As we shall see later, molecular biologists have studied her genetic make-up and are able to show how Margaret Blackwall 300 years ago was able to contract the plague and survive. It had nothing to do with bacon fat.

Mysterious resistance to the disease

It is clear from our reconstruction of the events at Eyam that some people were resistant to the disease. Unwin, Marshall Hole (Howe?) and Margaret Blackwall all contracted the disease but survived. Mary Hadfield must have been in close contact with her family members and would have nursed them through their final illness. Elizabeth Hancocke buried her entire family.

Rector Mompesson was very active among his dying parishioners and his wife died in his arms. Afterwards he wrote,

> During this dreadful visitation, I have not had the least symptom of disease, nor had I ever better health. My man had the distemper, and upon the appearance of a tumour I gave him some chemical antidotes, which operated, and after the rising broke he was very well. My maid continued in good health, which was a blessing; for had she quailed, I should have been ill set to have washed and gotten my provisions.

Mary Hadfield, Elizabeth Hancocke and Mompesson also escaped unscathed.

Progress of the epidemic

George Viccars, the tailor, was originally infected on 1st August 1665 at a place where a typical summer epidemic was raging. Where on earth was this? How far had Viccars travelled? There is no trace of any epidemics in Derbyshire and the surrounding area at this time, but the Great Plague of London was getting up a head of steam by then and it is certainly possible that George was infected there.

As we have seen, the outbreaks at Eyam and Penrith began in the autumn and were composed of two separate epidemics, rising to a small peak in October–November and then dying down and limping along during winter. They erupted again the following spring and peaked around August, after which they started to fizzle out, with the final extinction being accelerated by the onset of the second winter.

We later studied scores of plagues and found that this pattern was completely typical of epidemics that began in the autumn in England. The disease did not have time to get going at full throttle before the cold weather intervened, when onward transmission *out-of-doors* was well-nigh impossible. It then struggled through the winter months with very great difficulty. There must have been many unrecorded epidemics in England in which the infection was extinguished during January–February and the community escaped lightly.

A northern winter

Weather conditions in the Peak District were severe and in 1665 'in December a great snow is said to have fallen, with a hard and severe frost ... The weather at the commencement of 1666 was exceedingly cold and severe.' A cold winter in Eyam in the Little Ice Age was *really* cold by today's standards. With the sparing use of fire and badly fitting windows, the stone cottages would have been very cold and completely unsuitable for the establishment of a colony of black rats, which demand cosy conditions and thatched roofs. It is impossible that fleas would have been active under these conditions.

The popular story of the start of the Eyam epidemic cannot be explained as an outbreak of bubonic plague. Viccars could conceivably have been bitten by an infected flea from a box of cloths, *but he could not have infected anyone else directly* (i.e. via pneumonic plague) because the next victim (little Edward Cooper) did not die until 15 days after him. We remember that pneumonic plague victims die within six days.

The villagers at Eyam were quite correct in assuming that this was an infectious disease that could be successfully contained by the well-established practice of a *cordon sanitaire*. Obviously, such measures would have been completely ineffective against an outbreak of bubonic plague – rodents are unaffected by human ring-fences. However, the most cogent reason for accepting that the plague at Eyam was an outbreak of haemorrhagic plague passed person to person lies in the completely predictable spread of the infection that we, acting as historical detectives, have elucidated.

Postscript

When William Mompesson announced that the epidemic was finished and the ordeal was over, the survivors must have breathed a sigh of relief; they were lucky to be alive. There was no rejoicing, too many of the little community had died and so many of the cottages were closed and desolate.

Rector Mompesson ordered that all woollen clothing and bedding should be burnt and he set an example by burning his own effects so that, as he said in a letter to his uncle, he had scarcely enough to clothe himself:

> The condition of this place hath been so dreadful that I persuade myself it exceedeth all history and example. I may truly say our Town has become a Golgotha, a place of skulls; and had there not been a small remnant of us left, we had been as Sodom and like unto Gomorrah. My ears never heard such doleful lamentations. My nose never smelt such noisome smells and my eyes never beheld such ghastly spectacles.

A terrible obituary for the village, but one that must have been repeated over and over again during the age of plagues.

And what became of Mompesson? He married Elizabeth, the widow of Charles Newby, in about 1669 and she bore him four more children, two girls and two boys, although both the latter died in infancy. His patron presented him with the living at the parish of Eakring, 30 miles (47 kilometres) to the east of Eyam, where his arrival in 1670 is said to have terrified his flock. He was much preoccupied with rebuilding the church there. Within a year he was also appointed Prebend of Normanton and later a Prebend at York. Since he now held three livings, he was reasonably well off and he died on 9th May 1708, aged 70 years, and was buried at Eakring.

14

The Surprising Link between AIDS and the Black Death

When the Black Death struck first in 1347 and swept through Europe, it seems that almost everyone who made effective contact with an infectious person caught the disease and died. The reason for this was because nobody had been exposed to the disease before. Three hundred years later, in the seventeenth century, there is evidence that in towns where the plague had struck previously, some of the inhabitants had a form of in-built resistance. We have seen that the apprentices and servants in London, who had come from the countryside and small provincial towns where there had rarely (if ever) been a major epidemic, were often the first to be struck down. On the other hand, a proportion of the inhabitants, whose families had been in the metropolis for some generations, seemed to have some resistance to the infection.

Detailed inspection of parish registers shows that many people must have been in close contact with infectives indoors but did not contract the plague, and this indicates that by that time a proportion of the families, particularly those long resident in London, had a resistance to the disease. Samuel Pepys continued about his business in London (although he took some elementary precautions) and was not stricken during the major outbreak of 1665–66. And we have seen that some of the people at Eyam and Penrith were in close contact with victims but never succumbed.

What was going on here? We can obtain some clues concerning the molecular genetics of plague resistance 600 years ago from a surprisingly different and remarkable source today.

HIV and AIDS

Everybody has heard of the HIV pandemic, but it is not so well known that a considerable proportion of people of European origin do not catch the disease, even after continued exposure. They are resistant to HIV infection.

When the primary human immunodeficiency virus (HIV) enters the human body, it homes in on certain white cells in the bloodstream and then gains entry via a special molecular complex in their surface membrane, which is termed in technical jargon the *CCR5* receptor. This acts as an entry port (or chemical doorway) for the virus into the blood cell. Once inside, it can remain dormant for many years before its victim finally shows the symptoms of AIDS. However, once inside the virus quickly begins its dirty work and, unknown to anybody, the victim soon becomes fully infectious. Therein lies the major problem in controlling the spread of HIV. We see that the disease has an exceptionally long incubation period, which is measured in years. The *CCR5* receptor also acts as the means of entry for the pox virus that causes myxomatosis in rabbits, and it is probable that several other infectious agents that use it as a doorway will soon be discovered.

The *delta*-32 mutation

Europeans who have a resistance to HIV infection have inherited a genetic mutation in the *CCR5* receptors on their white blood cells that prevents them acting as an entry port. This is called the $CCR5$-$\Delta 32$ mutation, and individuals who have inherited a pair of mutated genes from both parents have nearly complete resistance to HIV infection, whereas those who have only one copy of the mutation delay the onset of AIDS.

Although this mutation occurs at a high frequency in Eurasian ethnic populations today, it is absent among native sub-Saharan African, American Indian and East Asian ethnic groups. This might explain the rapid spread of HIV in sub-Saharan Africa, whereas possession of the mutation may have delayed its progress in Europe.

When did the protective mutation appear?

When and why did this mutation arise in the first place? After all, HIV/AIDS emerged to scourge the human race only a few decades ago (no time at all in evolutionary terms) and presumably, before that time, the mutation would have been of no selective advantage in the rat race of human evolution.

We can put this another way. Any new mutation has a very high likelihood of being lost within a few dozen generations unless it confers a clear selective advantage on those individuals who have it. Possession of the $CCR5$-$\Delta 32$ mutation is of obvious benefit today: it confers protection against the killer disease HIV. But what could possibly have been gained by having the mutation before HIV/AIDS emerged and spread across the world in the twentieth century? It is highly unlikely that a mutation in the $CCR5$ receptor that conferred no selective advantage on individuals in whom it occurred could spread randomly through the people of Europe. In simple terms, if a new mutation does not provide an advantage in the struggle for survival, it will eventually disappear from the population.

Molecular biologists, using their extremely sophisticated techniques, have estimated that the $CCR5$-$\Delta 32$ mutation may have first appeared in Europe some 2000 years ago. There is general agreement that its frequency must have been driven up to present-day values in Europe of 5–20 per cent by a historic event that occurred approximately 700 years ago, probably an epidemic of an infectious disease that, like HIV-1 today, used the same entry port on white blood cells.

The Black Death is obviously an excellent candidate for such a catastrophe. The timing is right and it has been widely suggested and agreed that those very few fortunate individuals in Europe during the Black Death who possessed the CCR5-Δ32 mutation escaped with their lives and bore children who then also carried the mutant gene. The incidence of the CCR5-Δ32 mutation in Europeans at that time has been estimated at 1 in 40 000. All those who did not possess the CCR5-Δ32 (the great majority) and who made effective contact with an infected person inevitably died. In this way, the proportion of the population who carried the mutation would have been raised dramatically. Some individuals who carried the mutation may have caught haemorrhagic plague but recovered; they lived to fight another day and continued to have children, most of whom carried the Δ32 mutation.

What is wrong with this suggested origin of the Δ32 mutation?

Scientists who discovered that the CCR5-Δ32 mutation appeared around the time of the Black Death firmly believe that this was an epidemic of bubonic plague. Consequently, to make their story fit the facts, they have had to assume that the bacterium *Yersinia pestis* enters the white cells of the blood via the CCR5 receptor. We have already seen conclusive evidence that there never was an epidemic of bubonic plague in Europe, but there is further compelling confirmation that their theory is all wrong:

- Bacteria like *Yersinia* do not penetrate via the CCR5 receptor, an entry port used by some viruses. This points to a virus, and not a bacterium, being responsible for haemorrhagic plague.
- Mortality in epidemics of bubonic plague is always low: insufficient to have a major effect in forcing up the frequency of any protective mutation.

- The *CCR5-Δ32* mutation occurs only in people of European origin – the only area that was ravaged by plagues. In contrast, the mutation is not found in people from eastern Asia, sub-Saharan Africa nor American Indians, areas where bubonic plague has been rampant. Further evidence, if any were needed, that bubonic plague was not responsible for the Black Death.

At last: the explanation of resistance to the plague

So there is good reason to suggest that an epidemic of viral haemorrhagic plague during the Black Death suddenly conferred a strong selective advantage on those few lucky individuals who possessed the *CCR5-Δ32* mutation and thereby sharply increased its frequency. Nevertheless, this popular explanation is much too simplistic. A single epidemic like the Black Death could not have had such far-reaching and long-lasting effects, but it did presage the age of plagues. We suggest that each successive wave of outbreaks over the next 300 years steadily increased the numbers of individuals who had inherited the *CCR5-Δ32* mutation; if you were not carrying the mutation there was a good chance of dying when the disease next came round.

However, this again is an oversimplification of the situation. The major epidemics of haemorrhagic plague were largely confined to communities that were above a certain minimum size, and there were vast rural areas of Europe practising a scattered agricultural economy where the disease rarely, if ever, struck. The continuing strong selective pressures forcing up the frequency of the *CCR5-Δ32* mutation would operate only in the towns, particularly London, because haemorrhagic plague became ever-present there after 1580. Consequently, the overall distribution of the *CCR5-Δ32* mutation in Europe must have been patchy in the seventeenth century: the frequency of resistant individuals in the towns must have been very much higher than the current 20 per cent, and in rural areas very much lower.

The frequency of the mutant gene in Europe today is the result of a great deal of mixing and migration over the last 350 years since the plague disappeared – a general levelling-out process in the course of which the distinctions between rural and urban life have disappeared.

As we have seen, plague was persistent in London in the seventeenth century, with major outbreaks at irregular intervals, albeit with a relatively low percentage mortality. Having suffered from this continuous onslaught, in addition to a low grumbling endemic level of infection, a sizeable proportion of the population of London probably carried the mutation and was resistant. Mortality levels had fallen below 15 per cent by this time, and those who died from plague in London in the seventeenth century were frequently incomers, apprentices and servants. Each epidemic or famine crisis brought fresh waves of naive immigrants from the countryside who were not resistant and who made up a substantial part of those dying in the plagues.

The Eyam inheritance

Remember the story of Margaret Blackwall of Eyam, who survived the plague apparently by drinking warm fat? Molecular biologists visited Eyam in 2001 and took swabs from the mouths of 100 villagers 'who could trace their ancestry back the furthest' and found that the *CCR5-Δ32* mutation was present in 14 per cent of them – probably a little above the average European rate. Much more importantly, Joan Plant, who is living in Eyam today, is a direct descendant of the plague survivor Francis, the brother of Margaret Blackwall: she carries the *CCR5-Δ32* mutation.

We interpreted this news as follows: Margaret Blackwall carried the *CCR5-Δ32* mutation; she contracted the disease but did not die of it, as we have seen. Her brother Francis did not get the plague at all and was completely resistant. Copies of the mutation were handed on to his descendant, Joan Plant.

But the full story of Eyam is not clear. We have been unable to trace any record of the plague striking in Eyam before 1665, so there is no evidence of an event that would force up the frequency of the $CCR5\text{-}\Delta32$ mutation there. We conclude that the families at Eyam (or their parents) who were resistant at the time of the plague had been previously exposed to it elsewhere and had then moved into the village. It had struck violently at Thorpe 18 miles (29 kilometres) to the south in 1538 and at nearby Curbar 30 years before. Derby was repeatedly ravaged by plague, starting with the Black Death, which moved through the county and was recorded in the village of Crich, 17 miles (27 kilometres) to the south of Eyam. Rector Mompesson seems to have been resistant and it is reported that he had seen the plague elsewhere earlier in his life.

A number of those who survived at Eyam thus carried the $CCR5\text{-}\Delta32$ mutation and so the proportion of the population that was resistant would rise in the next generation. But they would have no selective advantage, because the disease had now gone. People would move into the village to fill the vacant niches and, during the next 300 years, there would have been a tremendous amount of immigration and emigration of both resistant and nonresistant individuals. The result of all this stirring up is the 14 per cent of resistant persons found in Eyam today.

The people of Eyam were unlucky because the epidemic there was very nearly the last outbreak ever. They had escaped for 300 years by being small and remote, only to be caught by the final strike.

What happened to the mutation after the plagues?

Once the pestilence had disappeared completely from Europe by 1670, there would apparently have been no benefit to anyone possessing the mutant gene. The mutation therefore probably changed from being advantageous to being neutral and, over the next 300 years (and some 12 generations), the frequency in European populations would be expected to fall slowly. Present-day frequencies are 5–20 per cent but they were probably higher than this in the seventeenth century, unless the *CCR5-Δ32* mutation conferred some other selective advantage on those lucky individuals who carried it ...

Fascinating and exciting news was announced in September 2003. Several earlier reports had proposed links between protection against smallpox and against HIV – older people who had been vaccinated against smallpox were less likely to contract HIV. Now, preliminary experiments with human blood cells at George Mason University, Virginia have shown that vaccination confers, on average, a fourfold reduction in infectivity of HIV. Myxoma poxvirus, a relative of the smallpox virus, also uses the *CCR5* receptor to gain entry to its target blood cells.

When the plague disappeared, smallpox replaced it as the dreaded scourge. Is it possible that possession of the *CCR5-Δ32* mutation in the eighteenth century in Europeans may also have provided at least partial protection from either infection or death from smallpox? If so, then the mutation would have been maintained or even modestly pumped up until 1900 when smallpox was effectively eliminated in Europe. On this argument, non-European races, which were never exposed to plague, might historically be expected to be particularly susceptible to smallpox – both North and South American indigenous populations were particularly badly hit when smallpox was introduced by conquering Europeans.

Thus those ethnic Europeans who today are resistant to HIV owe their good fortune to a chance genetic event in their ancestors, which provided them with protection against the plague.

15

Assembling the Jigsaw Puzzle

Today, when a crime is witnessed and a suitable description of the felon is available, the next step is to have an identity parade. But to do that, we must decide who is to be included in our gallery of suspects.

Of all the infectious agents, bacteria and viruses are the most important kinds for our purposes. These tiny organisms are sometimes called *microbes* and in the immortal words of Hilaire Belloc:

The microbe is so very small
You cannot make him out at all.
But many sanguine people hope
To see him through a microscope.

Bacteria

Bacteria are single-celled organisms that are between one-half and one-ten-thousandth of a millimetre in length: too small to be seen by the naked eye. Looked at under a microscope, they may be shaped like rods, spirals or spheres but, in spite of their small size, their structure is highly complex. They are the most abundant of all organisms and have many essential roles to play in the maintenance of life on earth. However, only a minority of species can infect humans and cause serious diseases.

Some bacterial diseases are spread by the intervention of insects, ticks or lice and these include bubonic plague (spread by a flea) and epidemic typhus, which was once a major killer in crowded conditions with poor sanitation. It is transmitted from human to human via lice and, unless treated with antibiotics, about 20 per cent of cases are fatal. Historians have (erroneously) sometimes tried to explain outbreaks of plague that could not possibly have been caused by bubonic plague as typhus.

Viruses

While viruses vary in size, they are all much smaller than bacteria and can be seen only under an electron microscope. Unlike bacteria, viruses can reproduce and multiply only within other living cells, which may belong to animals, plants or even bacteria. Since viruses cannot reproduce independently, they are not regarded as truly alive.

All viruses, then, are parasites that can wreak havoc on human populations by causing serious epidemic illnesses. They start by cleverly gaining entry to certain cells in our bodies and, once inside, the virus proceeds to take over the cell's genetic machinery, which then has to obey its commands. We have seen how HIV can enter certain white blood cells via the *CCR5* doorway, whereupon it sets about its dirty work.

An infecting virus is simply a set of instructions, like a computer program. The working of any cell in our body is normally directed by commands encoded in its DNA, but an invading virus can introduce a new set of instructions, so that the cell stops its normal work and puts all its efforts into making copies of the introduced program. In this way, the virus makes the host cell its slave, forcing it to provide all the raw materials and energy necessary for propagation. And viruses reproduce at a phenomenal rate. A single common cold virus can create 16 million copies of itself in a day.

The following is a small 'rogues gallery' of viral diseases:

- *HIV/AIDS*. The HIV virus destroys the body's immune defences and, eventually, the victim dies from another infection or from cancer. It is transmitted directly by body fluids or semen. There is, as yet, no cure.

- *Influenza*. This disease is spread by direct transmission and mutates readily; in the past, some strains have been major killers. It often emerges from animals – the major reservoirs are ducks, chickens and pigs in Asia. Again, there is no cure, but vaccines are now available.

- *Measles*. This very infectious disease is usually spread by droplet infection and can be fatal in children in developing countries with poor nutrition. There is no cure, but a vaccine is available.

- *Poliomyelitis*. This was the great epidemic disease of the developed world from the late 1940s to the early 1960s. It is an acute viral infection of the central nervous system, with serious effects including paralysis and sometimes death. It is incurable, but a vaccine is now available.

- *Smallpox*. In the past this was a major killer of children, but a worldwide vaccination programme has eliminated the virus completely, except for some stocks held in laboratories. Smallpox is regarded as a possible terrorist weapon. It is often fatal and there is no cure, but a vaccine is available.

Medical science has enabled us to gain effective control of many infectious diseases (but not all – look at AIDS). An extensive range of antibiotics has been developed that can cure many bacterial infections, although the appearance of resistant strains of bacteria is causing problems. However, there are few really effective drugs to treat viral diseases. Nevertheless, prevention is better than cure and the development of vaccines, beginning with the work of Edward Jenner on smallpox in the eighteenth century, has transformed our ability to cope with these killer infections.

The hidden dangers of animal reservoirs

All animals carry parasites, which have evolved together with their hosts over hundreds of thousands of years and have established a way in which they can coexist, if not in perfect harmony, at least without causing too much harm to each other. But occasionally, parasitic viruses or bacteria escape from their normal mammalian hosts to be transmitted to other species – including humans. Many human diseases originated in this way.

Some of these – such as Lyme disease (where the animal host is a deer) and bubonic plague (where the animal host is a rodent) – are not usually passed on further by person-to-person infection. Their spread is critically dependent on the animal rather than on the human population. The mechanisms of infection are therefore much more complicated than in 'simple' viral infectious diseases such as measles, chickenpox or smallpox – and haemorrhagic plague.

Other viral diseases – such as AIDS, influenza and Ebola – have emerged from animals to infect humans and, most importantly, they can then *be directly transmitted from one person to another*. These pose a much more serious problem; they are often lethal and, once established in a human population, their spread is governed by the same factors as for any other directly transmitted infectious disease. Their origins in animals are immediately forgotten. These are called emergent viral diseases.

Narrowing the field of suspects

From our investigations, can we make an informed guess as to whether haemorrhagic plague was a bacterium or a virus? Its characteristics, summarized in the previous chapters, suggest that the causative agent was a virus. This hypothesis is supported by the observation that in the population of medieval Europe, there seems to have been very strong genetic selection in favour of the CCR5-Δ32 mutation, which is known to protect against the human immunodeficiency virus.

The infectious agent also appears to have been remarkably stable. In the 300 years of plagues following the Black Death, the characteristics of the infectious agent seem to have changed very little. There may have been some minor mutations, but these had little effect on the time course of the disease, on its infectiousness, on its symptoms or on its lethality.

Most changes in the pattern of the disease from the fourteenth to the seventeenth century can be explained as alterations in the behaviour and genetics of *human* populations, rather than as any change in the virus. Thus, the gradual increase in levels of the human CCR5-Δ32 mutation throughout Europe increased the proportion of resistant individuals and so modified the spread and mortality rate of plague epidemics.

Many respiratory viral diseases are spread directly from one person to another by droplet infection. Dr Thomas Stuttaford, medical correspondent for *The Times*, explains that droplet infection is a euphemism used by doctors to describe the spread of a disease by small drops of spittle and nasal discharge which, laden with a pot-pourri of organisms, viruses and bacteria, are scattered with every cough and sneeze. A sneeze can produce millions of droplets, which can travel at anything up to 90 mph (145 kph). Kissing delivers an even larger dose. Or an infected person sneezes into his or her hand, then shakes yours and you rub your eye, a virus can travel into your nose and throat through your tear duct. We remember that haemorrhagic plague was believed to have been passed by droplet infection; it was considered to be safe if one kept at least 13 feet (4 metres) away from an infected person out-of-doors.

We can now compare haemorrhagic plague with two other viral diseases, influenza and HIV, that have emerged from animal reservoirs to attack humans. The viruses responsible for these three diseases have evolved very different strategies to

Disease	Infectious period	Mode of transmission	Infectiousness	Duration of epidemic
Influenza	2 days	Droplet	High	3 weeks
Haemorrhagic plague	4 weeks	Droplet	Moderate	9 months
HIV	10 years	Body fluids	Low	Infinite

maximize their chances of survival and spread. The above table summarizes their basic characteristics.

Influenza persists because it is highly infectious and is transmitted to many other people even during its short infectious period. HIV continues to spread slowly because of its very long infectious period, which compensates for the low infectiousness associated with its difficult mode of transmission.

Haemorrhagic plague lies somewhere in between: its infectious period was long enough for the disease to be transmitted over long distances, and it was infectious enough for an epidemic to get going easily, given a sufficient number of susceptible people and suitably warm weather.

What kind of virus caused the plague?

We now have a general category in which we can place our villain, but can we narrow this down further by looking at the symptoms of its victims?

Later descriptions of plague symptoms, in the seventeenth century, accord with earlier accounts from the first outbreak. A victim usually displayed the symptoms for about five days before death although, from reading contemporary accounts, we came to the conclusion that this period could be anything between two and twelve days. However, we found one exceptional report of a victim in London who survived twenty days.

The main diagnostic feature was the appearance of haemorrhagic spots, often red, but ranging in colour from blue to purple and from orange to black. They often appeared on the chest, but were also seen on the throat, arms and legs and were caused by bleeding under the skin from damaged capillaries. These spots were the so-called God's tokens and Dr Hodges, an apothecary, wrote:

the sign most feared was that to which the people gave the name of 'the tokens'. The devout and superstitious accepted them as God's sign – 'the heathen are afraid of Thy tokens'. Some called them 'God's marks'. They were the almost certain forerunners of death. Medical observation agreed that very few with these marks upon them recovered health. 'The tokens' were spots upon the skin, breaking out in large numbers, varying in colour, figure, and size. Some, where they had run together, became as broad as a finger nail, others were small as a pin's head, till they enlarged and spread. The colour might be red, with a surrounding circles inclining towards blue; in others a faint blue, the circle being blackish; others again took a dusky brown tone. Often the flesh was found to be spotted when no discoloration was visible on the skin. No part was immune from these round spots, though the neck, breast, back and thighs were the most common places for them. 'The tokens' sometimes were so numerous as to cover all the body.

Daniel Defoe wrote:

Many persons never perceived that they were infected till they found, to their unspeakable surprise, the tokens come out upon them, after which they seldom lived six hours; for those spots they called the tokens were really gangrenous spots, or mortified flesh, in small knobs as broad as a little silver penny, and hard as a piece of callus ... there was nothing could follow but certain death.

Dr Hodges also described in 1665 'the case of a maid who had no idea that she was attacked by Plague, her pulse being strong and senses perfect, and she complained of no disorder or pain, but on examining her chest I discovered the tokens there. Within two or three hours she was dead. The tokens sometimes first became visible after death.' He mentions, as being most strange in his experience, that many persons came out of delirium as soon as 'the tokens' appeared, believing that they were in a recovering and hopeful condition. The poor sufferers did not realize that their fate had been sealed.

Various swellings were also characteristic of the disease: these included carbuncles, blains and the buboes, which were swollen lymph glands in the neck, armpits and groin. In the seventeenth century, it was believed that those cases in which buboes did not appear were the most dangerous. Dr Hodges reported that if the growth failed to break naturally, the surgeon opened it by incision. 'Unhappily the rising of Plague buboes was attended by such severe pain, and feeling as of intolerable burning as the time for suppuration approached, that the sufferers often became raving mad.' The incision (without anaesthetic, of course) and the subsequent cleaning were so painful that patients often collapsed under the procedure. If the buboes failed to rise and burst, there was little expectation of life, but if they broke the fever apparently declined. Some physicians believed that lancing the buboes would stop the disease from progressing to the development of the dreaded tokens.

A surgeon, serving in the garrison at Dunster in Somerset in southern England in 1645, bled all sick soldiers showing the first signs of the disease until 'they were like to drop down', and it was reported that all his patients recovered. Presumably, this bleeding would have taken place when the symptoms first appeared, some 30 days after infection. Is it possible that these treatments, whereby swollen lymph nodes were lanced or perhaps a large proportion of the infected white blood cells was removed, could have allowed the immune system to defeat the infection?

Along with the swellings, victims experienced fever and high temperature, continual vomiting, diarrhoea and prolonged bleeding from the nose. Physicians in Milan in the fifteenth century regarded blood-tinged urine, in addition to the haemor-rhagic spots, as evidence of plague. The onset was also often accompanied by a burning thirst and acute fever, in some, was accompanied by madness and delirium, 'so much so that many hurled themselves out of windows'.

This is confirmed by the eye-witness account of Chester in 1647:

> The plague takes them very strangely, strikes them black on one side and then they run mad, some drowne themselves, others would kill themselves; they dye within a few hours; some run up and down the street in their shirts to the great horror of those in the City.

One contemporary account of the agonies suffered by victims of the 1665–66 plague in London describes

> the vomit running out from the side of the mouth, prolonged bleeding at the nose, the sores decreasing and turning black on a sudden ... Some of the infected run about staggering like drunken men, and fall and expire in the streets; while others lie half-dead and comatous ... Some lie vomiting as if they had drunk poison.

Dr George Thompson carried out an autopsy of a youth who had died in this plague:

> The surface was stigmatised with several large ill-favoured marks, much tumified and distended, from which, on section, there issued sanious, dreggy corruption and a pale ichor destitute of any blood. The stomach contained a black, tenacious matter, like ink. The spleen gave out on section an ichorish matter. The liver was pallid and the kidneys exsanguine. There were obscure large marks on the inner surface of the intestines and stomach. The peritoneal cavity contained a virulent ichor or thin liquor, yellowish or greenish. There was a decoloured clot in the right ventricle, but not one spoonful of that ruddy liquor properly called blood could be obtained in this pestilential body.

W. G. Bell reported laconically that this dissection showed that the disease produced far-reaching alterations in the internal organs, as well as affecting the skin by a multitude of blue or black spots that contained congealed blood. 'In fact, no organ was found to be free from changes.'

The following reports of two autopsies of victims of the plagues in 1656–57 in Rome and Naples respectively confirm the widespread degradation of the internal organs.

> The exterior part of the body was found to be covered by black petechiae ... the omentum rotten, the guts all black, the peritoneum cyanotic, the stomach very thin, the spleen rotten, the liver doubled in size but of bad colour and consistency, the gallbladder full of black bile ... the pleurae were rotten, the pericardium very hard, the mediastinum and the sagittal septum livid, the heart livid with its tip black, both ventricles full of very dark blood. The lungs, of bad consistency and colour, were all covered with black petechiae.
>
> It was noticed that all the organs – namely, the heart, lungs, liver, stomach, and guts – were covered with black spots. Moreover, the gall bladder was found full of black bile, which was very thick and fattish ... Especially, however, the major vessels of the heart were full of blood, which was clotted and black.

We have uncovered the key characteristic of haemorrhagic plague: death was preceded by a generalized necrosis of the internal organs. It was as if the insides of the victim were being dissolved away. It was, without doubt, a grisly way to die.

The signs, symptoms and autopsy reports of victims of bubonic plague are entirely different from these: they do not display God's tokens, nor is there widespread necrosis of the internal organs.

The following account gives a good description of the spread of plague through a household and illustrates the medical features described above:

> We were eight in the family – three men, three youths, an
> old woman and a maide; all which came to me, hearing of
> my stay in town, some to accompany me, others to help me
> [he was a celebrity in the religious world with a large
> following]. It was the latter end of September before any of
> us were touched ... But at last we were visited ... At first our
> maid was smitten; it began with a shivering and trembling
> in her flesh, and quickly seized on her spirits ... I came home
> and the maid was on her death-bed; and another crying out
> for help, being left alone in a sweating fainting-fit. It was on
> Monday when the maid was smitten; on Thursday she died
> full of tokens. On Friday one of the youths had a swelling
> in his groin, and on the Lord's day died with the marks of
> the distemper upon him. On the same day another youth
> did sicken, and on the Wednesday following he died. On
> the Thursday night his master fell sick of the disease, and
> within a day or two was full of spots, but strangely
> recovered ... The rest were preserved.

We can be sure that the virus responsible for the Black Death is
not one that is known today; indeed, it is possible that it does not
even belong to any of the known families of viruses. However, the
symptoms most nearly resemble those of Ebola, Marburg and
the viral haemorrhagic fevers and, although it was certainly not
identical to any of these, of all the diseases known today they
seem to be the most similar to it.

The causative agents of these diseases are called filoviruses.
They have a high fatality rate and tend to occur in explosive
epidemics driven by person-to-person transmission. Outbreaks
occur unpredictably; there is no treatment and, as yet, their
animal reservoir is unknown. The term 'viral haemorrhagic fever'
covers several different and diverse diseases that are characterized
by sudden onset, aching, bleeding from the internal organs, fever,
shock and spots – comparable to 'God's tokens' – that result from
bleeding under the skin. The symptoms of Ebola start with a

sudden fever and the victim is killed by the liquefaction of the internal organs.

Other identifiable features of haemorrhagic plague

Seasonality

The disease struggled to survive the winter months in England, particularly during the Little Ice Age. Even in southern France, the virulence of the plague was demonstrably reduced during the colder months. It was generally appreciated by the seventeenth century that it was much less infectious in cold weather. W. G. Bell, who in 1924 wrote the definitive history of the Great Plague of London, recorded that on 6th February 1666:

> All men declared [it] to be one of the coldest days they had ever experienced in England. In two separate months ice blocked the Thames, stopping the river traffic. But Plague occasionally showed its head even through the frost. There is Dr Hodges' testimony that very few died that season, but he himself in January attended a case in which the Plague spot was apparent and the patient recovered. Josiah Westwood in the continuance of the frost also attended patients in whose conditions he recognised Plague; they obtained a cure, 'the air then being so friendly to nature, and an enemy unto the Pestilence'. Other indications suggest that instances of Plague were not uncommon, but in the cold the disease never became severe, and the deadly symptoms afterwards so familiar were suppressed.

It was probably almost impossible to be infected out-of-doors in a cold winter and even indoors the transmission rate was low, in spite of families being huddled together in their cold and draughty cottages. Evidently, this virus did not enjoy being exposed to cold air.

Transmission was much easier in warmer climates and this observation gives us a clue as to the source of the disease, which is discussed in the next chapter.

Confinement to Europe

Prior to 1670, the regions afflicted by haemorrhagic and bubonic plague overlapped only on the Mediterranean coast. The former became established in Europe, with occasional forays into North Africa and the eastern Mediterranean, while the latter had its stronghold in Asia and the north African coastlands, with rare outbreaks in Italy, southern France and Barcelona that did not persist.

Why did they hold these separate territories? We have already listed the reasons why bubonic plague has never become established in Europe, but why was haemorrhagic plague confined there, where the climate varied so much from the southern Mediterranean to the Arctic Circle? Why did it not spread to central Asia or to sub-Saharan Africa?

There were probably several reasons. The main trade routes in these places, like the Silk Road and the routes across the Sahara, included very long stretches without any major towns, so that infected travellers were more likely to perish on the journey without initiating an epidemic. The absence of conurbations along the way also prevented epidemics from being established and any infections would soon die out completely.

Trading was less intense when compared with the internal routes in Europe, so that fewer potential infectives would be passing to and from Asia and it would have been impossible to establish a persistent focus. Finally, the climate en route may have been too hot and dry for droplet transmission to be effective.

Persisting as a reservoir only in France?

Conditions in France were uniquely suitable for the continuous maintenance of the plague because the warmer temperatures, particularly in winter, and relatively high humidity there facilitated the persistence and spread of the infection. The area was large enough for the plague to circulate between the large towns and there was a good internal communications network.

In contrast, areas where outbreaks of the plague were irregular lacked some or all of these conditions:

- Italy was too small a country to act as an effective reservoir; the summers were hot and dry and strong public-health measures were instituted and enforced, including strict quarantine regulations at the ports.

- In the Iberian peninsula, the summers were hot and dry; internal communications were poor; and the infections were introduced only by sea. The Pyrenees formed an effective barrier to the north.

- North Africa was hot and dry; the inhabited area was small; the population was scattered; and communications were poor.

- In the Holy Roman Empire, the winters were cold, and Scandinavia and Iceland were too cold all year round.

- In England, winters were also cold and the infection could arrive only by sea.

We have used all the evidence from the previous chapters to bear on the question: what were the characteristics of the virus that caused the devastation of the plagues? It will always remain something of a mystery because, obviously, the disease is not around today, but we have already revealed many of its secrets. We go further in the next three chapters towards answering the question of where the Black Death had come from when it appeared in Sicily and comparing it with other mysterious viral diseases that have suddenly emerged over the last three millennia.

16

The Black Death in Hiding

As long as people believed that the Black Death was an outbreak of bubonic plague, there was no mystery concerning its origins: they assumed that it must have come from western Asia, almost certainly courtesy of the famous galleys from the Crimea, as we saw in Chapter 1.

But now that we are certain that the Black Death was an outbreak of a lethal and directly infectious disease, we are faced with an entirely new problem: where on earth had this terrible disease really come from? A full-blown viral disease cannot have come out of thin air. If it had originated from the known western world at that time, surely the terrible mortality would have been noticed and recorded.

The origin of the Black Death

Let us begin our search for the origin of the Black Death by backtracking from its arrival in Sicily. We may remember that the traditional story tells of how the disease was brought by the healthy crews of Genoese galleys when they arrived at Messina. The sailors had been at sea for many weeks and had docked with a clean bill of health. When they disembarked, anyone who met them was immediately stricken with the plague.

This account is completely inconsistent with the behaviour of any infectious disease and, if there were any truth in the story, the galleys must have arrived in the port at Messina coincidentally when the epidemic in Sicily had already passed through the first stage and was just about to get into full swing. Superstition, the desire for a scapegoat, no medical knowledge and exaggerated and embroidered story-telling would have all combined to provide a case against the inoffensive sailors. The epidemic in Sicily must have begun some weeks earlier in the summer.

However, it is a pretty good bet that the Black Death was originally started by one or more infected people coming by boat. After all, Messina and Catania are seaports on the east coast of Sicily – important entry points for boats trading from the eastern Mediterranean and the North African coast.

But where did the infection originate from? The Genoese galleys are traditionally believed to have come from the Crimea, where some form of plague was raging. Did haemorrhagic plague really start here? We searched the literature on epidemics in the Mediterranean area in the fourteenth century and came to the conclusion that there were two possible places in 1347 from which the Black Death could have come, the Crimea and the Levant.

We discovered many records of plague epidemics in the Levant on the eastern Mediterranean coastline both before and after the Black Death. Syria and Iraq were literally plagued by the disease in the eighth and ninth centuries and we concluded that outbreaks sporadically developed in this area over very many years. It seems that the lands around Egypt and Syria were a plague hotspot that was capable of putting out its tentacles to destroy European civilizations for over 1000 years before the Black Death. But this remarkable conclusion immediately leads to the next problem: how did the plague establish its base in the Levant in the first place? To answer this question we have to go back to the very origins of humanity in east Africa.

Out of Ethiopia

It is probable that our hominid ancestors appeared in eastern central Africa and that the cradle for human evolution was the

Great Rift Valley, which stretches from what is now Mozambique northwards to Ethiopia and thence to the Black Sea. Fossilized remains of an extinct, human-like ape, named *Australopithecus*, have been found in eastern Africa, particularly in Ethiopia and

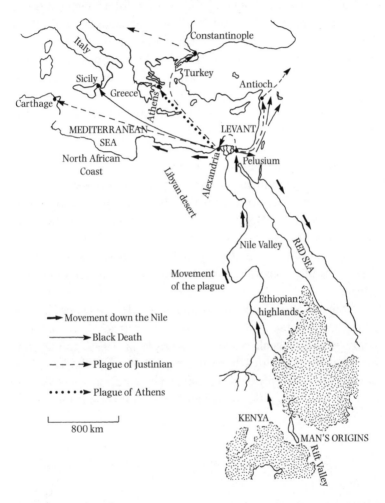

Origins of haemorrhagic plague in the Great Rift Valley. It moved down the Nile Valley and established a base in the Levant. It made three major historical strikes from here: the plagues of Athens and Justinian and the Black Death.

Kenya. The genus *Homo* probably evolved from *Australopithecus* and *Homo erectus* then gradually spread out of Africa, moving northwards down the Nile valley or the Great Rift Valley, to Europe and Asia.

Our own species, *Homo sapiens*, evolved from *Homo erectus* in Africa between 100 000 and 200 000 years ago. It was destined to colonize all the continents of the world except Antarctica and it probably began by following the Nile northwards to Egypt and Syria, then branching eastwards to Asia and westwards to Europe.

These early ancestors were hunter-gatherers who gradually, about 10 000 years ago, changed to a dispersed agricultural way of life. They suffered sporadically from infectious diseases but were safe from major epidemics, which can be established only when large numbers of people are living together.

A number of writings from the fifth century BC have traced plagues back to Ethiopia. Several Arabic sources mention the persistence of plague in this area of Eastern Africa from the seventh century AD and they tell how epidemics spread by caravan traffic from there to Sudan and then to Egypt and North Africa.

Is it just a coincidence that humans and these plagues all seem to have originated in the same region of Africa? W. H. McNeill, who wrote the book *Plagues and People* in 1997, thinks not: he suggests that Africa harbours more human pathogens than anywhere else simply because that is where humans evolved and that is where they have existed for the longest period of time.

How haemorrhagic plague emerged from Africa

Most of the diseases that suddenly emerged in the twentieth century had their origins in animals, usually mammals or birds. We may tentatively suggest the following scenario. Originally, the virus of haemorrhagic plague infected other primates, but only in a mild way, otherwise all their hosts would have been killed. Probably the primates would have been outwardly unaffected. Occasionally, it may have been transmitted to our hominid ancestors and it may, or may not, have been lethal to them. In any case, the infection would not have spread far in these primitive, loose and scattered communities of early humans and a few deaths would have had no significant consequences. The virus, multiplying steadily while safe in its animal reservoir, would have been completely unaffected and would have continued to reproduce prodigiously.

As humans evolved, they became more and more separated from the animal hosts. When groups of people left Africa to colonize Europe and Asia and eventually to found the great civilizations and city states, with busy traffic between them, they created ideal conditions for establishing and propagating devastating epidemics. Fortunately for them, the sources of plague were now hundreds of miles away and separated by the vast Mediterranean sea.

However, there were several occasions in history when haemorrhagic plague reached those civilizations. Presumably one or more Africans became infected from the animal host, and the virus was then transmitted by infected people travelling down the Nile Valley. The disease established a base in the Levant and then it was only a lengthy sea voyage away from the centres of civilization.

Thus, the area around the eastern Mediterranean becomes pivotal to our story: it may have acted for hundreds of years both as a sink for the infection coming from central/eastern Africa and as a staging post for onward transmission to western civilizations.

The plague of Athens in the fifth century BC

The devastating epidemic that struck Athens in 430 BC has been discussed by many scholars, but it remains one of the great medical mysteries of antiquity.

The Athenian civilization was then at the height of its glory, but it was locked in a major series of wars with Sparta – the Peloponnesian Wars – a territorial and ideological struggle which lasted from 431 until 404 BC. On one side was Athens, dedicated to democracy, and on the other was Sparta, an oligarchy, which restricted the franchise to a few individuals. In 443 BC, Pericles emerged as the political, military and cultural leader of Athens and he became the architect of its military strategy.

The first cases of plague appeared in Piraeus, which was a port and base for many travellers and merchants who brought the disease from abroad. It quickly spread to the upper city where entire households were killed; mortality among doctors and other attendants of the sick was especially high.

Thucydides was an upper-class Athenian writer who suffered from the plague and recovered, and is now famous for his history of the Peloponnesian Wars. Afterwards, he wrote an invaluable eye-witness account of those terrible days, with the express purpose of providing an accurate description of the disease so that it would be recognized if it should ever recur.

Thucydides relates that people were suddenly stricken with severe headaches and inflamed eyes and began to cough blood. Coughing, sneezing and chest pains followed; then stomach cramps, intense vomiting and diarrhoea, and an unquenchable thirst. The skin was flushed and broken with small blisters and open sores. The victims suffered from an extreme fever and could not tolerate being covered, choosing rather to go naked. Consumed by thirst, they felt an overwhelming desire to throw themselves into cold water and many jumped into public cisterns. Most became delirious and died on the seventh or eighth day. Of those who recovered, many had lost the use of their extremities, their memory or their eyesight.

The Athenians were fully aware that the disease was infectious: the healthy avoided the sick and did not observe the customary burial rites for family and friends; dead bodies were left lying in the streets and temples.

Thucydides' descriptions are remarkably similar to eye-witness accounts of the Black Death and they are certainly not descriptions of bubonic plague, nor of any other disease that exists today. It is probable that this was an early outbreak of some form of haemorrhagic plague.

Pericles, fearing an attack by the Spartans, ordered the people in the surrounding countryside to move inside the fortified walls of the city. These people were crowded together in an already overpopulated city and had nowhere to live. The summer was hot and the city was under siege, ideal conditions for the spread of the infection.

The disease continued at a low level through 429 BC – when Pericles died of it – and returned in force in the summer of 428, during another Spartan siege. It was quiescent from the winter of 428 until the summer of 427, but broke out again, for the last time, in the autumn of that year.

The plague of Justinian in the sixth century AD

According to the historian Procopius, the plague of Justinian originated near Ethiopia. It moved down the Nile valley in AD 541, all the way to the Mediterranean port of Pelusium in Egypt, and from there it ripped through Egypt and onwards to Syria and Palestine. It then 'seemed to spread all over the [known] world; this catastrophe was so overwhelming that the human race appeared close to annihilation'. The plague mostly followed trading routes, which (most significantly) provided an 'exchange of infections as well as goods'.

Procopius added that the disease always started from the coast and then moved into the interior of a country; apparently it usually arrived by boat. It seemed to move 'by fixed arrangement, and to tarry for a specified time in each country'; that is, like all infectious diseases, the epidemics followed a characteristic pattern and time course.

When it arrived at Constantinople in AD 542, it put a catastrophic end to the Byzantine emperor Justinian's dream of reestablishing the Roman Empire. The peak of the epidemic lasted some four months and the death toll rose from 5000 to a staggering 10 000 a day; 300 000 people were said to have died in Constantinople in the first year alone, although these figures may be exaggerated. Officials were overwhelmed by the task of disposing of the dead bodies: trenches were dug but were soon filled to overflowing, and an evil stench pervaded the city.

Merchant ships and troops then carried the pestilence through the known western world and it flared up repeatedly over the next 50 years, causing terrible mortality. Procopius relates that people were terrified, knowing that they could be struck without warning. The first symptom was only a mild fever, but bubonic swellings followed within the next few days. After the swellings appeared, most sufferers either went into a deep coma or became violently delirious, sometimes paranoid and suicidal. When the physicians opened the swellings, they found a carbuncle inside them. Black pustules the size of lentils broke out in some victims, who invariably died within 24 hours. They were overcome by thirst and many plunged into the sea. Most were vomiting blood and died a few days after the appearance of the symptoms. The black blisters were regarded as a certain sign of impending death but otherwise doctors could not easily predict the course of the disease, or the success of the various treatments they tried. Apparently, not all the victims died.

Contact with those displaying symptoms was apparently not dangerous. This agrees with our conclusions about haemorrhagic plague, where transmission more often took place early in the infectious period rather than during the final days after the first signs had appeared.

Unlike the plague of Athens, the plague of Justinian continued for many years, with epidemics flaring up repeatedly. It is interesting that it recurred in cycles of about nine to twelve years and during the period AD 541 to 700 the decline in the Mediterranean population has been estimated at 50 per cent.

A historian writing of a second outbreak in AD 558 related that it had never completely abated after the first epidemic, it had simply moved from one place to another – a similar story to that of haemorrhagic plague in France. That it could be carried from place to place on the slow merchant ships of the time again points to a long incubation period. Once more, it was certainly not bubonic plague.

There are striking similarities between this plague, the plague of Athens nearly 1000 years earlier and haemorrhagic plague: a suggested origin in Ethiopia, swollen lymph glands, delirium, fever, black blisters, person-to-person transmission, a short period of symptoms before death and raging thirst. Everything suggests that these were early outbreaks of haemorrhagic plague.

The power base of haemorrhagic plague in the Levant

Plague was well known to Middle Eastern peoples long before the Black Death, so that the disease was recognized when it reappeared in the middle of the fourteenth century. The plague of Justinian was one of its earliest strikes. Muslims could recall the macabre history of the disease, dating from their conquests of the Middle East in the seventh century. The chroniclers record that there were five great plagues in Islamic history, the first strike being in AD 627. About 25 000 Muslim soldiers died in AD 638 in the second epidemic, which spread through Syria and to Iraq and Egypt. The next strike was named the violent plague because it swept through Basrah 'like a flood' in AD 688 and the fourth major epidemic struck this city again in AD 706. Iraq and Syria experienced the 'plague of the notables' in AD 716 and Syria experienced further outbreaks about every 10 years from AD 688 to 744.

When epidemics ravaged the early Islamic Empire, the Muslims had responded to the danger; they sought to explain it and to treat its victims. The epidemics held special religious connotations because of its association with the Prophet and came to determine the cultural attitudes of traditional Muslim society. The records of these pandemics reveal that it was comparable to the Black Death (which struck 600 years later) in its transmission, social and economic consequences and cyclical reappearances.

Evidently haemorrhagic plague was alive and well and doing very nicely in its stronghold in the Levant and the Middle East for hundreds of years before the Black Death. As ever, it was carried around by trade.

The elusive Yellow Plague

A lethal epidemic known as the Yellow Plague struck Europe in the sixth century AD, reappeared in the seventh century and continued for many years. It broke out in southern England in AD 664, from where it eventually spread to Northumbria and to Ireland. It was noteworthy that this plague was active during the summer months. There are also contemporary accounts of it in Italy, France and Spain. There are few facts to go on, but the Yellow Plague certainly persisted for a long time (possibly 600 years), although the epidemics in England seem to have been sporadic. Perhaps the disease was endemic in southern continental Europe and only occasionally crossed the English Channel to initiate summer outbreaks in England.

Were the plagues of Athens and Justinian, those of the early Islamic empire and the Yellow Plague forms of haemorrhagic plague? If so, did they (particularly Yellow Plague) gently force up the frequency of the $CCR5$-$\Delta32$ mutation to its estimated level of 1 in 40 000 before the arrival of the Black Death? This seems to us to be a probable scenario.

Haemorrhagic plague rampages in the Crimea

The pestilence did not stand still in the Levant, as we have seen: it was frequently pushing northwards to Antioch and thence progressively through Turkey, Asia Minor and the Ukraine and striking regularly at the Islamic Empire.

In 1266, Caffa (now called Feodosiya) was established in the Crimea by the Genoese and became the main port for their great merchant ships. A coastal shipping industry to Tana (now called Azov in Russia) developed on the Don River, and trade was continued along this waterway to Central Russia and thence by caravan routes to Sarai.

By the 1340s (immediately before the Black Death) Caffa was a thriving city, heavily fortified within two concentric walls: the inner wall enclosed 6000 houses and the outer 11 000. The highly cosmopolitan population included Genoese, Venetians, Greeks, Armenians, Jews, Mongols and Turkic people.

The Mongols besieged Caffa and Tana in 1343. The Italian merchants in Tana fled to Caffa, where the siege lasted

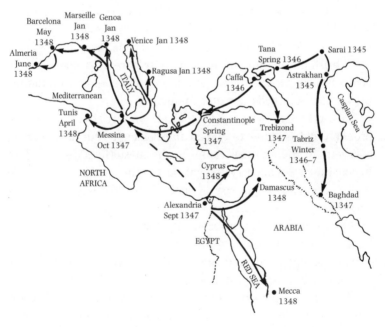

Movements of haemorrhagic plague around the Levant and the Crimea prior to and during the Black Death.

until February 1344 when an Italian relief force killed 15 000 Mongol troops and destroyed their siege machines. The Mongols renewed the siege of Caffa in 1345, but a year later were forced to lift it because a deadly epidemic devastated their forces.

We have already encountered the notary Gabriele de Mussi of Piacenza in Chapter 1. He also wrote an account of events in the Crimea, although he was probably not an eye witness. He described how, in 1346, in the countries of the East, countless numbers of Tartars and Saracens were struck down by a mysterious illness that brought sudden death. The Tartars besieged Caffa for nearly three years but that army was stricken by a disease that 'killed thousands and thousands every day'. Surely this is an exaggeration. They died as soon as the signs of disease appeared on their bodies: swellings in the armpit or groin followed by a putrid fever.

The Tartars placed the corpses of their comrades in catapults and lobbed them inside the walls of Caffa, supposedly in the hope that the intolerable stench would kill everyone there. In response, the Christians within the besieged city threw as many of the bodies as possible into the sea, but the rotting corpses soon tainted the air and poisoned the water supply.

This primitive form of biological warfare by the Tartars probably did nothing to spread the epidemic, but soon almost everyone in the area fell victim to the mysterious disease. 'One infected man could carry the poison to others, and infect people and places with the disease by look alone.' We have heard this sort of comment before.

Some sailors who had been infected escaped from Caffa by boat; some went to Genoa and others were bound for Venice. When the sailors arrived there, 'every place was poisoned by the contagious pestilence and their inhabitants died suddenly'. And when one person contracted the disease he poisoned his whole family 'even as he fell and died'. Presumably, this is another account of the arrival of the Black Death in northern Italy in 1348.

Did the Black Death come from the Crimea?

It is quite clear from the account of Gabriele de Mussi that this mysterious epidemic in the area around the Crimea was not an outbreak of bubonic plague. Was it haemorrhagic plague? Allowing for the usual exaggerations, the descriptions, although sparse, strongly suggest that it was, and de Mussi clearly links the epidemic with the appearance of the Black Death in the north of Italy.

So did the Black Death come directly from Caffa following the well-established trade routes? The first objection is the length of the voyage. Graham Twigg has made a special study of shipping at that time and he concluded that the galleys could not have completed the journey from the Crimea to Genoa via Sicily in less than four or five weeks and might have taken three months. We believe that this is too long even for an infectious disease with an incubation period of 32 days.

Instead, it is more probable that the epidemic at Caffa in 1346 spread across the Black Sea and reached Constantinople a year later in spring 1347. It would then have been a shorter voyage to hop across to Sicily, bringing the Black Death to Messina six months later in October 1347, although it may have travelled via Greece. This scenario is more convincing with respect to the timing of events.

We can therefore plot the sequence of events during the terrible epidemic of south-western Asia. It seems to have started close to the Caspian Sea at Astrakhan and Sarai in 1345, two years before the appearance of the Black Death. It spread to Tana in spring 1346 and was quickly transmitted to Caffa. These towns were besieged by the Tartars who rapidly succumbed to the disease, which spread like wildfire through their troops. So many died that the Tartars eventually gave up the siege and the movement of refugees and troops probably promoted the transmission of the epidemic throughout the area.

During the next year, this lethal disease spread across the Black Sea to Constantinople in the spring and to Trebizond in the autumn of 1347. Simultaneously, it moved southwards from Astrakhan to Tabriz in present-day Iran, arriving there in winter 1346–47, and it continued from there, appearing in Baghdad on the Tigris some time in 1347. It is clear that this disease could move great distances along the trade routes and again, it certainly was not bubonic plague.

The Black Death could have been brought to Messina by trading vessels from Constantinople, probably via Greece. But it was also reported at the port of Alexandria in September 1347, one month before it arrived in Sicily.

We are still left with unanswerable questions. Did the Black Death come to Sicily from Constantinople or from Alexandria? Did the outbreak in Alexandria also originate from Constantinople? It is impossible to judge, but the epidemic in Egypt did not stand still: it followed its usual paths along the trade routes and arrived in 1348 at Damascus to the north and Mecca in Arabia to the south. The plague was covering vast distances in Eurasia during the three years from 1345 to 1348 and by 1350 it had arrived at the Arctic Circle.

After 1348, the disease seems to have died out in south-western Asia forever. The chains of transmission were broken, probably during winter, the epidemics ceased and were not started up again.

After the Black Death

The evidence suggests that after the Black Death haemorrhagic plague persisted in the Levant, at a variable but generally low level. In Egypt alone, plagues were reported every five years after the Black Death for 150 years.

Several outbreaks of haemorrhagic plague certainly came to Italy through the ports. As we have seen, the vigilant health authorities of the northern city states were particularly wary of boats arriving from the Levant and they evidently perceived a strong risk of haemorrhagic plague coming from this area.

A single epidemic might last in the warm climate there for three or four years, but the habitable coastal strip of Syria, Lebanon, Israel and Egypt is relatively small and the disease would eventually die out. Therefore, if this region was perceived as a constant threat, it was probably because there were frequent sporadic epidemics there, each started afresh by an infected person arriving from the Nile valley.

However, the Nile is some 1500 miles (2400 kilometres) long, so the transmission of the disease could hardly have been accomplished during the incubation period of a single infected person, even travelling by boat downstream. Rather, there were probably chains of infections and epidemics that constantly moved up and down the valley by boat or caravan.

17

Why Did Haemorrhagic Plague Suddenly Disappear?

The plague in England and in northern continental Europe survived the winter only with difficulty and, as we have established, its persistence over the centuries was completely dependent on repeated introductions from France. It disappeared from Scotland in 1649 and quickly fizzled out in England after 1666 because it could not persist through the winter months and there were no further introductions from continental Europe because it had disappeared from there. So the big question now becomes: why did the plague eventually disappear from its stronghold in France?

There is probably no single answer to this question. Rather, a number of factors, some more important than others, must have combined to eliminate the disease from its reservoir in France. After that, there was no long-term hope for the pestilence – it was simply a matter of time.

The Little Ice Age

The global climate cooled significantly in the sixteenth and seventeenth centuries and the beginning of the Little Ice Age was marked by low sunspot activity, the advance of the glaciers and lower temperatures. The main period of cooling did not begin until 1560, but even as early as 1506 southern France experienced a severe winter and the Mediterranean froze at Marseille.

In Europe, it was March that reflected the climatic change most consistently. That month became cold and wintry, with low rainfall, and probably the weather at that time of year was dominated by blocking anticyclones and northerly winds. In addition, the spring months that followed were cold and dry, and June was cool and wet.

Thus the persistence of the cold weather through the spring and early summer may have been the important factor that reduced the ability of the plague to reestablish itself after the winter, so stamping out many incipient epidemics.

These colder conditions would have contributed to its disappearance in England but, more importantly for our purposes here, it may also have constrained the spread of the plague and contributed to its demise in southern France.

However, the 1630s were an exception to the general climatic pattern of the Little Ice Age because the weather was relatively warm during this decade. It was then that the plague in continental Europe was at its worst, with widespread epidemics in France and Germany. The 1640s, in contrast, were the coldest decade of all in the age of plagues and it was then that the disease became much less severe, with only a few minor outbreaks on the continent.

Public-health measures

Gradually throughout Europe the health authorities became more efficient at detecting the disease and preventing epidemics from starting and spreading. By the seventeenth century, even in the provinces, cases were quickly recognized and appropriate measures were introduced, which included isolation in designated pest houses, ring-fencing and quarantine.

A regular, informal information service between towns was established and boats entering ports, as well as strangers arriving by road, were regarded with great suspicion if they came from a place where it was known that the infection was raging. In France, clean bills of health were required from travellers entering cities.

These measures were not very successful in containing the epidemics, although they probably reduced the mortality. Nevertheless after 1646, when the disease was already declining in France, they may have helped to curtail its spread markedly and thereby accelerate its decline.

Disappearance of the plague from the Levant

If there was a plague focus in the eastern Mediterranean, it may have died out because the disease was no longer regenerated and reinforced by a stream of infected travellers coming down the Nile valley. There would then have been no chance of any new introduction of the disease into southern France to reinforce the epidemics there.

Improved nutrition

A general improvement in nutrition, particularly in southern France, may have created a stronger, healthier population, with immune systems better able to resist the disease. This would be comparable to the reduction in the lethality of whooping cough in England in the nineteenth century, which was clearly linked to a better diet.

In 1628–29 there was a widespread famine in northern Italy: grain became very expensive and there followed the greatest outbreak of plague of all in continental Europe. After 1662 grain became much cheaper in France, and this would have resulted in improved nutrition for the bulk of the population.

Development of resistance

This was the most important factor that led to the disappearance of the plague. By the seventeenth century, some fortunate members of the European population were either completely or partially resistant to the virus because, as we have seen, they possessed the $CCR5$-$\Delta32$ mutation. This proportion of protected individuals would have been increasing steadily over the years, particularly in the crucial towns on the trading routes in France. As a result, the number and density of susceptible people in these key locations would have fallen.

For a major epidemic to be maintained, there must be a sufficient density of susceptible people. With the rise in the number of resistant individuals, it became increasingly difficult for epidemics in the major towns in France to get going and to produce a supply of travellers to carry the infection elsewhere and so the plague lost its foothold in France. It was the beginning of the abrupt end for haemorrhagic plague.

The end of an age

This progressive rise in levels of resistance in the French towns probably acted cooperatively with the other factors listed above. Together, they finally led to the apparently sudden disappearance of the virus. The chain of infection had only to be broken completely in one year for it to disappear. After that, epidemics could only occur following a new introduction of the disease from outside Europe.

18

The Dangers of Emergent Diseases

Throughout this book we have continually used the word 'plague', although in truth it has no precise definition. It has been applied to a wide variety of unpleasant events, from the 'plague of locusts' in the Old Testament to the influenza pandemic of 1917–19. The word is part of the common name of some diseases (like 'bubonic plague') and it is also used to refer specifically to the sequence of epidemics in Europe following the Black Death.

Nevertheless, there is an interesting and important class of diseases that more or less corresponds with our intuitive notion of a plague. These are the *emergent diseases*, on which we touched in Chapter 15.

Once we accept that the Black Death was not caused by bubonic plague, it becomes obvious that no known infectious agent was responsible and that it was just one (although certainly the most terrible) of a long line of emergent diseases that have afflicted humanity since the dawn of civilization. These lethal infections appear mysteriously from nowhere, run their course and then disappear. Sometimes, they can reappear.

We must, then, take on board the frightening possibility that the Black Death could emerge again from wherever it is hiding; such an event could potentially destroy our civilization.

It was obvious to us that we must now examine thoroughly the biology of known diseases that have emerged from animal hosts in the twentieth century. Everyone has heard of the unstoppable pandemic of HIV/AIDS and we discovered that many other completely new diseases have emerged in the last 30 years. If there is any chance of the Black Death – the most awful killer that has ever struck humankind – emerging again, we need to be prepared.

The hidden menace of emergent diseases

In this chapter, we shall give an overview of some of the plagues that afflicted humans after the Black Death. Emergent diseases continue to appear today, most worryingly with increasing frequency. What are their salient features? Before answering this question, let us consider some well-known examples of infectious diseases that are *not* plagues.

Diseases such as measles have been around for a long time. Measles is highly infectious and epidemics spread like wildfire among susceptible children. It is not a danger to well-nourished children in the developed world, but in previous centuries – and in poor countries today – perhaps 15 per cent of cases were fatal. If an infected child recovers, they become immune and will not be infected again. This virus can be viewed as a successful parasite that is in balance with its host, humans. As long as children continue to be born, the virus will coexist with humans unless it is eradicated by a vaccination programme.

Smallpox probably first appeared as a rather benign disease having come from domestic animals, but it mutated in about 1630 to become much more deadly, and it was the most feared disease in Europe after the disappearance of the plague. As with measles, recovery brought immunity and hence only children were infected. It was less infectious than measles, but much more lethal.

Smallpox was slowly brought under control, first by means of inoculation with the virus itself and then by vaccination. Then another deadly mutation occurred in Europe in 1869, resulting in a terrible loss of life in spite of vaccination. Smallpox was eventually eliminated by a carefully controlled worldwide vaccination programme. However, now that vaccination is no longer compulsory, if smallpox were released, either accidentally or by terrorists, only a small proportion of the population would have any effective resistance or immunity.

Cholera is a potentially lethal infection of the gastrointestinal tract acquired by drinking contaminated water. It kills many people in refugee camps today and the death toll in the nineteenth century was grim: 10 per cent of the population of St Louis died from it in three months in 1849, half a million in New York in 1832. Cholera is a well-understood disease: it is not spread from person to person, it does not appear from nowhere and the epidemic ceases if the drinking of contaminated water stops.

One-fifth of the inhabitants of London in 1665 had active tuberculosis and the rates continued to climb. London was a very unhealthy place. The disease was brought to the United States by immigrants and was firmly entrenched in the northern cities by the time of the Civil War. It caused heavy mortality in Europe and the USA in the nineteenth century, and continues to do so in poor countries today. Tuberculosis is not highly infectious and does not produce genuine epidemics. It was almost eliminated by improved nutrition and living conditions, even before the invention of antibiotics, but is again on the increase.

Despite the severity of some of these diseases, they do not count as plagues. They usually persist in a population at low levels, with occasional epidemics, have been around for a very long time and their modes of transmission are well understood. We have learnt how to live with them and in some cases we have conquered them by vaccination programmes, but some are potential weapons for bioterrorist attack.

How can we recognize deadly emergent plagues?

In contrast, emergent plagues have the following characteristics: they have a high lethality, often close to 100 per cent; they seem to appear from nowhere although, by the second half of the twentieth century, epidemiologists were usually able to determine their probable animal origins; they are directly infectious from person to person; they are usually viral; they often produce epidemics.

Emerging plagues of the twentieth century were usually traced back to animal origins and here lies the clue to their success. Since they kill their human host they could, at first sight, be regarded as an unsuccessful parasite. An epidemic ends once all available victims have been killed and then the parasites also, inevitably, die out. But with emergent diseases, the infectious agent continues meanwhile living harmoniously in its animal host, which it affects only slightly – an example of a truly successful parasite. The disease lies dormant in its reservoir and (here lies the danger to us) is potentially able to strike again if humans accidentally come into close contact with an animal carrying the parasite.

The strange Sweating Sickness

In the autumn of 1485, a strange disease appeared in England that was said to have been introduced by mercenaries who had just returned from France. It lasted only during the autumn and early winter and became known in Europe as the 'English Sweat', because of the high susceptibility of the people in England.

The mysterious Sweat reappeared four more times – in 1508, 1517, 1528 and 1551 – after which it disappeared from England forever. Most of the surviving accounts of these outbreaks are confined to London, an exception being the last epidemic, which began in the town of Shrewsbury in Shropshire and then proceeded to London 'with great mortality'. However, an analysis of the records of 680 parishes shows that this was in fact predominantly a rural disease, capable of very rapid transmission along the main thoroughfares, killing about 30 per cent of the population of the towns that it struck.

The Sweat seemed particularly to affect the affluent. Cardinal Wolsey contracted it three times in 1517, but survived. Many people in Henry VIII's court fell sick with the Sweat, and the King developed such a morbid fear of the disease that he would change residences every other day in an attempt to avoid contact with those of his court who had become infected.

An attack of the Sweat would begin without warning, generally in the night or early morning. Chills and tremors were followed by a violent inflammatory fever with profuse sweating, often accompanied by a rash; the victim suffered sudden headaches and muscle pain and had difficulty breathing. It lasted no more than 24 hours and, if the victim was lucky, the perspiration diminished and was replaced by an abundant flow of urine; recovery was complete within a week or two. Otherwise, the intense headache and convulsions were followed rapidly by coma and death. Many victims died a few hours after the symptoms appeared, although most lingered for 24 hours. The Sweat did not affect infants, small children or the elderly, and surviving the disease was no guarantee of immunity.

In 1528, the French ambassador to the English court wrote:

One of the *filles des chambre* of Mlle Boleyn was attacked on Tuesday by the sweating sickness. The King left in great haste, and went a dozen miles off ... This disease is the easiest in the world to die of. You have a slight pain in the head and at the heart; all at once you begin to sweat. There is no need for a physician; for if you uncover yourself the least in the world, or cover yourself a little too much, you are taken off without languishing. It is true that if you merely put your hand out of bed during the first 24 hours ... you become as stiff as a poker.

The epidemics were of short duration: 'It attacked a community suddenly and then was gone. The disease swept through a parish in the space of a very few days, a fortnight at most.'

Whatever the cause, it was not bubonic plague; nor was it haemorrhagic plague, with which it coexisted. But of interest are the questions of where it went in the inter-epidemic years; and whether it, somewhere, had an animal host.

A central Asian 'black death'

Graham Twigg has kindly drawn our attention to a report by the Governor-General of Turkistan that appeared in the *British Medical Journal* in 1892. Turkistan covers a large area of central Asia and, according to the report, the region had been 'severely visited by an epidemic of the black death', which appeared suddenly at Askabad in September 1892. The Governor-General explained:

> Black death has long been known in western Asia as a scourge more deadly than cholera or [bubonic] plague. It comes suddenly, sweeping over a whole district like a pestilential simoom [a hot, dry desert wind], striking down animals as well as men, and vanishes as suddenly as it came, before there is time to ascertain its nature or its mode of diffusion.

In Askabad it killed 1303 people in six days, out of a population of 30 000, and then disappeared, 'leaving no trace of its presence but the corpses of its victims. These putrefied so rapidly that no proper *post-mortem* examination could be made.' The attack began with rigors of intense severity, the patient shivering literally from head to foot; the rigors occurred every five minutes for about an hour. Next an unendurable feeling of heat was complained of; the arteries became tense and the pulse more and more rapid, while the temperature steadily rose. Convulsions alternated with syncopal attacks and the patients suffered intense pain. Suddenly the extremities became stiff and cold and in between 10 and 20 minutes the patient sank into a comatose condition, which speedily ended in death. Immediately after the victim had ceased to breathe, large black bullae formed on the body and quickly spread over its surface. Decomposition took place in a few minutes.

What was this strange disease of central Asia, which could appear so suddenly and disappear so soon afterwards? And why did the corpses decompose so rapidly? Could this possibly be a mutated form of haemorrhagic plague?

The worst pandemic after the Black Death

Influenza is a disease of animals that can be transmitted to humans and it mutates readily. A strain of the influenza virus emerged in 1917. Beginning in the USA, as a mild form of influenza, it swept over the world, but only a few people (mostly young adults) died of it. However, in August 1918 the virus mutated, unleashing the deadliest influenza epidemic of all time. It appeared almost simultaneously in three ports where troops and supplies from all over the world were being gathered and dispatched to the trenches of the Western Front: Boston in North America; Freetown in Sierra Leone; and Brest in Brittany.

Helped by rapid twentieth-century transport, this epidemic killed half a million people in the USA; Britain reported 2000 deaths a week; in India, 20 million people died. Worldwide, the final death toll is estimated at 30 million and at least 200 million became ill with the disease. Later blood tests showed that it touched the majority of the human race. This frightening epidemic began to subside after the end of the First World War and soon vanished completely.

The weak, the very young and the elderly are usually particularly vulnerable to influenza. However, surprisingly, this epidemic struck hardest at healthy people in their twenties, and the usual symptoms of influenza (headache, severe cold, fever, chills, and aching bones and muscles) were augmented by complications such as severe pneumonia, purulent bronchitis and heart problems. Regarded as 25 times more deadly than ordinary influenzas, this strain in effect drowned its victims by filling their lungs with blood.

New strains of the influenza virus that are capable of engendering epidemics are caused by radical genetic mutations, which usually originate in Asia. These occur in a virus infecting an animal – often a duck, chicken or pig – and then pass into the environment and to human beings.

In 1998, fragments of the influenza virus were found in victims of the 1918 pandemic: in the lungs of a woman whose body was preserved in Alaska, and in the lungs and brains of Spitzbergen coal miners who were buried in the permafrost. Scientists have decoded the complete sequence of one important gene of the virus, which proved to be closely related to the standard form of influenza that affects pigs.

There is always the danger that the strain that caused the 1918 epidemic may resurface, perhaps in just as virulent a form. Avian influenza A virus has recently been shown to be transmitted from patients to healthcare workers in Hong Kong and, worryingly, it has been suggested that this finding may portend 'a novel influenza virus with pandemic potential'.

In February 2003, an outbreak of 'bird flu' in a Hong Kong family who visited Fujian province in southern China fuelled fears that that country will be the source of the next global flu pandemic. Flu experts are fearful because the Chinese practice of keeping large numbers of different birds in close proximity to humans favours the emergence of new strains of the disease. The family had visited Fujian for the Chinese New Year and was struck by tragedy when the eight-year-old daughter became ill and died. The father and son also fell ill with similar symptoms. The father died shortly after the family returned to Hong Kong and the son was admitted to hospital, where health officials diagnosed his illness as the bird flu virus H5N1.

The outbreak of bird flu in several East Asian countries in early 2004 caused considerable anxiety and some consumer panic. Although 18 people had died by mid-February, fortunately the virus had not so far developed the mutation that would allow influenza to spread directly from one person to another.

Why the flu virus sometimes turns lethal is a mystery, but the worst outbreaks have happened when a human flu virus picks up new genes from fowl flu viruses, or jumps directly from chickens to humans.

An outbreak in a remote African town

First described in the 1950s, Lassa fever is an acute emergent viral disease of one to four weeks' duration, and the symptoms range in severity from nothing at all to an extremely dangerous illness that may be fatal. It now occurs mainly in West Africa where it is persistent in some areas and there are between 100 000 and 300 000 infections each year, which cause about 5000 deaths.

Lassa fever is transmitted to humans from a wild rodent known as the multimammate rat. These animals live near human settlements and transmission is usually through direct or indirect contact with their excrement, which is deposited on floors, beds, food or water. The incubation period is between six and twenty-one days. Person-to-person infections also occur by direct contact with blood, throat secretions or urine, or by sexual contact.

HIV/AIDS

This is now a worldwide epidemic and is of particular interest to us because, as we have seen, like haemorrhagic plague, HIV uses the CCR5 receptor as its port of entry into human cells. This lethal emergent disease originated in chimpanzees in west central Africa and hunters were exposed to infected blood while killing and dressing the animals. One in six monkeys eaten as bush meat in

Cameroon are also now known to be infected with a variant of HIV and this has raised fears that new strains of the disease could develop.

It is believed that HIV was born more than a million years ago, out of a union between two viruses that infected different species of monkey. The virus had probably been living harmlessly in primates for hundreds of years and scientists think that it crossed over to humans sometime after 1700 and then mutated into its current form around 1930. The changed socioeconomic conditions in Africa meant that HIV began to be spread widely by sexual intercourse in the 1960s and 1970s.

The origins of the disease are now of no practical consequence and have been forgotten, and it is simply regarded by most people as a deadly infectious disease of humans.

The HIV epidemic is different from most other emergent disease outbreaks, partly because of the exceptionally long incubation period of the virus and partly because of the low rate of infection. However, modern means of travel have allowed the disease to spread all over the world. Nevertheless, even in the worst-hit areas, it is advancing fairly slowly and it is unlikely that the epidemic will burn itself out in the foreseeable future. Scientists have been trying for nearly two decades to produce a vaccine that will combat the disease, with no success. They are continually thwarted by the virus's ability to change its structure. Yet the spread of HIV was theoretically preventable, given clinical measures – such as sterile hypodermic needles – and proper precautions during sexual intercourse.

However, an estimated 40 million people around the world are now living with HIV or AIDS, including 2.5 million children below the age of 15. There were 5 million new infections and over 3 million deaths in 2003.

Sub-Saharan Africa remains the worst-affected region, with 27 million people HIV positive and 11 million AIDS orphans. The threat of mass starvation and death in southern Africa caused by acute shortages of food has been largely averted, announced the head of the United Nations World Food Programme in

2002, because of the rapid reaction by humanitarian workers and aid agencies with generous gifts from international donors. However, Africa is now confronted by something very different from anything the world has witnessed recently. Botswana has the highest HIV infection rate in the world, where 39 per cent have the virus, while South Africa has the highest number of sufferers: 5.3 million. The Ministry of Health in Zambia expects that half the population will die of AIDS and some 25 per cent of the people of Zimbabwe are HIV positive. The pandemic is spiralling out of control and threatens to tear apart the fabric of society: hospitals are swamped, businesses are losing employees and agricultural production is falling.

In August 2003, the Indian National AIDS Control Organisation announced that the number of people in that country with HIV/AIDS had risen by half a million in the last year alone and the total infected stood at an estimated 4.6 million. The disease is no longer confined to high-risk groups living in the cities, such as drug injectors, but is starting to spread to rural regions. The pandemic is worsening severely in countries that have so far escaped lightly, particularly China, Russia and Indonesia, driven largely by intravenous drug use and unsafe sex.

The longer-term prospects are even more frightening: the United Nations has revised down its forecast for world population growth because it expects nearly 300 million people to die of AIDS over the next half-century, a figure comparable to the population of the United States. In 2001, the UN Population Division said that it expected the world population to grow from 6 billion to 9.3 billion by 2050. It is now expected to reach only 8.9 billion. The HIV pandemic illustrates all too clearly the terrible dangers of emerging diseases if they are not quickly checked when they first appear. Draconian measures may be necessary.

An intriguing observation about HIV has recently emerged: the number of AIDS cases per head of population in Saudi Arabia is just one-hundredth of that in the USA. This is not explicable by a high frequency of the CCR5-Δ32 mutation there because, of 105

Arab blood donors resident in the country, none had the double mutation and only one had the single mutation. Other (at present unknown) protective effects must be at work. Could it be that haemorrhagic plague scourged Saudi Arabia hundreds of years ago and the people there developed a different form of genetic resistance? After all, early humans moving northwards along the Great Rift Valley from Ethiopia and the Sudan would pass along the shore of the Red Sea and could have entered Arabia via the Sinai peninsula and Aqaba. And we have already seen that haemorrhagic plague penetrated into Arabia in the 1340s.

A postscript on HIV: in little more than a dozen years, the African lion population has plummeted from 230 000 to 20 000 today because their immune systems are being destroyed by the lion version of HIV. This is good news for zebras, but the lions face extinction. It is not only humans who are at risk from an emerging virus.

The most gruesome way to die today

Ebola and Marburg are fatal emergent diseases, characterized by widespread tissue infection and destruction, haemorrhaging and fever. The Ebola filovirus appeared in 1976 in northern Zaire, where there were 318 cases with a fatality rate of 90 per cent; Ebola then caused 150 deaths among 250 cases in Sudan. Smaller outbreaks continue to appear periodically, particularly in eastern, central and southern Africa. In 2002, the European Commission in Brussels warned that increasing numbers of tourists from Africa were bringing the Ebola virus to Europe.

Ebola is arguably the most gruesome way to die today and it is frighteningly like haemorrhagic plague. The patient vomits endlessly, bringing up a liquid known as the black vomit, which is actually a speckled mix of degraded tissues and fresh red arterial blood, the result of internal haemorrhaging. The vomit is loaded with virus and highly infectious. Again, it originates from animals:

gorillas and chimpanzees are the main suspects. In March 2003, there was news that over 100 people had been killed in a remote forest region of the Congo Republic in a spreading outbreak of suspected Ebola virus, which is thought to be linked to the consumption of infected monkey meat. In the Lossi gorilla sanctuary alone, some 500 of the 800 animals died. To try to stop the virus from spreading, all schools and churches in the area were closed and people were told to stay at home, but cordoning off the entire region was difficult because of the network of tiny forest trails.

An epidemic with symptoms similar to Ebola killed 63 people in May 1999 in the war-ravaged eastern border region of the Democratic Republic of Congo, but the medical authorities claimed that the haemorrhagic fever was not caused by the Ebola virus. The region had suffered similar outbreaks previously in 1994 and 1997. The outbreak in 1999 centred on the gold-mining town of Durba, close to the borders with Uganda and Sudan. Most of the victims were believed to be illegal miners living in unsanitary conditions. Presumably, these outbreaks were yet another emergent disease in Africa.

The most feared disease today?

Crimea–Congo haemorrhagic fever belongs to the broad category of viral haemorrhagic fevers that, with their dramatic symptoms and high mortality, are among the least understood and most feared of all diseases today. First described in the Crimea in 1944 and later identified in the Congo in 1956, this virus is circulated over a vast area of the world by ticks, which transmit it to humans and ruminant animals. Humans can also be infected by direct contact with blood or other infected tissues from livestock.

Patients usually die six days after the onset of the illness and the list of symptoms has a familiar ring: fever; headache; vomiting; diarrhoea; swollen lymph glands; bleeding from the nose, throat, gums and colon; and bleeding into the skin, causing an extensive haemorrhagic rash.

The mystery virus

The perplexing organism that struck Native Americans in 1993 is now known as Sin Nombre virus (literally 'without name'). It would take three months and about forty deaths before experts got a grip on the situation, identifying the common deer mouse as the reservoir for the virus. It had jumped from the rodent to human beings and is classified as a hantavirus.

Worryingly, *new hantaviruses turn up each year*, some colonizing geographic areas previously unblemished by the scourge. Sin Nombre virus may have struck before: Navajo folklore tells of two mystery epidemics in 1918 and 1934 and warns against the dangers of getting too close to rodents.

A sleeping dragon

When humans first started living closely together in cities, with busy trade routes between them, conditions were exactly right for the inevitable emergence of fatal diseases of animal origin, and we have described just some of the most infamous examples. In the United States, West Nile virus has been a problem for some years and the disease is now endemic in many parts of the country, having emerged from Uganda in 1937. US Air Force aircraft spray standing water and swamps where the mosquitoes that carry the virus live in an effort to stop the disease in its tracks. Infected birds are spreading the infection and are being followed by the mosquitoes. Scientists at Oxford University reported in autumn 2002 that they had identified antibodies to the virus in a number of dead birds in England – a sure sign of either past or current infection.

In the twenty-first century, the world is progressively getting smaller and we are moving into more and more areas that have previously been virgin. When large numbers of people engage in ecotourism or enter the rainforest to chop down trees, they come into contact with thousands of viruses that have never been near humans before. While the great majority of these will not be able to jump across the species barrier, a handful will.

If the plagues of Athens and Justinian and of the early Islamic empire and the Yellow Plague were forms of haemorrhagic plague, as we suggest, then the virus responsible for the Black Death must have been dormant in animal populations for centuries, breaking out occasionally over a period of more than 2000 years. There is no reason to suppose that it departed for good in 1670.

Now, with ever more people travelling at great speed from place to place, the situation has become critical. Since the mid-twentieth century we have seen over 30 terrible diseases emerge from their animal hosts with alarming frequency. What will be next? Will the Black Death return?

19

The Return of the Black Death?

Haemorrhagic plague finally disappeared in 1670. Or did it? When Danish TV was making a programme about our work, the producer told us about the plague of Copenhagen in 1711 – everything in that epidemic corresponded with our descriptions of the spread of haemorrhagic plague, he said. This really set us thinking because, if this were true, the disease had not disappeared completely in 1670 as we and everyone else had supposed, but had reemerged 40 years later – and probably on more than one occasion, as we judged from our subsequent reading. If it had succeeded in frequently reemerging over a period of 2000 years from wherever it was hiding, why should it not do so again?

Using our imagination and what we have already learnt so far, we can suggest how this disease has been lying in wait and could suddenly pounce again on the human race. The scenario below reads like a screenplay for a horror film, but would it be too far from the truth?

Sometime in the twenty-first century

Haemorrhagic plague was brought back to the western world by biologists who had been working closely with primates in the high forest of central Africa. They returned home to London and unwittingly spread the infection widely when travelling daily on crowded public transport. The London Underground, packed with constantly changing fellow passengers, allowed transmission of the virus to a great many victims coming into the metropolis over a 25-mile radius. Some were visitors from all over the world. Trips to sporting venues, theatres and cinemas all disseminated the infection widely before the symptoms appeared in any of the victims.

When the primary cases died, the health authorities realized that their patients had contracted a serious, unknown disease. They took proper precautions with full protective clothing when nursing victims during their final days and the bodies were sealed into special bags. Beyond that, there was nothing else they could do.

It was only when the multitude of secondary and tertiary cases began to appear all over the UK that the scale of the epidemic became apparent. Eventually, the Chief Medical Officer announced that there was a major epidemic of an unknown lethal disease, which was spreading rapidly and widely, and that the situation was out of control. It was thought to have come from Africa as a new emergent disease and was probably spread by droplet infection. Beyond that, people knew nothing of its epidemiology. It was too late, the damage had been done. Britain was totally isolated. Nothing came through the ports or the Channel tunnel. Nobody in the rest of the world would risk coming to a hotbed of such a terrible disease. The British were alone and had to fend for themselves.

It proved impossible to quarantine the vast suburban sprawl of London and, in any case, it was pointless, because the disease was spreading rapidly through the provinces. It was uncontrollable. There were too many people crammed into too small an island.

The terrible bug particularly favoured discos, shopping malls, cinemas, football matches, centrally heated offices and pubs, and these were all closed by law. Given a few weeks, the infection could kill most of the children in a school who, during the long incubation period, went home and carried the bug to their families. All educational establishments were closed.

The hospitals eventually refused to admit any victims of this horrible and mysterious disease: they were completely full, they did not want any more infectious people and anyway it was pointless; they could not cure these patients.

A number of people in England were, surprisingly, resistant to infection (we now know why). They did not catch the disease, even after repeated close contact with those who were infectious. Even more surprising was that some people were catching the disease and, although they were very ill indeed, they were making a full recovery. Shaken and gaunt, they were emerging from their houses and looking at a transformed world outside. They soon had other pressing problems about which to worry.

One unforeseen problem was the disposal of the bodies of the victims. Were they infectious? Everything had developed so quickly that the medical microbiologists had been unable to answer this fundamental question. Healthy people refused to come near either the cadavers or the houses where they died. Bodies were therefore merely dragged into the gardens in the suburbs and countryside and at first buried in shallow graves, but people were soon overwhelmed and struck with a dreadful apathy. They were all going to die horrible deaths anyway and they simply left the corpses to the mercy of the elements, stray dogs and rats. This was not an option for city dwellers, particularly those living in high-rise flats. In desperation, the corpses there were thrown on to the streets and left to rot. The results were indescribable.

Cholera and typhoid epidemics then broke out in many towns and millions of brown rats boldly emerged from the sewers. They were going to take over.

Everything started to come to a standstill and most offices and factories were closed. Since almost everyone had been employed in nonessential work this did not much matter, but catastrophically, the means of supply and distribution also stopped.

Panic buying and frantic stockpiling of food began instantly. Prices were raised tenfold and the supermarkets were crammed with people trying to empty the shelves – ideal conditions for spreading the disease.

Once this food was eaten, there were only limited further supplies. Rationing was not introduced because there was very little food to distribute and there had been no time to establish an infrastructure of food production and supply. It was not possible to hide away and isolate yourself, because it was essential to get out and about and search for any source of food if the family were to survive. Looting and petty thieving were rife. Gangs armed with knives and whatever other weapons they could lay their hands on roved the streets seizing any food they could find.

Many rural communities resorted to the wholesale killing of lambs and sheep and there was little the farmers could do, although they freely shot anyone they caught. This gave temporary relief from the famine conditions, but was of little benefit to city dwellers. They were unable to reach the country-side and, even if they had been able to capture a lamb, would have been incapable of slaughtering, skinning and butchering the carcass.

The authorities, very sensibly, issued advice to the effect that it was dangerous for people to congregate at their places of work. However, when the power workers refused to report for duty, the electricity supplies failed. The government's promise of greatly inflated wages was to no avail: money now had no value whatsoever. Electricity, not petrol, was the life-blood of this developed economy and many people were now unable even to sterilize drinking water by boiling.

The complex fabric of life in the twenty-first century had collapsed completely. The rugged independence and self-sufficiency of people's ancestors had long gone and they had been living a completely artificial existence based on computer technology, which was driven by international finance and a world economy. They had been cocooned by central heating, refrigerators, television, rapid transport, convenience foods, microwaves, an array of electrical goods and the pharmaceutical industry. There was no problem that could not be solved by technology.

People were adept at surfing the Internet, but had lost the basic instinct to survive. They had moved too far from their roots and had lost their self-sufficiency. They were grossly overcrowded and consequently were extracting too much from the soil and were heavily dependent on supplies of food from overseas. Few people in the twenty-first century had seen food at the point of production and many children probably believed that the chicken on the dining table originated in a deep-freeze, wrapped in plastic.

The global technology civilization was precarious and any spanner in the works would have caused a catastrophe. This mysterious and horrific epidemic was an accident that was waiting to happen.

In contrast, Australia escaped almost completely. The authorities there closed all entry points and went into total isolation when the news of the outbreak came through.

The single infected person who flew to Melbourne was identified and isolated. More importantly, every contact he had made on Australian soil or on the flight was meticulously followed up and quarantined. Then, in turn, all their contacts were traced and quarantined. In this way, the health authorities kept a tight control on the disease. They then delineated areas where it was felt there might be some residual risk of infection. People were instructed to wear masks at all times when in public. Schools, cinemas, discos and pubs were temporarily closed in these areas.

Such draconian measures were completely successful and the incipient epidemic quickly fizzled out. A total of 20 people died.

Australia covers a vast area and has many natural resources. Its people are thin on the ground so that even in complete isolation, they were easily able to fend for themselves. They were self-sufficient and good at DIY. Some adjustments had to be made and rationing of certain foods and goods had to be introduced. Later they were able to negotiate a limited supply of oil. When this terrible pandemic eventually disappeared (if it ever did) would the world be recolonized by Australians?

In contrast, the effects when the pandemic spread to India and China were truly catastrophic. It was unstoppable. The emergency health measures were limited and largely ineffective and supplies of painkillers and sedatives were rapidly exhausted. Nobody showed any sign of resistance to the disease (unlike the situation in Europe, where one in seven people were, surprisingly, resistant) and it went through the crowded population like a blowtorch.

Terrified, everybody showed the usual response and fled by bus and train, carrying the disease far and wide. When the authorities prohibited all forms of transport, the people tried to flee on foot, dragging handcarts behind them. But it was no use: they carried the disease with them and each epidemic spread steadily and remorselessly from its centre in a radial fashion, like waves on a pond when a stone is thrown in – an inexorable, gigantic, evil wave of terror and agonizing suffering. Then the people fleeing met the wave of refugees coming from the opposite direction. The conditions were ideal for the bug and the teeming millions provided a seemingly endless supply of susceptible people. It was later estimated that the final death toll would eventually be counted in billions. It was impossible to bury the bodies which decomposed rapidly in the heat, leading to scenes of unimaginable horror.

The Black Death had returned, 700 years after its first appearance. Its pattern of spread in underdeveloped countries was broadly similar to that of the original pandemic, except that there was now an endless supply of victims all tightly packed together. Transmission was ridiculously simple and the economy of developed countries collapsed completely.

Could the world recover from such a catastrophe?

Is the time ripe for the reemergence of haemorrhagic plague?

Many apocalyptic scenarios have been suggested for the end of the world as we know it, including global warming, meteor impacts, mega tidal waves, volcanic eruptions and, of course, all-out nuclear war. Governments invest varying amounts of money and effort in preparing for these potential threats, but few have taken seriously the possibility that a killer viral disease, such as the Black Death or something like it, could emerge without warning – probably from a mammalian host in Africa, as we suggest above – and destroy our civilization.

The circumstances of human life in the twenty-first century – so different from those of medieval Europe – would, as we have suggested above, facilitate rather than hinder the progress of such an epidemic and the devastation would be on a vastly greater scale. Tourists are now flocking to Africa and air travel would spread the virus rapidly around the world; it was only when HIV escaped from Africa to Haiti, and thence to the USA, that the AIDS epidemic took off.

Our story began with the emergence of humans in the Great Rift Valley in eastern Africa about a quarter of a million years ago, at a time when our species was living in close association with a great variety of wild animals. Even after the first agricultural revolution about 12 000 years ago, when farming replaced hunting and gathering as the mainstay of human life, people lived in small settlements and did not suffer from epidemics. It was only when they began to congregate in cities that lethal infectious diseases started to emerge. Even so, over a period of some 3000 years there were only a handful of such outbreaks. Most probably emerged from Africa and caused grievous mortality, but the survivors were strong and resourceful and they soon rebuilt their societies. Even after the horror of the Black Death in the fourteenth century, Europe was almost back to normal in a few years.

Then came the second agricultural revolution in the eighteenth century. Mechanization and more sophisticated crop management led to greater productivity, necessary to feed a fast-growing population. The plague had disappeared by then, but the large towns were very unhealthy places. Smallpox, measles, whooping cough, diphtheria and other infectious diseases killed about a quarter of all children in England; many adults died from tuberculosis and influenza. Nevertheless, people learned to live with these diseases and in spite of them, the population continued to grow.

Then in the twentieth century came the technological revolution. Thanks to incredible advances in medical science, the invention of antibiotics and the development of vaccines, the developed world is now virtually untroubled by infectious diseases. This is not the case in poor countries, where infections caused by animal parasites (such as malaria) continue to kill large numbers of people.

Nowadays, we in the developed world are much more worried about cancer, heart disease and growing old than about infectious diseases. We may be living in a fool's paradise. Microbes reproduce at a prodigious rate and are continually evolving and coming up with new weapons in the biological war of survival – the speed with which they develop resistance to antibiotics is proof of their ingenuity.

We are completely defenceless against a new virus until it can be characterized and a vaccine developed. If it happens to be highly lethal and infectious, it can wreak havoc. Worse still, if it has a long incubation period it can establish a pandemic before anyone knows of its appearance.

With the help of the internal combustion engine, most of us now travel great distances every day. Air travel, for both business and pleasure, has widened people's horizons even further. By contrast, in the fourteenth century only the lucky few had a horse, tourism was unheard of and travel by boat was slow and haphazard. It is not surprising that in those days, emergent diseases escaped from Africa so rarely.

The Black Death was confined to Europe. It set up its stronghold in France and regularly sent out epidemics to the rest of the continent. However, if it were to return, the situation today would be very different.

Parts of the southern United States, India, China, Australia and the Mediterranean coast would provide ideal conditions for the virus to set up strongholds where it could persist. With global warming, there are now more such areas. Air travel would ensure that it reached these places: one infected person would be enough to introduce the disease, which would then spread remorselessly, aided by central heating and air conditioning and unchecked by cold winter conditions. There would be few resistant individuals with the $CCR5$-$\Delta32$ mutation outside Europe and, once strongholds were established, infected people would soon be travelling regularly, by land and air, to other parts of the world.

The planet is vastly more crowded than Europe was in the fourteenth century. In particular, the billions of people living in Asia would provide an ideal home for the virus; we must remember that two-thirds of the deaths in the 1918 influenza epidemic were in India. Also, a very much larger proportion of people today are crowded together in towns: they congregate in supermarkets, cinemas and football matches and commute on public transport. An epidemic would escalate rapidly in such conditions.

We now live in a global economy, both financially and socially. Stock markets everywhere react instantaneously to any event, in any part of the world, that traders believe will affect the value of shares. And the effects of any perturbation in the complex global society – such as a major epidemic – are instantly felt throughout the world.

Finally, because of the technological revolution, people in the developed world have become separated from nature. We are not as strong, resilient or self-sufficient as our ancestors. The production and distribution of goods are dependent on a bewildering array of technologies, particularly electricity and the internal combustion engine. If large numbers of people started dying from the Black Death and others took evasive action, the fabric of our complex technological society would come apart, so exacerbating the effects of the epidemic. And how could the survivors start up their lives again? Most of us would be unable even to light a fire without matches.

Lines of defence

Is it possible to prepare for such an eventuality?

Knowledge is power. We now know that the standard view of the Black Death is wrong: it was not an outbreak of bubonic plague and it was not spread by rats and fleas. If it had been and it returned to Europe, we should have nothing to worry about because bubonic plague is readily treatable and any epidemic could easily be contained. However, the Black Death was in fact caused by an unknown virus that could potentially reemerge at any time. Nevertheless, it would not be completely new – we hope that anyone who has read this book would know what to expect.

If the Black Death did reemerge, the first victims would display symptoms similar to those described in the various accounts that we have quoted earlier. Hopefully, those signs would be recognized immediately as haemorrhagic plague and not casually categorized as 'just another emerging disease', because the success of any defence against the Black Death would depend on early diagnosis and immediate action.

Unfortunately, nothing could be done for the victims, but draconian health measures should immediately be imposed to try, if possible, to contain the initial infection. These measures would be: isolation of the victims; widespread and compulsory use of masks (since transmission is by droplet infection); cancellation of all public congregations over a wide area; a 40-day quarantine for anyone suspected of infection; wearing of protective clothing; and a ban on all movements in and out of the affected area, particularly by plane.

However, as we have shown, haemorrhagic plague's secret weapon, which made it so hideously effective, is its exceptionally long incubation period. Because of this, it would be almost impossible to trace everyone who might have become infected – health authorities would not be properly prepared. The above procedures alone would not be adequate, as the people of Europe found to their cost in the fourteenth century.

Public-health officials would need to adopt more radical strategies. The first symptoms would not appear until at least a month after the first victim was infected – probably in Africa – and in that month he or she would probably have travelled great distances and unwittingly infected many people.

So a second line of defence would be needed. As we have described, the dates when the victims were infected and when they became infectious can be accurately determined from the date of death. Their movements from the day when they became infectious must be rigorously checked and all possible contacts traced. That would be a Herculean task, requiring full and active international cooperation. In the best possible case, where the victims had not moved around much during the time when they were infectious, blanket isolation techniques would control the outbreak.

More probably, the victims would have moved over a wide area, and even infected passengers on the international flight home from Africa. They may have travelled on crowded public transport and attended sporting events and other congregations. Tracing all contacts would be impossible, and blanket isolation and prohibition of all movement in any areas where they had travelled would need to be implemented urgently. Health authorities throughout the world would be on the alert for secondary and tertiary infections and, knowing the character-istics of the virus, they would know the approximate dates when these symptoms would be expected. The same measures – isolation, wearing of masks and tracing of contacts – would have to be rigorously applied every time a new case came to light.

Inevitably, the virus would escape and spread far and wide, killing many people, but it should be possible with the right measures to capture and control it eventually. The first objective would be to restrict the rate of spread in each area where it started. When an outbreak was completely isolated, there would have to be a major mopping-up operation, based on a 40-day quarantine period. The task would be enormous and armies of health officials would be required to act quickly, to trace contacts and to enforce the necessary measures. But if we were vigilant and acted quickly and sensibly, whole continents might escape.

If the virus is not contained in this second phase, it would be too late and the disease would eventually spread across the planet.

The price of safety

It is not only humans who are vulnerable to deadly emergent diseases. In the second half of the twentieth century, elm trees were all but wiped out in England by a fungal disease transmitted by small beetles, thereby irrevocably transforming the countryside. Some other trees may soon suffer a similar fate: sudden oak death, a fungal disease that kills viburnums and rhododendrons, was identified in England in May 2002 and could have catastrophic repercussions. Stringent control measures were introduced, including a team of nearly 100 plant-health inspectors. The disease has wiped out large numbers of tan oaks in coastal California and southern Oregon. In December 2003, the UK Government issued a new alert because the fungus had been found for the first time in beech, sweet chestnut, sitka spruce and Douglas fir, as well as in camellias, *Kalmia*, lilac, *Pieris* and potted yew plants in garden centres. The disease appears to have been spread to trees from infected rhododendrons and vast banks of these bushes may have to be destroyed.

Foot-and-mouth disease infected sheep and cattle in Britain in 2001 and spread dramatically and frighteningly in spite of a massive containment exercise in which thousands of uninfected animals were slaughtered – a public-health intervention that is (fortunately) not available when killer diseases of humans emerge.

Bluetongue is a viral disease of sheep that is carried by a small biting midge. It leaves the animals so debilitated that they cannot see, feed or move and 70 per cent of infected flocks are killed. It is just as deadly as foot-and-mouth disease. The midge, common in North Africa, crossed the Mediterranean and moved into southern Europe in 1998. Outbreaks across Spain, Italy, Greece and Bulgaria have caused the deaths of more than half a million sheep. A spokesman for the Institute for Animal Health said that he believes that the spread of bluetongue virus may be caused by the changing climate. With every one degree Celsius rise in yearly average temperatures, the midge, on average, extends its range 56 miles further north. More ominously, the range of the midge now overlaps with a closely related species that can live much further north, potentially bringing the threat of the disease into much cooler climates.

To return to humans, nature is capable of wreaking much greater havoc on humanity than is almost any terrorist attack or environmental catastrophe. Infectious diseases account for over 40 per cent of the global disease burden and millions die each year from HIV/AIDS, tuberculosis and malaria. About 70 000 people die in England each year because of infections – disturbingly, 5000 of these are acquired in hospitals.

Viruses and bacteria coexist with people and share a common environment, but the problem is never static and is predicted to worsen considerably. A recent report by the UK's Chief Medical Officer outlines the reasons why the prevalence and control of infectious diseases are unpredictable, and why they will become more difficult to manage:

- Increase in global travel – the rising trend in travel to more exotic locations and the boom in adventure travel have been mirrored by a rising trend in infections, such as the more severe type of malaria.

- The impact of technology – new technologies can have unforeseen effects on human health (for example, there is a direct link between air conditioning and Legionnaires' disease).

- Environmental change – future climate shifts may produce an increase in some water-borne diseases as well as in cases of food poisoning, which in the UK are linked to the warmer weather and have already become much more common.

- Changes in human behaviour patterns may facilitate the spread of an epidemic. (For example, recent increases in the levels of sexually transmitted diseases, including HIV, have been directly attributed to changes in sexual behaviour.)

- Drug-resistant organisms – diseases that have become relatively insignificant threats to human health can reemerge because the agents concerned develop resistance to the drugs that have been devised to treat them. The MRSA bacterium (or methicillin-resistant *Staphylococcus aureus*) is a superbug that can be resistant to many antibiotics and has long been a serious problem in hospitals and nursing homes, where it infects the wounds of patients weakened by disease or injury. Even more disturbingly, it has now escaped from the hospitals where it developed and lurks all around us. Random sampling found the bacteria on a pen in a high-street bank, on the seat of an underground train, on the button of a pedestrian crossing and on the floor of a clothing shop.

  It now appears that a new strain of MRSA is emerging that disperses through skin contact and can even infect healthy people. It spreads like wildfire in crowded jails and there have also been numerous smaller outbreaks in towns and cities across the US recently. Most of those infected are gay men, but the superbug is certainly not restricted to this group: athletes, schoolchildren and newborns have all fallen victim. Those involved in contact sports are also at risk. In Texas in September 2002, for instance, there were 50 cases among schoolchildren in Pasadena, some on the football team.

  The superbug has spread to domestic animals, prompting fears that they could infect their owners. Cases in cats, dogs, guinea pigs and horses have been confirmed in the USA and a report in December 2003 said that it has been detected in cats, dogs and a rabbit in the UK.

- Existing microbes can mutate to more virulent forms. For example, there is an ever-present risk of another lethal influenza pandemic like that of 1918 because of the arrival of a new strain.

The report makes clear that today's patterns of human behaviour are turning infectious diseases into a global threat, not just to the health, survival and well-being of populations, but to the economies of many countries and, in some parts of the world, to social stability and security. The scale of the danger is disguised by the fact that these changes are occurring gradually. Apparently, most people are still confident that the standard procedures for controlling infectious diseases will be able to cope. Staggeringly, some 400 diseases that can be transmitted from animals to humans have already been identified, but patient and meticulous work by epidemiologists and microbiologists means that we can now deal with them and sleep easily in our beds at night.

However, a much graver danger is the emergence from animals of new and terrible viral diseases. At least 30 previously unknown infectious diseases for which there is no fully effective treatment have appeared since 1970. This is more than are known to have emerged in the preceding 3000 years – though, of course, recent advances in medicine and biology have made them easier to identify. Many diseases – including haemorrhagic plague – have probably emerged at various times from African animals to infect small villages and tribes, causing mysterious deaths, which were unreported and then forgotten. This would certainly be the case before the time of Dr Livingstone.

An unidentified disease appeared in an Afghan village in March 2002 and killed 40 people. The real cause for alarm is that it is considered *inevitable* that more lethal diseases will emerge in the coming years. Herein lies the problem: we can contain and cope with even the really awful diseases like Ebola and nvCJD – although West Nile Fever and the haemorrhagic fevers still cause some concern and are being vigilantly monitored – but the example of HIV/AIDS stands starkly before us. This emerged, escaped and spread worldwide before it was fully recognized and even then, people shied away from imposing the necessary measures of mass testing and control. The health authorities in Britain, for example, relied on an advertising campaign. The world is now paying the price: 42 million children in 27 countries will lose one or both parents to AIDS by 2010. And this is a disease that is not readily transmitted – droplet infection is vastly more effective.

It is unlikely that HIV can be eradicated now: it will continue to spread slowly and kill more and more people. However, the world population continues to grow even more rapidly and the mortality from HIV is negligible compared with what would follow from a sudden strike of a new, highly infectious disease similar to the Black Death.

Panic

Even trivial epidemics can cause widespread panic with international repercussions – if the outbreak is of an unknown disease. A mysterious pneumonic virus emerged in Guangdong province in southern China in December 2002 and two months later there was widespread panic even reaching Shanghai, which is a day's train journey away. Millions of Chinese swamped chemists and shops, stockpiling antibiotics, anti-inflammatory medicines, vinegar and surgical masks, supplies of which all ran out, even with inflated prices.

The panic affected regional stock exchanges and caused shares of drug companies to rise – but these were outdone by the vinegar manufacturers. Many Chinese believe that if a pan of vinegar is boiled until it evaporates, the steam will be an effective disinfectant against disease. Four extra deaths were reported as a result of the vinegar being boiled over coal-burning stoves, which gave off lethal fumes.

All this furore arose because 300 people were in hospital with pneumonia caused by the virus, one-third of them doctors, nurses and other health workers. But only five people had died by February 2003.

Although the identity of what was believed to be a virus was not known, an official of the provincial Disease Prevention and Control Centre announced: 'The disease is under control. The priority now is to figure out what caused it. We did not realize it was a serious epidemic, so we did not take it seriously at the beginning.'

Governments in Macau and Hong Kong pleaded with residents not to panic, but they knew better: southern China has repeatedly been struck by deadly new viruses in recent years.

This outbreak in Guangdong province probably escalated into the mini-epidemic of SARS. We tell the unfolding story in the diary below:

- *26th February 2003*: A Chinese–American businessman flew to Hanoi, Vietnam, after spending time in Shanghai and Hong Kong. Two days later he fell ill and on 6th March he was taken into hospital, where his condition deteriorated and he died on 13th March. He left behind in Vietnam an outbreak of a deadly type of pneumonia, which became known as Severe Acute Respiratory Syndrome (SARS). He had infected workers at the Hanoi French Hospital where he was treated.

- *5th March*: In Toronto Sui-chu Kwan, an elderly woman, died and her son, Chi Kwai Tse, aged 44, died on the following day; they had been visiting Hong Kong. Four relatives and a close family contact were also infected. Two people in British Columbia were reported as victims of the same mystery illness.

- *6th March*: The disease spread to Singapore, where three people who had visited Hong Kong were reported to have developed the symptoms. By 16th March, ten of their relatives and friends and seven health staff who cared for them had been admitted to hospital with the illness.

  There was no cure because medical workers at this point did not even know whether the disease was caused by a bacterium or a virus. They concluded that the disease is transmitted from one person to another and has a short incubation period, of two to seven days. It normally involves a high fever of more than 38 °C, accompanied by a respiratory problem such as coughing, shortness of breath or breathing difficulties, or muscle aches. Other symptoms may include headaches, muscular stiffness, loss of appetite, malaise, confusion, rash and diarrhoea.

- *10th March*: In Taipei three people became ill, including a 64-year-old woman who had arrived home via Hong Kong after visiting the Chinese mainland. Hong Kong was sensitive about being seen as the source of the disease because of the potential devastation to its tourist industry. Shoppers in the former British colony stripped shelves of surgical masks and the traditional Chinese flu remedies as 42 people, many of them medical staff, were taken into hospital. Three hospital wards were cleared, a specialist heart clinic had to reduce its services and nonurgent operations were cancelled to keep intensive-care beds free. Eight days later the total of people who had fallen ill in Hong Kong, mostly medical staff, had risen to 100.

- *15th March*: The disease reached Europe when a doctor flying home from a conference in New York became ill before his plane stopped over in Frankfurt, Germany. He had treated some of the victims in Singapore. German officials (sensibly) took the unprecedented measure of keeping passengers in quarantine for much of Saturday before releasing them to continue their journeys.

- *18th March*: A man who had travelled to Manchester, UK from Hong Kong was admitted to hospital suspected to be suffering from SARS, the first case in Britain. The World Health Organization issued an alert concerning the spread of the disease, calling it a 'global health threat'. It advised travellers from China, Hong Kong and south-east Asia who developed symptoms of the bug to contact their local health services.

- *19th March*: The bug was tentatively identified as a paramyxo-virus, but six days later this diagnosis was changed to a novel type of coronavirus. Until then, the common cold was the only human ailment known to be caused by a coronavirus.

- *1st April*: *The Times* suggested that the spread of SARS may now be unstoppable. Analysts commented that the economy of the Far East could be the next victim of the virus – tourism had slumped and business activity had been hit hard.

- *2nd April*: Banks around the world introduced emergency measures in an attempt to prevent employees from coming into contact with SARS. UBS, a Swiss bank that employs thousands of people in the City of London, introduced quarantine conditions for employees returning from the stricken area. They were told to stay at home for 10 days. Standard Chartered, one of the biggest investment banks in Hong Kong, banned its staff from travelling to and from the Far East.

- *3rd April*: The *Daily Mail* carried the headline: 'Could this be an early warning of something even deadlier?'

  Hong Kong moved more than 200 residents of the Amoy Gardens housing complex in Kowloon into isolation camps after an outbreak of SARS, because the World Health Organization announced that 'bodily secretions' containing the virus might somehow enter common systems that link rooms or flats.

  On a flight from Hong Kong to Beijing, 22 people caught the disease from a single infected person.

- *4th April*: Qantas, the Australian airline, cut up to one in five of its international flights because of a fall in bookings, with customers not travelling by plane following the outbreak of SARS. British Airways also announced that passenger numbers were down by 11 per cent as a result of the epidemic. The International Air Transport Association predicted that airlines could face a loss of a staggering £6.5 billion.

- *7th April*: Wall Street experts predicted that the SARS outbreak could trigger a global downturn and so tip the world economy into recession.

- *15th April*: Scientists reported that many animals can play host to SARS, so increasing the chance that the disease was lying low somewhere. They predicted that the disease was in Asia to stay.

Although serious, this outbreak was only a mini-epidemic: the infectivity was low and only 4 per cent of the victims died, as the table below shows. This is minor compared with an outbreak of the Black Death, should it reappear.

As the epidemic continued in south-east Asia, the disease was brought under control by sound public-health measures in the other parts of the world where it had appeared, courtesy of airline travellers. Scientists gradually established some of the features of this new disease. The incubation period is variable, from two to ten days, and individuals are probably not infectious during this time, unlike haemorrhagic plague, so

	Cases	Deaths
Australia	1	0
Belgium	1	0
Brazil	1	0
Canada	69	0
China	1220	49
Hong Kong	800	20
Taiwan	15	0
France	3	0
Germany	5	0
Ireland	1	0
Italy	3	0
Romania	1	0
Singapore	100	5
Spain	1	0
Switzerland	2	0
Thailand	7	2
UK	3	0
United States	100	0
Vietnam	59	4
Total	2392	87

SARS should be easier to control by the prompt isolation of cases.

Also, the disease is spread by droplets rather than by aerosol and seems to involve much closer contact through bodily fluids and secretions. You may catch the virus simply by touching a contaminated table top, lift button or doorknob. It can be transmitted via a sewage pipe or the air in a plane. But the Health Protection Agency in London has stated that if SARS were spread by aerosol there would be 10–100 times as many people affected.

The mini-epidemic of SARS brought home several important warnings. First, new diseases are emerging all the time and health authorities throughout the world have to be continually on their guard. The SARS virus is believed to have appeared first in a cat-like animal called the masked palm civet and then jumped across the species barrier to infect humans. The meat of the civet is prized as a delicacy in Guangdong province.

Second, a new disease can spread rapidly to all corners of the globe by air travel.

Third, an epidemic always causes panic – because at this stage, the infectious agent and the consequences are unknown. This has serious knock-on effects, such as the predicted staggering losses by the international airlines and the suggestion of the possibility of collapse of the world economy.

Finally, immediate action is essential once an outbreak has been identified. A report in the *Journal of the American Medical Association* points out that the SARS epidemic in Beijing was quickly brought under control once the Chinese authorities stopped concealing its existence. In just six weeks, the epidemic declined to zero from a peak of 100 new patients a day being admitted to hospital.

Have we learnt our lessons?

Health authorities throughout the world are well aware in general terms of the dangers of emergent diseases, and international teams are standing by to deal with any reported outbreak. But have the lessons of HIV/AIDS been learnt? If a disease were to emerge with a lethality and ferocity comparable to the Black Death it would be not simply idiotic but suicidal for governments to pussyfoot around with advertising campaigns, or for anyone to think 'it could never happen in my country'. Once the means of transmission had been identified and the nature of the disease determined, strict control and security measures would be immediately necessary. The key lies in the determination of the incubation and infectious periods. Full international aid and cooperation should be made available without question. Teams of epidemiologists and microbiologists would have to work around the clock to determine the characteristics of the new disease, so that the spread and outcome of the epidemic could be predicted and appropriate measures taken.

As ever, the price of safety is eternal vigilance.

20

Is There Something more Terrible than the Black Death?

We know that the great powers of the world have been secretly working with biological weapons for several decades. The development of the requisite technology was an inevitable consequence of the discovery in 1953 of how DNA governs heredity and controls the working of all living things, from microbes to man. An immense amount of time and money has been spent on devising ways of attacking and killing people *en masse* by releasing lethal organisms or their toxins, as well as on preparing defences against such attacks.

Germ warfare is the poor man's atom bomb because nuclear weapons are expensive to produce, difficult to deliver and easy to detect. Saddam Hussein's resistance to stopping Iraq's biological weapons programme, which cost him billions of dollars in forfeited oil revenues, shows the importance that he attached to this method of attack. A terrorist organization, unless it is backed by a superpower that can provide nuclear weapons and the means of delivering them, will fall back on germ warfare, and a trained microbiologist could easily teach such a group of fanatics how to make devastating biological weapons – 'from a few handfuls of backyard dirt and some widely available laboratory equipment' (noted in *Germs: The Ultimate Weapon*, see below).

For the terrorist, a further advantage of biological weapons lies in the uncertainty of their effects. Once a conventional bomb has exploded, the scale of the devastation and the mortality can be determined, but in a biological attack the health authorities would know neither the nature nor the scale of the strike, and would be unable to predict future developments or the final death toll. All they could do would be to prepare for a worst-case scenario, which might be an over-the-top response to a minor attack.

Early bioterrorists

The history of biological warfare is a long and undistinguished one. The story told in the Old Testament (Exodus 9:8–9) of the Lord advising Moses to sprinkle ashes in the face of Pharaoh is considered to be an example of germ warfare and an account of an outbreak of anthrax: the dust must have been converted into an aerosol of bacilli because it became 'a boil breaking forth with blanes upon man, and upon beast'.

In the sixth century BC the Assyrians contaminated the wells of their enemies with rye ergot, a type of fungal disease. Solon, the sage of Athens, used the herb hellebore to poison the water supply of the Cirrhaeans.

More than 2000 years ago, Scythian archers dipped arrow-heads in manure and rotting corpses to increase the deadliness of their weapons. As we have seen, the bodies of plague victims were thrown over city walls in the hope of infecting the enemy during the plague of Athens and the siege of Caffa.

Smallpox became a way of subduing Indian tribes in North America. In one case, during the French and Indian War in Canada, Sir Jeffrey Amherst is said to have presented tribal leaders with blankets contaminated with smallpox crusts, which infected the population and aided the British advance. The British also used smallpox-laced blankets to infect tribal members at Fort Pitt on the Pennsylvania frontier in 1763.

All this has returned to haunt us. Gregg Bourland, chairman of the Cheyenne River Sioux tribe in South Dakota, is a descendant of one of the American Indians who died of smallpox, called Blue

Earrings. He claims that unlike the Europeans, the native North Americans did not build up immunity against the disease and he is demanding mass vaccination for his people in case of a bioterrorist attack.

In 1797 Napoleon infected the citizens of Mantua with swamp fever. There are accounts of soldiers during the American Civil War poisoning water supplies by deliberately dumping dead animals in ponds.

A present-day nightmare

But these primitive efforts at germ warfare pale into insignificance beside today's methods. In their book *Germs: The Ultimate Weapon*, Judith Miller, Stephen Engelberg and William Broad describe how during the Cold War, the USA and Soviet Union devoted enormous amounts of money and manpower to the development of biological weapons; by the early 1980s, the Pentagon was secretly spending $91 million a year on so-called bio-defence. The legacy of this secret arms race was a windfall for terrorists.

All nations signed a treaty in 1972 that banned the development of biological weapons but, in direct conflict with the spirit of the agreement, the Soviets secretly decided to expand their programme on a vast, industrial scale. Miller, Engelberg and Broad give the following staggering industrial capacities for germ production (in *metric tons per year*) at peak levels:

	USA	Soviet Union
Anthrax	0.9	4500
Venezuelan equine encephalitis virus	0.8	150
Yersinia pestis	0	1500
smallpox virus	0	100
Marburg virus	0	250

There were therefore two terrible consequences of the Cold War: first, a literally unimaginable stockpile of germs; second, an army of trained scientists capable of producing and manipulating microbes to order. Projects included work on making a biological attack harder to diagnose and on enabling germs to defeat vaccines.

Both the stockpiles and the scientists were available for purchase by unfriendly countries and by terrorist groups. Until 1989, US security was so lax that an American company was selling strains of anthrax to Iraq by mail order. In a recent security exercise, a team of American agents was able to set up a functioning germ warfare factory for a mere $1 million without the CIA knowing what they were doing. After the collapse of the Soviet Union in 1991, it was discovered that former Soviet scientists had helped Iraq to acquire stocks of Clostridium, botulinum and anthrax.

The Aum Shinrikyo cult attacked the Tokyo underground in 1995 with a nerve gas, sarin, killing 11 people and injuring 5500 others. Investigators subsequently found a research laboratory for biological weapons in the cult's compound; its adherents had already tried to unleash anthrax and botulinum toxin on the population, fortunately without success. Members of this cult had visited Zaire, during the 1992 Ebola outbreak there, in an attempt to obtain samples of the virus for cultivation and weapons development. The investigators discovered that an even more serious attack was planned, with devices that could pump biological and chemical agents into the streets of Tokyo.

Germ warfare research, occasional bioterrorist activity and contingency planning against the risk of the deliberate release of a biological agent in the UK and USA have been continuing for many decades without attracting a great deal of public interest. However, the events on 11th September 2001 changed all that and brought home to everybody the reality of the situation. The emergence of the USA as the world's most powerful nation made a biological attack there more likely. The technological revolution of the twentieth century (including the building of mega-skyscrapers) and the high density of people moving incessantly in cities have led inevitably to modern society's extreme vulnerability.

The western world reacted swiftly, at last, and the threat of a biological attack against a civilian population is now recognized as a current and ongoing danger. An analysis in 1997 estimated in some attack scenarios an economic impact of \$26 billion per 100 000 persons exposed to anthrax, and the threat of biological weapons is considered sufficiently serious to warrant the creation of an unprecedented civilian stockpile of medicines and vaccines.

US President Bush announced \$11 billion of new spending in the health budget for the financial year 2003 to combat bio-terrorism, and the German army intends to triple its investment in research into protection against biological weapons. But Professor Reinhard Kurth, president of the Robert Koch Institute, believes that civilian vaccination programmes should be developed independently of what the army is doing, thereby creating a buffer of vaccinated people in a localized outbreak. He concludes,

> In my opinion, and it is the general opinion of experts in this field, the potential threat through biological weapons is worse than that from chemical and atomic weapons.

In January 2002, the UK's Chief Medical Officer announced plans for the establishment of a new protection agency with wide powers to streamline the services involved in the containment and control of infections, including future emergent diseases (which are regarded as inevitable) and those created by terrorists. Anthony Fauci, director of the National Institute of Allergy and Infectious Diseases, wants 'to include bioterrorism in the big umbrella of emerging and re-emerging infections'.

However, as Madeline Drexler says in *Secret Agents: The Menace of Emerging Infections*, we should not underestimate Mother Nature, perhaps the most savage bioterrorist of all. Whatever the infectious agent may be, including some new microbial horror that we have yet to detect, the bottom line is that keen surveillance and rapid response are really the only weapons in our arsenal.

Operation Doomsday

A nightmare vision of Britain under terrorist attack was conjured up in February 2003 when the British Government unveiled the biggest shake-up of emergency planning since the Cold War. In blood-curdling detail it spelt out how the emergency services would decontaminate those caught in a chemical, biological or nuclear attack.

Under these doomsday plans, specialist fire crew in protective suits will operate mass decontamination units in which survivors will be stripped and then walk or be stretchered through warm showers to remove traces of hazardous material at a rate of 15 seconds per person. Watches, spectacles and hearing aids will be confiscated and the victims will then don white overalls and be sent to casualty clearing stations.

A sum of £56 million has been committed for mass decontamination and monitoring equipment and the number of gas-tight protection suits is being doubled to 4000. Police cordons with armed military back-up will be assigned to stop the inevitable panic and ensure that the injured are cleaned up before they are given treatment.

Biological warfare

About 25 microbes or bacterial toxins have been identified as potential biological weapons. The most serious threats are considered to be anthrax, smallpox, bubonic plague and the viral haemorrhagic fevers, either because they are easily disseminated or transmitted from person to person, or because they cause high mortality, or because they might cause widespread panic and social disruption. The Center for Disease Control and Prevention, very significantly for our thesis, has cited the viral haemorrhagic fevers as possibly posing the highest threat if used as a bioweapon, because of their potential for aerosol transmission and high mortality rates. The manufacture of these agents is now straightforward, but to produce them in a form that can be easily delivered and would harm large numbers of people is technically more difficult at present.

The fear of anthrax

So what happened after 11th September 2001 that completely changed everybody's thinking and appreciation of the possibility of a bioterrorist attack and led to the reallocation of prodigious sums of money? The chosen weapon on that occasion was anthrax spores delivered via the US postal system that left five dead, with considerable attendant inconvenience and public alarm.

In addition to the fear of another mail attack, experts suggest that the tiny airborne spores could be introduced into air-conditioning systems in apartment blocks or shopping precincts, and at government buildings such as the White House or the Capitol. Such an attack would not only kill thousands of people but could create mass panic across America.

Patrick Kelley, director of the Pentagon's Global Emerging Infections Surveillance Response Systems, compared the attack with the effects of HIV and malaria the world over: 'You cannot expect them to care about five deaths from anthrax'. And yet this seemingly trivial terrorist campaign has had enormous and far-reaching consequences. A letter sent to members of the American Society for Microbiology by the FBI in January 2002 suggested that the anthrax used in these attacks may have come from a US laboratory that was conducting research into *defence* against biological weapons. Radiocarbon dating has now proved that the anthrax sent through the post to two senators and two prominent journalists was made and milled into a fine powder within the previous two years.

Certainly there are thousands of tonnes of anthrax spores hidden in stockpiles around the world: more than enough to wipe out humanity if they could be appropriately delivered. Russian scientists have already produced a vaccine-resistant strain of anthrax. Only 100 kg of spores released as an aerosol upwind of a major metropolitan region could kill a million people. Furthermore, the spores are remarkably resilient and it would be very difficult to eradicate them and to disinfect the area under attack, so that the disruption to services and the normal pattern of life would be profound and long-lasting.

In spite of the justifiable fears about the deliberate mass release of anthrax spores, the overall effects on the world would be negligible compared with the return of the Black Death or a similar emergent disease. There would certainly be a terrible loss of life, but anthrax is not an ideal weapon because it is not transmitted from person to person and barrier isolation precautions would be sufficient. The outbreak would be largely confined to the area downwind of the point of release and the rest of the world would not be affected. There should be no pandemic. Furthermore, health authorities are now geared up to combat an anthrax attack and would be able to reduce the mortality substantially.

Yersinia pestis

What of bubonic plague, however? During the Second World War, the Japanese are said to have dropped fleas infected with bubonic plague on Chinese cities and may have succeeded in killing some people, presumably by initiating localized outbreaks of pneumonic plague. During the cold war, the Soviet Union invested heavily in research into *Yersinia pestis* as a potential weapon and it is high on most governments' lists of infectious agents against which defences have to be prepared. But why is this?

Nobody, but nobody, should be the slightest bit alarmed by the prospect of a terrorist attack with bubonic plague. The United States have lived with the disease for the last 100 years and it causes only a handful of cases annually. The delivery and establishment of an epidemic of bubonic plague would be very difficult because, as we show in Chapter 11, so many factors would critically affect the outcome and spread of the epidemic would be impossible. In any case, bubonic plague is readily treated with antibiotics.

So why have governments committed so much effort and money to producing *Yersina pestis* as a biological weapon? The answer is obvious: they believe that bubonic plague was the cause of the Black Death, which killed half of Europe at a stroke – in their minds it must surely be the ideal weapon.

Of course, this is nonsensical. There has been no consideration of the basic biology of bubonic plague. The situation has worsened considerably because mind-boggling sums of money are freely available for anyone working on anything remotely connected with bioterrorism. Consequently, several teams are now modelling the effects of an epidemic of bubonic plague that might be initiated by a terrorist. In our opinion this is a complete waste of time and resources. These research scientists should read Chapter 11. But they have a vested and financial interest in maintaining the present fiction. We believe that it is essential that everybody, particularly those needlessly handing out large sums of public money, understands the true nature of bubonic and haemorrhagic plague, and the real problems of germ warfare.

The deadly viruses

We should be far more concerned about the potential use of viral diseases by terrorists. They are cheap and easy to deliver and the infected people themselves do all the work of multiplication and dispersal. The virus multiplies within the victim at a fantastic rate and is soon ready for onward transmission to infect many others. With modern air travel, the result would be a global epidemic.

The smallpox virus has long been considered as a possible biological weapon. Stockpiles are known to be ready for use and in November 2002, the USA identified four nations that have undeclared secret samples of the virus: Iraq, North Korea, Russia and France. A terrorist would only need to send one infected person travelling continuously, say on the London Underground, to start a major epidemic. This imaginary scenario was presented in a 90-minute BBC television programme broadcast in February 2002, in which the final death toll was estimated at 60 million. Governments have been working clandestinely to predict the outcome of a smallpox attack and to organize their defences via suitable public-health measures.

We have spent several years researching historical smallpox epidemics. Although an outbreak of this disease would be dreadful, we do not believe that a terrorist strike with the standard virus would spell total disaster. The strain of the virus that existed in England in the seventeenth and eighteenth centuries killed only about 20 per cent of infected children.

Once the disease had been identified following a terrorist attack, transmission could be greatly reduced by the use of masks and, most importantly, a protective vaccine is available. This viral, infectious disease is well understood and with forward planning, good emergency health measures, early diagnosis, rapid response and mass vaccinations, a smallpox epidemic produced in a major city by a terrorist strike could be contained and eventually controlled.

The Government of the United States has decided to manufacture and stockpile enough vaccine for its entire population: a formidable task that will cost hundreds of millions of dollars. President Bush began operations on 13th December 2002, when he announced that half a million civilian health workers as well as half a million troops would be vaccinated by 15th March 2003. Fortunately, so far severe reactions have been rare. However, it seems to be unlikely that the US will reach the target of 10 million vaccinated by July 2003.

However, there is an enormous proviso. Dr Vivienne Nathanson from the British Medical Association has warned that civil defence preparations can help counter attacks only with *known* biological agents.

> No medical response exists to counter unknown biological weapons or genetically engineered strains of superbugs for which there is no vaccine available. The only real defence against the use of biological or chemical weapons is to prevent their development in the first place.

To conclude: the enormous amount of time and money currently being devoted to combating infectious diseases released in a terrorist attack are necessary and welcome. But it should be remembered that this incredible activity was stirred up only when five people died after anthrax spores had been sent via the US mail, and there is more than a hint of overkill in the response. There never has been – and there certainly is not now with all these welcome precautions – any suggestion that a bioterrorist attack or a germ warfare strike with any of the known bugs in the world today would have more than a fraction of the impact of the return of the Black Death.

Apocalypse?

Why, then, is bioterrorist activity included in this chapter as a way in which the Black Death, or something very like it, could return? The answer lies in the biotechnology revolution. When the outbreak of SARS in the Far East was first reported, bioterrorism was considered as a possible cause and was taken seriously on both sides of the Atlantic. The UK Department of

Health said: 'The pattern of infection certainly looks like a naturally occurring illness but obviously we are keeping an open mind. It would be ridiculous for us to rule anything out at this stage.'

There remains the frightening possibility that terrorists could manufacture something very like the Black Death. There are now many microbiologists, veterans of the Cold War, who have moved on from manufacturing bulk stocks of anthrax spores and developing vaccine-resistant variants of known diseases, to the production of designer super-germs to order. The possibilities of biotechnology are awesome and it is becoming ever easier to create new biological entities. Microbes and toxins that attack the human immune system or nerve sheaths are already available, and both the Americans and the Russians have succeeded in producing more deadly versions of anthrax, smallpox, Ebola and bubonic plague.

In November 2003, it was announced that a scientist funded by the US government had deliberately created by genetic engineering an extremely deadly form of mousepox, a relative of the smallpox virus.

American scientists have recently demonstrated how easy it would be to create deadly germs for biological weapons. They have assembled a man-made version of the polio virus by using DNA and a genetic blueprint for the pathogen that is available on the internet. This is the first time that a scientific team has used the available technology to make a completely artificial virus from scratch. To test its efficacy, it was injected into mice, which first suffered paralysis and then died.

In fact, using a new emergent disease or a biologically engineered super-bug would be a cunning ploy on the part of terrorists. It might not raise suspicions for a long time during which a global pandemic could be established, whereas a smallpox outbreak anywhere in the world would be immediately recognized as being man-made.

Inevitably, some day soon, someone, somewhere will start tinkering with the viral haemorrhagic fevers. Imagine an engineered super-germ that is even more ferocious and infectious than the Black Death. Transmission would be by droplet infection and only one person need be infected (although the terrorist would hope and work for more, preferably in different countries, to give a margin for error) for apocalyptic oblivion to beckon. That is the danger of playing with fire, and is a direct consequence of the biotechnology revolution that followed the fateful discovery of the structure of the double helix of DNA. Thus, the blueprint of life becomes the blueprint for death.

A wake-up call

Our quest is complete. We have turned history upside down. From our chance discovery of the record of an epidemic in a market town in the north of England, we now know that the Black Death and the plagues were caused by the most fearsome emergent infectious disease of all time. Escaping from Ethiopia about 3000 years ago, travelling as always by the movement of infected traders, haemorrhagic plague established its base in the Levant. From there it struck at the Greek and Byzantine civilizations and the early Islamic Empire. Flourishing city states were its preferred victims.

Finally, in the mid-fourteenth century, haemorrhagic plague devastated the population of Europe, the greatest human tragedy in history. In the days of very limited transport, it was able to make these long-range strikes only because of its remarkably long incubation period. For the next three centuries, Europe was held in its relentless grip and it is probably only the presence of a genetic mutation in a few lucky individuals that led eventually to its disappearance.

We must realize and take on board the terrible dangers of emergent infectious diseases. These occurred only rarely until about 1970, when our way of life changed rapidly and completely and a new disease was reported every year. Nevertheless, while these are serious and lethal, at present they in no way approach the ferocity of our medieval serial killer. The accounts that we have uncovered show all too clearly the devastating mortality – nearly half of the western world was killed in the single epidemic of the Black Death, an event that is without parallel. The descriptions of the agonizing and lonely deaths make our hair stand on end and send shivers down our spines.

We owe it to ourselves and to those who died to be continually on our guard against the reappearance of haemorrhagic plague, to make sure that it is not allowed to establish a stranglehold once again through ignorance and misrepresentation. In this way, the suffering and deaths of millions will not have been in vain.

Further Reading

There have been many books written about plagues and in particular about the Black Death, but most promulgate the theory that bubonic plague was responsible or are concerned with the social consequences of the pandemic.

Twigg, G. (1984) *The Black Death: A Biological Appraisal*, London: Batsford Academic. This was the first book to assemble the evidence and to show convincingly that bubonic plague was not responsible for the Black Death.

Shrewsbury, J. F. D. (1970) *A History of Bubonic Plague in the British Isles*, Cambridge: Cambridge University Press. This gives a comprehensive account of the epidemics in England, although it is a rather boring read. Shrewsbury believed whole-heartedly that *Yersinia pestis* was responsible for the pestilence but, as a medical microbiologist, realized that this was an impossibility in many of the epidemics. His repeated attempts to rationalize the situation spoil an important compendium. A must if you want to find out about recorded plague epidemics in your local area.

We have presented a new, scientific and mathematical approach to the epidemiology in Scott, S. and Duncan, C. J. (2001) *Biology of Plagues: Evidence from Historical Populations*, Cambridge: Cambridge University Press.

McNeill, W. H. (1977) *Plagues and People*, Oxford: Blackwell gives a general account.

An account of events during the arrival of the Great Pestilence is given in Ziegler, P. (1969) *The Black Death*, London: Collins.

Biraben, J. N. (1975) *Les hommes et la peste en France et dans les pays Européens et Méditerraneens, Vols 1 and 2*, Paris: Mouton & Co and École des Hautes Études en Sciences Sociales. An invaluable compilation of the recorded plagues in Europe, listed by geographic area. There is a comprehensive bibliography. Biraben also gives an authoritative account of true bubonic plague at Marseille in 1720–22.

Pepys, S. (1665/1906) *Diary of Samuel Pepys*, London: J. M. Dent. The Great Plague of London in 1665–66 is the best documented of all the epidemics in Europe. Samuel Pepys stayed in London throughout and went about his daily business. His diary is lively and provides an invaluable eye-witness account.

Defoe, D. (1722) *Diary of a Plague Year*, London: Everyman's Library. Daniel Defoe was six in 1665 and did not write his very readable story of the Great Plague until

1722. It has been criticized as being fictional, but checking against contemporary sources suggests that this is an accurate account of life during one of the terrible epidemics.

Bell, W. G. (1924) *The Great Plague in London in 1665*, London: John Lane. Probably the definitive account.

Creighton, C. (1894) *History of Epidemics in Britain*, Cambridge: Cambridge University Press. Creighton is the doyen of epidemiologists. Although medically qualified, his approach in this classic work, which was to provide a chronicle of death and disease in the people of the UK, was that of a professional historian and he worked with great care on his sources.

An account of the epidemic at Eyam published 30 years before Yersin's work on bubonic plague is given by Wood, W. (1865) *The History of Antiquities of Eyam*, 4th edn, London: Bell and Daldy. It contains no confusing mention of rats and fleas.

The plagues of Iceland are of particular interest because they were constrained within this isolated island community and were initiated by the arrival of a single ship. Karlsson, G. (1996) 'Plague without rats: the case of fifteenth century Iceland', *Journal of Medieval History*, 22: 263–84. It would be particularly interesting to measure the frequency of the *CCR5-Δ32* mutation in Iceland today.

An erudite account of plagues in the early Islamic Empire is Dols, M. W. (1977) *The Black Death in the Middle East*, Princeton, NJ: Princeton University Press.

The effect of the plagues in controlling the demography of Europe is covered in two of our books: Scott, S. and Duncan, C. J. (1998) *Human Demography and Disease*, Cambridge: Cambridge University Press, and Scott S. and Duncan, C. J. (2002) *Demography and Nutrition*, Oxford: Blackwell.

There are many papers or books that cover specialized aspects of our story, for example:

Davis, D. E. (1986) 'The scarcity of rats and the Black Death: An ecological history', *Journal of Interdisciplinary History*, XVI: 455–70.

Dyer, A. (1997) 'The English Sweating Sickness of 1551: An epidemic anatomized', *Medical History*, 41: 362–84.

Taviner, M., Thwaites, G. and Grant, V. (1998) 'The English Sweating Sickness, 1485–1551: A viral pulmonary disease?' *Medical History*, 42: 96–8.

Furness, W. (1894) *The History of Penrith from the Earliest Period to the Present Time by Ewanian (William Furness)*, Penrith: William Furness.

Hughes, J. (1971) 'The plague at Carlisle 1597/8', *Transactions of the Cumberland and Westmorland Antiquarian and Archaeological Society*, 81: 52–63.

Longrigg, J. (1980) 'The great plague of Athens', *History of Science*, 18: 209–25.

Pfister, C. (1980) 'The Little Ice Age: Thermal and wetness indices for Central Europe', *Journal of Interdisciplinary History*, 10: 665–96.

Twigg, G. (1978) 'The role of rodents in plague transmission: A worldwide review', *Mammal Review*, 8: 77–110.

Twigg, G. (2003) 'The Black Death: A problem of population-wide infection', *Local Population Studies*, 71: 40–52. Covers evidence that the black rat was not present in rural England during the plague.

A detailed account of the array of newly emerging diseases in a world out of balance is given by Garrett, L. (1994) *The Coming Plague*, New York: Penguin Books.

Miller J., Engelberg, S. and Broad, W. (2001) *Germs: The Ultimate Weapon*, New York: Simon & Schuster. Comprehensive coverage of biological weapons of mass destruction and current fears of bioterrorism.

Index

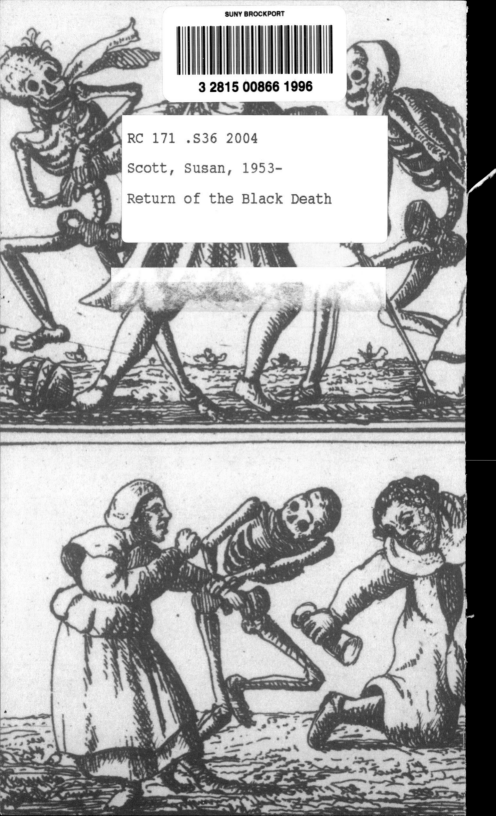